CLACTON — APR 2015

1 3 JUL 2015

Please return this book on or before the date shown above. To
renew go to www.essex.gov.uk/libraries, ring 0845 603 7628 or
go to any Essex library.

Essex County Council

First published in the UK in 2013 by Golden Guides Press Ltd.

10 8 6 4 2 1 3 5 7 9

ISBN 978-1-78095-017-4 (Paperback)
ISBN 978-1-78095-046-4 (Kindle)
ISBN 978-1-78095-047-1 (ePub)

Typeset in Palatino by Mac Style, Driffield.
Cover design by Mousemat Design Ltd.
Edited by Melanie Marshall.
Printed and bound in Great Britain by
Marston Book Services Limited, Oxfordshire
Ebook produced by ePubDirect.

Golden Guides Press Ltd
P.O. Box 171
Newhaven
E. Sussex
BN9 1AZ
UK
admin@goldenguidespress.com
www.goldenguidespress.com

# MILITARY AIRFIELDS
# IN BRITAIN
## During the Second World War

WAR IN BRITAIN SERIES

## Jon & Diane Sutherland

# Prisoner of War Camps in Britain During the Second World War

## by Jon & Diane Sutherland

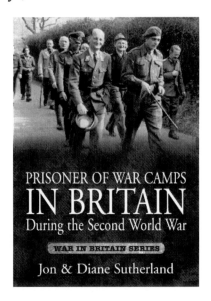

At the beginning of the Second World War, there were two prisoner of war camps in Britain. By the time the war ended, there were over 600. This book explores the role of the camps, their prisoners and workers, together with their impact on the local community. It reveals why locations were chosen and how they were turned into prisons for the enemy, including who got locked up and why, from a famous footballer and artist to infamous escapees.

You'll discover the people behind the names and their stories, including how some fell in love, either with local girls or their new country and stayed after the war, integrating into their former enemies' community. It's a fascinating study of a story rarely told and will also compare the treatment of prisoners of war compared to British prisoners of war overseas.

This is the first in the War in Britain Series for Golden Guides Press.

**Available from all good booksellers and as an eBook for all eReaders (ISBN 978-1-78095-013-6, £16.99)**

*For more details and to see our other books, visit*
*www.GoldenGuidesPress.com*

# Contents

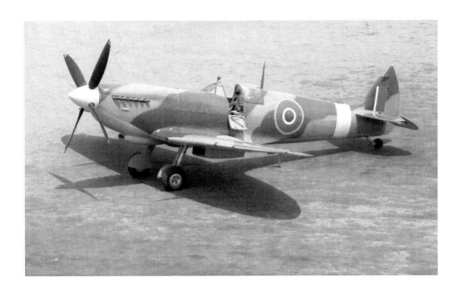

# Introduction

A BRIEF look at the index of this book will reveal the fact that there are literally hundreds of former airfields that were used during the Second World War. It is almost impossible to travel more than 50 miles without being close to an airfield. It may give the impression that Britain, as some have suggested, was rather like an enormous, immobile aircraft carrier. This could certainly have been the case when the United States Army Air Forces (USAAF) began arriving in 1942.

## Types of airfield

In the detailed listings of all of the airfields that have been researched for this book you will encounter some semi-technical terms. These are really shorthand descriptions of the type of airfield and how it was used:

- Satellite station or airfield – these were built close to an existing major airfield, often a bomber or fighter base. The satellite airfield could be used if the capacity of the main base had been reached, or there was a need to disperse the aircraft over a greater distance to make a less tempting target for the enemy
- Relief landing ground – this means that the facilities at the airfield were relatively primitive and that the airfield tended to be used if there was a major problem at the main airfield close by; perhaps an aircraft had crashed on the main airfield or a large amount of aircraft were returning to the area at the same time

- Emergency landing ground – these again had fairly primitive facilities, often only tents. Usually, if bomber crews' aircraft were in trouble, these would be pointed out as the location that they should try to land instead of their main base. Some of the emergency landing fields were incredibly busy after the bombing missions from 1943 onwards
- Forward or advanced landing ground – these were usually temporary airfields set up in requisitioned farmland. The majority of these were in the south of England. Fighter and fighter bomber squadrons were shifted here temporarily from their stations further north. These landing grounds provided the basics for the squadrons to operate for a short period of time, particularly in the run up to the Normandy landings in June 1944. Some were also used for other major land support efforts, such as Operation Market Garden and the crossing of the Rhine.

## Who built the airfields?

Obviously the Royal Flying Corps or civilian operators had already developed some of the airfields, but these tended to be grass airfields only. As aircraft became more sophisticated, particularly with the use of retractable wheels, more permanent runways were needed. This meant that concrete or mesh was needed and that the land had to be levelled and properly prepared. The construction tends to fall into three different categories:

- British military construction – either RAF or, more commonly, army engineers
- Private contractors – many of the major contractors that would go on to build motorways, housing estates and other infrastructure in the post-war period were involved in the building of airfields and their facilities
- US Army engineers – as we will see, the USAAF was actually a part of the American Army and not strictly speaking a separate organisation. US Army engineers moved into specially designated sites and carried out extensive work in preparation for the arrival of the American squadrons

## Who used the airfields?

Each airfield has its own distinct history. Whilst some of the airfields were barely open a matter of weeks, others can trace many decades of association with aviation, either military or civilian. As far as the British airmen (and air women) were concerned, these fall into the following categories:

- Royal Flying Corps and Royal Navy Air Service – these were First World War organisations. They were separate and essentially the Royal Flying Corps was a part of the British Army. The Royal Naval Air Service was part of the Royal Navy. The two groups were merged in 1918 with the birth of the Royal Air Force
- Civilian flying clubs and airlines – many pioneering aviators were involved in either private flying or were pilots for the very early scheduled flights run by the very first airlines. In many cases these individuals were actively involved in the development of flying from airfields in the interwar period. Of course many had close links with the Royal Air Force and would go on to fly military aircraft during the Second World War
- Royal Air Force flight training – it was of course extremely important to train both pilots and crews in order to compete in the air with the Luftwaffe. Many airfields focused on this aspect and would train pilots, navigators, observers, bomb aimers, radar operators, aviation mechanics and other trades
- Royal Air Force Air Sea Rescue and Coastal Command – it was of course incredibly important to try to retrieve pilots and crews that had been shot down. In fact these men were in many respects far more valuable than the aircraft that they were flying in. It was a practical decision to try to ensure that experienced crews were saved from either drowning or becoming prisoners of war. Many of the airfields around the coast had not only seaplanes and other aircraft whose sole purpose it was to pick up downed aircrews (be they Allies or enemy), but also fast launches that would respond to sightings of crews and try to reach them before the ditched crews succumbed to the elements. Coastal Command was involved in patrolling the waters around the British Isles, attacking enemy shipping, particularly U-boats and searching for downed crews

- RAF fighter bases – these are, perhaps, the most romantic of all of the aspects of the Royal Air Force and would have been home to legendary aircraft such as the Spitfire and Hurricane, as well as world famous pilots such as Douglas Bader. Many of the more established bases were involved in the Battle of Britain, but they were also of vital importance in taking the war to Germany over Europe
- RAF bomber bases – these were the larger, purpose-built sites that saw a steady progression of ever-more successful and effective British bombers over the course of the war. They would launch incessant offensives against German industry, military targets and, controversially, civilian targets such as Hamburg or Dresden. Of all of the branches of the RAF it is undoubtedly Bomber Command that took the highest casualties
- USAAF – particularly in the eastern part of England, the 8th Air Force established itself to take part of the strain of Bomber Command's offensive against Germany. The Americans would fly huge formations of large bombers during daylight hours, supported by long-range fighters. At night the task would be taken up by RAF Bomber Command. Many purpose-built airfields were constructed across the east of England. Other parts of the country were covered by the 9th Air Force. This had a slightly different role; it was there to support ground offensives rather than carry out their own aerial bombardment of the enemy. Many of the early arrivals to the 9th Air Force were transferred to the 12th, which was operational in North Africa and the Mediterranean. Many of the airfields that the USAAF used were located far to the west of the British Isles, notably in Northern Ireland. Effectively these were transit airfields. Aircraft would fly in from North America, land, refuel and then proceed to their allocated squadron either in the south or east of Britain.

## The USAAF

As the name suggests, this was the United States Army Air Force. The Americans had had a long-standing and close relationship with the Royal Flying Corps and the Royal Air Force since the First World War. It was a component of the US Army. At its peak there were 2.4 million in the organisation in March 1944 and they had around 80,000 aircraft.

Not all of these, of course, were based in Britain, but the USAAF had 1.25 million stationed abroad and were operating from 1,600 airfields. It was a vast organisation and it had many thousands of female members. This was also true of the RAF, who of course had the Women's Auxiliary Air Force (WAAF).

The first of the US aircraft began arriving in the summer of 1942 and within two years they had upwards of 3,000 aircraft, 200,000 personnel and over 120 airfields.

## A typical airfield

It is true enough to say that there was no such thing as a typical airfield, but many of them did follow a pattern. It very much depended on the location and the use to which the airfield was being put. There were also marked differences between airfields used by the USAAF and those used by the RAF. Some of the airfields never developed further than being glorified, tented encampments. Others would be fully developed and would have the following types of features:

- Permanent concrete runways – the length of these would depend on the types of aircraft using the airfield. There would often be more than one runway and these would be configured so that the maximum use could be made of them at any one time
- Control tower or watch office – this would be a tall building with large windows. From here a ground-based air traffic controller would liaise with the pilot or crews of taking off or landing aircraft. They would also receive information from command headquarters and, importantly, from weather forecasters
- Hangars – some airfields never received hangars and all their aircraft would be left out in the open and often they could be camouflaged under trees. The hangars would serve the dual purpose of providing shelter for the aircraft, but more importantly a place where mechanics could work on them
- Accommodation – probably the most common were the Nissen huts. These were semicircular, often prefabricated buildings. Some of these would serve as sleeping quarters whilst others would be used as canteens, medical facilities, storage and even the airfield cinema

- Dispersal pens – these were basic, concrete, roofless, walled structures in which the aircraft would be housed. They would afford some protection from enemy attack and would be placed far enough apart so that a cluster of bombs would not be able to destroy several aircraft at a time

- Anti-aircraft and other protection – many of the airfields were ringed with barbed wire and had pillboxes, in order to protect the site from being attacked from the ground or penetrated by enemy agents. They would also have anti-aircraft guns, although this was only for local defence. There would be major anti-aircraft positions protecting factories and some protecting vital airfields.

### The legacy of the airfields

A huge number of airfields, whether they were temporary or far more permanent, have all-but disappeared from the British landscape. The vast majority of the sites are now covered by farmland. Even the concrete runways were broken up in the post-war period. More often than not they were used as hardcore for the construction of roads and motorways.

Other airfields, by sheer luck, have retained many of the features that were constructed during the Second World War. Perhaps they were too remote or the land was of insufficient value to warrant clearance? In latter years some of these sites have come to be protected by English Heritage and other organisations that recognise the importance of retaining some notable examples.

Of course, the Second World War just acted as another phase in the development of other airfields. Since then the airfields have embraced civilian aviation and today they are the sites of the major London and regional airports across the British Isles.

Other airfields have regressed; they were originally small, private flying clubs and were intensely developed during the Second World War. After the RAF left them in the late-1940s many of the facilities were demolished and, once again, they have only basic facilities.

Some of the sites are now completely gone and are beneath factories, housing estates, sports fields, leisure parks, golf clubs and racing tracks. Others had so very little of a permanent nature that they have been erased, such as the numerous seaplane bases and many of the emergency landing fields in the south.

There is a small and highly dedicated group of individuals who have visited as many of these sites as possible and, at times, have been able to photograph the last vestiges of these airfields before they are lost forever. It is still possible to visit many of the sites and find, amidst farmland and in overgrown areas, structures that were of vital importance to the defence of this country and, ultimately, as a springboard to victory in 1945.

Chapter One

# The Battle of Britain Airfields

## The fall of France

ON 10th May, 1940 German troops invaded France. Although the attempts to defend Britain's closest geographical ally failed and the losses suffered by the RAF were huge, there was an even greater danger. Despite the fact that Hitler wanted to negotiate peace with Britain it was clear that he was planning an amphibious assault across the English Channel. There were two key forces that aimed to prevent him from achieving this goal. He needed to gain air superiority over the English Channel and the southeast of England. Having achieved this would make it impossible for the vastly superior Royal Navy to risk trying to stop the German landings. This meant that the German Luftwaffe had to create the conditions under which Operation Sea Lion, as it was known, could take place.

A raid against the Luftwaffe that had swept Polish, French and British aircraft out of the skies over mainland Europe had left a seriously depleted Royal Air Force. In the summer of 1940 the RAF could muster around 9,000 pilots and 5,000 aircraft. The problem was that the majority of these aircraft were bombers and trained fighter

On 1st July Britain could muster around 1,103 fighter pilots. Many of these had very little flight training and were largely inexperienced. The Luftwaffe had at least 1,450 highly experienced pilots.

pilots were in seriously short supply. Britain was producing around 300 aircraft a week but only 200 pilots were coming out of training school.

## The Battle of Britain

In July 1940 the Luftwaffe resumed its aerial assault by hitting British convoys and ports. In the following month they shifted their emphasis and began attacking RAF airfields. They also attempted to destroy the aircraft industry.

It was not only British pilots that faced the onslaught; there were also Americans, Australians, New Zealanders, Czechs, Poles, Belgians, South Africans, French, Irish and British from Palestine and Rhodesia.

There were four distinct phases in the Battle of Britain:

- 10th July to 11th August – the Luftwaffe attacked shipping and ports around the English Channel
- 12th August to 23rd August – attacks on RAF airfields in the coastal areas
- 24th August to 6th September – RAF airfields across the southeast of England came under attack
- 7th September to the end of September – the Luftwaffe targeted towns and cities across the UK

## RAF Fighter Command

To cope with the air defence of Britain, RAF Fighter Command was split into four groups:

- 10 Group – largely located on airfields in order to protect Wales and the West Country
- 11 Group – covering the southeast of England and protecting London
- 12 Group – located around the Midlands and in East Anglia
- 13 Group – protecting the north of England, Northern Ireland and Scotland

It was 11 Group that saw the heaviest engagements during the Battle of Britain. In order to keep them up to strength, many pilots were shifted from other groups as replacements. Each of the groups operated from a number of different airfields. They were ably assisted by elements of Bomber Command and, crucially, the RAF Air Sea Rescue was on hand to save the valuable pilots and return them to their units as quickly as possible.

## 10 Group

### Boscombe Down, Amesbury, Wiltshire

Boscombe Down was home to RAF No 249 Squadron, although it had formerly been used to evaluate aircraft. It was actually opened in October 1917 and the Royal Flying Corps used it, along with American pilots. After the First World War some of the buildings were retained, but much of the field returned to farm use. It was reopened in 1930, during a period of expansion by the RAF, and Bomber squadrons trained there. The airfield was, therefore, designed for light bomber squadrons and for experimental work. It was bombed by the Luftwaffe on several occasions.

Royal Navy Gannet, XL472, parked on the grass at RAF Boscombe Down during the 1990 International Air Tattoo. Behind is the crowd line and the Red Arrows can be seen performing their display. [*Image courtesy of Martin Addison*]

> On 16th April, 1941 a German aircraft bombed the airfield, damaging 14 aircraft and destroying a 15th. The only casualty was an injured pig.

RAF No 56 and 249 Squadrons operated out of Boscombe Down during the Battle of Britain, and post-war new runways were opened up. The airfield returned to its role of experimental work. This is still the case today, where jet engines, helicopters and other equipment are all tested on the air base.

### Box, northeast of Bath, Wiltshire
This was also known as RAF Rudloe Manor. It was built on top of a honeycomb of caves that were created as a result of quarrying for Bath stone. It was, therefore, ideal as a storage point for ammunition. It was used as the headquarters for No 10 Group. Although not strictly speaking an airfield, Box was an important site for communications and administration. The station itself was used by the Royal Observer Corps until 1980. Some of the site was sold off, but some of it remains under the control of the Defence, Equipment and Support part of the Ministry of Defence.

### Colerne, Wiltshire
This served as a satellite field for Middle Wallop and a number of fighter squadrons were based there from 1940. It remained in use by the RAF for many years and was also used by the British Army. It is currently used by the Bristol University Air Squadron and the Royal Signals.

### Exeter, Devon
Originally this was a flying club built in 1937, but in July 1938 it opened as Exeter airport. In 1939 the landing area was enlarged and hardstanding was added. By 1942 there had been even more expansion and during the Battle of Britain period alone several different RAF fighter squadrons were based there. Later in the war it was used as a base by the US 9th Air Force to transport paratroopers landing around the Carentan area of Normandy on 6th June, 1944. During the Battle of

Britain alone RAF Nos 87, 213 and 601 Squadrons operated from the airfield. Immediately after the war, RAF Air Sea Rescue operated from Exeter and it was then home to Spitfires and Mosquitos. The last RAF unit, No 691 Squadron, left the airfield in 1946 when it once again became a civilian airport. Gradually it has built up to become Exeter International Airport, which handles in excess of one million passengers a year.

### Filton, north of Bristol
This was a major airfield during the First World War, being home to the Royal Flying Corps Nos 33, 42, 62 and 66 Squadrons. When the Second World War broke out it became home of the Filton Sector Operations Room and initially home to the Hawker Hurricanes of 501 Squadron. RAF No 236 Squadron was based there with Bristol Blenheim aircraft between May and July 1940. In February 1941, No 118 Squadron operated convoy patrols out of Filton until January 1943. Several other squadrons also operated there during the war and post-war the airfield became an important Royal Auxiliary Air Force base. The base finally closed down in the 1960s. The site is now known as Bristol Filton Airport and is currently under threat of closure, despite the fact that it is home to an air ambulance and a police helicopter. It is proposed that housing be built on part of the original airfield.

Filton came under a sustained attack at around noon on 25th September, 1940. Nearly 60 German bombers, with fighter escorts, were aiming to destroy the Bristol Aeroplane Company's factory on the south of the airfield. Two hundred people were killed in the raid. At that time there were no RAF fighter aircraft based at Filton.

### Middle Wallop, Wiltshire
RAF Middle Wallop is now the Army Air Corps Centre and the Museum of Army Flying. Construction began on the base in 1938 and it was used by a number of RAF squadrons, after initially being used

as a training school in 1940. RAF squadrons belonging to 10 Group, including Nos 238 and 609, flying Hurricanes and Spitfires respectively, were operational during the war. It was later used by Bristol Beaufighters of 604 Squadron, who helped defend Britain during the Blitz, until May 1941. RAF Chilbolton was a relief landing field for Middle Wallop. In November 1943 the US Army Air Force, in the shape of the 9th's 67th Reconnaissance Group, moved in. In July 1944 the Royal Canadian Air Force's 418 Squadron, in their Mosquitos, operated from the base. But in January 1945 Middle Wallop was transferred to the Royal Navy. The RAF got the airfield back in 1946 and it was used by No 164 Squadron and later it was home to 288 Squadron. The Army Air Corps took over in 1954, using it for helicopters. In 1957 the Army Air Corps set up the School of Army Aviation on the site, which is its use to this day.

### Pembrey, northwest of Llanelli, Wales

RAF Pembrey became a base for anti-aircraft gunners in 1936 and over the period 1938 to 1939 it was transformed into an airfield. One of the squadrons operating from there was the Polish crewed 316 Squadron, with their Hurricanes. There was a major factory at Pembrey, run by Royal Ordnance, and as such the area became a magnet for German aircraft attacks. By 1941 it was a training base, but by 1947 operations on the airfield began to slow down although it was still used until 1957. The RAF still uses the station but it is intended that the site will become Pembrey West Wales International Airport in the future.

On 23rd June, 1942 a German fighter pilot named Faber mistook the Bristol Channel for the English Channel. As he was running short of fuel he hunted for an airfield on which to land, still believing that he had just crossed the coast of France. He came in to land at Pembrey and the duty officer at the airfield recognised it as a German aircraft. He jumped onto the wing and took Faber prisoner, armed only with a flare pistol.

### Roborough, near Plymouth, Devon

This was an existing civilian airport and at the beginning of the war it was taken over as a Royal Navy air station. The first RAF aircraft arrived on 1st August, 1940 and they flew defensive patrols around the area. The airfield continued to be used by the RAF until the 1950s, but there were plans to transform it into a civilian airport and in the 1960s Dan Air operated from there until 1965. Jersey Airlines also ran there between 1961 and 1963 to the Isles of Scilly and for a short time, in the 1970s, it was possible to fly further afield from their airport. The airport closed at the end of December 2011.

### St Eval, Cornwall

St Eval was designed to be a Coastal Command base and work got underway in 1938. The airfield officially opened in October 1939. It was used as a base for Spitfires during the Battle of Britain. There was also a meteorological flight operating there throughout the war. Later RAF No 238 Squadron operated from St Eval in their Hurricanes. Aircraft from 22 Squadron, in Beauforts, launched an operation against the German battleship *Gneisenau* on 6th April, 1941 out of

RAF Coastal Command Memorial window at St Eval. [*Image courtesy of Peter Skynner*]

St Eval. In the following year anti-submarine operations began from the airfield, but by October 1942 the Americans were using the airfield in the guise of the 409th Bombardment Squadron, in their Liberators, and engaged on anti-submarine operations. Other American units continued to operate until at least 1943. St Eval, in the post-war period, was still useful for search and rescue, until it was closed in March 1959. What remains of the base is now a communications centre and housing has been built on much of the airfield.

### Warmwell, southeast of Dorchester, Dorset

When construction began in 1936 it was originally known as RAF Woodsford. But there was a 'Woodford' airfield in Cheshire and this name was deemed too similar, hence it became Warmwell. It was designed to accommodate over 1,600 personnel and was home to 609 Squadron during the Battle of Britain. From the period 1940 to 1944 no fewer than 33 different RAF fighter squadrons used Warmwell. Hence the airfield saw a wide range of aircraft, including Spitfires, Hurricanes and Typhoons. The base was designated for US use in August 1942, but it was still being used by RAF units. It was not ideal for bombers, so the idea was to use it as a USAAF fighter base with some 80 aircraft. In March 1943 the 474th Fighter Group arrived with their P-38s. The group consisted of the 428th, 429th and 430th Fighter Squadrons. As it would transpire the 474th were the last of the 9th Air Force's fighter groups to shift to France, which they did in August 1944. The RAF continued to use the base until around 1950. Some of the original buildings, including the hangars, still exist, but sites such as the rifle range have been demolished in recent years.

## 11 Group

### Biggin Hill, southeast of London, Bromley, Kent

Biggin Hill is one of the iconic airfields of the Battle of Britain. Approximately 453 aircrew based there were killed over the course of the Second World War, but the squadrons accounted for some 1,400 German aircraft. It was originally opened for use by the Royal Flying Corps during the First World War. Bristol Fighters of 141 Squadron were involved from 1917 in dealing with German bomber attacks and Zeppelin raids. In the interwar period, despite a period of closure

Lancaster bomber at Biggin Hill during Biggin Hill airshow. [*Image courtesy of Oast House Archive*]

between 1929 and 1932, it was used by a wide variety of different units and additional construction work took place. Biggin Hill was ideally placed as an airfield for the Battle of Britain and, as such, it came under sustained attack between August 1940 and January 1941. It was not until 1958 that the RAF ceased using Biggin Hill as an operational base. In the 1960s it was brought into local government hands and it is now leased as a regional airport. Several of the original buildings still survive, although the long-term future of the airfield is uncertain.

### Croydon, south of London, Surrey

During the First World War there were two airfields close to one another, known as Beddington and Waddon. Just after the First World War these two smaller airfields were combined under the name of Croydon Aerodrome. In the 1920s the airfield was developed to become a civilian air terminal and there were flights to Amsterdam, Paris and Berlin. It closed to civilian aircraft in September 1939 and became an RAF fighter station. Unfortunately for Croydon, after the war, housing encroachment had left little room for expansion and the runways were simply too small to take the type of aircraft and the space that they would need to land and take off. The last scheduled flight left Croydon in September 1959 and the airfield officially closed later that day. Since then the majority of the site has given way to housing and industry, although many of the historic buildings still remain. There is a significant RAF Battle of Britain memorial on the site.

### Debden, southeast of Saffron Walden, Essex

Debden opened in 1937, but it was not until 1940 that it had proper runways. It was an important operational centre during the Battle of Britain and a number of squadrons operated from Debden, including Nos 1, 17, 29, 65, 73, 80, 85, 87, 111, 157, 418, 504 and 601 Squadrons.

In September 1942 Debden was handed over to the USAAF 8th. This saw the transfer of the US crewed RAF Eagle Squadrons Nos 71, 121 and 133 to become the 4th Fighter Group. They would continue to operate from Debden until July 1945 when they moved to Steeple Morden. They were the most successful US fighter group with over 1,000 German aircraft destroyed for a loss of 241. The RAF took the airfield back in September 1945. It was first used for training and then bomb disposal and vehicle repairs. In 1973 one of the Second World War huts became a USAF museum. The station itself officially closed in 1975 and it is now used by the British Army as Carver Barracks.

On 4th February, 1941 a German pilot landed at Debden and headed for the control tower. At that point, he realised that he was not on a German airfield but on an RAF one. He took off again and flew home.

### Detling, northeast of Maidstone, Kent

Originally there was a Royal Naval Air Service base at Detling but the Royal Flying Corps also used it during the latter half of the First World War. It was opened as an RAF base in 1939 and remained open for 20 years. Over its short lifespan it was home to numerous RAF squadrons flying Spitfires, Mustangs, Hurricanes, Tomahawks and Blenheims.

During the Battle of Britain Detling primarily was used as a satellite airfield, mainly for Biggin Hill. The RAF Regiment used it in 1945 and then from 1955 it was used by the British Army, but a phased period of closure began in 1956 and ended in 1959. Some of the site is now the Kent County Showground and other parts have been built on.

> In May 1940 WAF Daphne Pearson saved an unconscious pilot onboard a burning Avro Anson. It still had its full bomb load and could have exploded at any moment. Pearson dragged the pilot clear and she was awarded the first ever George Cross to a WAF.

### Ford, southwest of Arundel, West Sussex

Ford Open Prison now stands on the site of the former airfield. Some of the hangars are now an industrial estate and the runway is used for Sunday markets. Construction of the airfield had begun in 1917 and the Admiralty took it over in 1939, calling it HMS Peregrine. It was still a Royal Navy airfield throughout the bulk of the Battle of Britain but eventually transferred over to the RAF. The RAF handed it back to the Royal Navy at the end of the war and the airfield officially closed in 1958. RAF 23 Squadron operated from the airfield from September 1940.

### Gosport, Hampshire

This was another Royal Naval airfield and primarily used to protect the important ports of Portsmouth and Southampton. Royal Naval aircraft were based there, as were RAF units. Much of the airfield has now been built over but some of the hangars still exist. Housing now covers most of the original air base. HMS Sultan, as the Royal Navy called it, is now used to store helicopters and to train engineers.

### Gravesend, Kent

This was used as a satellite station for Biggin Hill and it had a grass runway. During the Battle of Britain it was home to a succession of squadrons:

- May 26 1940 – 610 Squadron
- July 3 1940 – 604 Squadron
- July 25 1940 – 501 Squadron
- September 11 1940 – 66 Squadron

The airfield was extended over the period 1940 to 1941 and in 1943 the runways were enlarged so that they could handle Hawker

Typhoons. Mosquito squadrons used the airfield from August 1944. In 1956 activities on the airfield came to a close and it was sold off for housing.

### Hawkinge, Kent

This airfield had the distinction of being geographically closest to the Luftwaffe on their bases around the Pas-de-Calais. In fact the airfield was around 10 minutes away. It was also in range of the larger of the German shore batteries. Nonetheless during the Battle of Britain it was home to RAF No 79 Squadron, who arrived there in July 1940. Although the site was closed in December 1958 it is now home to the Kent-based Battle of Britain museum. Today, much of the rest of the site is covered in housing.

### Hendon, North London

Hendon had an association with aviation going back to the 1860s. It was from here that a balloon was launched and the first powered flight took place as early as 1909. The site was then developed into an airfield and in 1916 it was used to train pilots. The airfield was an active one during the Battle of Britain, being home to

Kent Battle of Britain Museum, Hawkinge. Some of the buildings used to house the exhibits. [*Image courtesy of Ron Hann*]

> In the 1920s there were aerial derbies held at Hendon. The race started and finished at the airfield. They were as popular as the horse racing at Ascot.

257 Squadron and 504 Squadron. Officially the airfield ceased operations in 1957. Some of the airfield became housing but in 1972 the RAF Museum opened, using some of the original hangars. Sadly, a unique watchtower was demolished to make way for the museum itself.

### Hornchurch, London borough of Havering

Hornchurch was originally developed to help protect London during the First World War. It was formerly known as Sutton's Farm and became operational in October 1915. It continued to be used throughout the First World War.

In 1920 the airfield was sold and returned to farming, but later in the 1920s it was decided that the site would be ideal for a new airfield. The new air base, which became RAF Hornchurch, opened in April 1928. Aircraft operating out of Hornchurch were controlled from Romford and by the end of 1940 alone the Luftwaffe had attacked the airfield no fewer than 13 times. There were a large number of different RAF squadrons that operated out of the base, but during the Battle of Britain the squadrons operating from Hornchurch claimed 411 enemy aircraft destroyed and the probable destruction of another 235. In the post-war years it was used as an RAF selection centre until the closure in 1962. It then became Hornchurch Country Park in the 1980s. A number of the original buildings still exist in the area.

> Pilot John Slessor, later Sir and Marshal of the Royal Air Force, made the first interception of a German Zeppelin on the very first day that he flew from Sutton's Farm on 13th October, 1915. Lieutenant William Leefe Robinson, also operating out of the airfield, was the first to shoot down a German airship on 2nd September, 1916.

## Kenley, Croydon, Surrey

Kenley was created in 1917 and was used originally by the Royal Flying Corps to test aircraft before they were sent to France for combat operations. Hangars were built that could also hold long-range bombers. The airfield was retained by the RAF and in 1924 there were two squadrons operating from Kenley. Prior to the Second World War there were further developments and two concrete runways were built. The site was attacked on many occasions during the Battle of Britain, the worst of which took place on 18th August, 1940, which wrecked 10 hangars and 12 aircraft. Some of the remaining buildings survive, although the control tower was pulled down in 1978.

The film based on the autobiography of Douglas Bader, *Reach for the Sky*, was filmed at Kenley, as was *Angels One Five*, starring Jack Hawkins and released in 1952.

## Lee-on-the-Solent, west of Portsmouth, Hampshire

Lee-on-the-Solent was originally HMS *Daedalus*, a Royal Naval air station. Flights began in July 1917 and it was seen as a useful addition to the nearby RNAS Calshot. After the First World War it was used for seaplane training. A new airstrip was built in 1931. The base was used during the Battle of Britain to help protect Portsmouth and Southampton. Occasionally RAF units also operated from the airfield and constructions and improvements continued throughout the war. The site was used in the post-war period by the Royal Navy for aircraft, including helicopters. It is now used for a variety of purposes such as a civil airfield and helicopter base for HM Coastguard and it is possible to see many of the original features, including an air watch office that was built in 1942.

## Lympne, south coast of Kent

This was a satellite airfield used during the Battle of Britain. It had been opened by the Royal Flying Corps in 1916 and after the First World War it became a civilian airport. In 1939 the Royal Navy Fleet

Air Arm took it over and named it HMS *Buzzard,* although it was later renamed HMS *Daedalus II.* The RAF took over the airfield in 1940 and it was used by several RAF squadrons during the Battle of Britain. It was used throughout the war and the last squadron left in June 1945. The RAF then handed back Lympne in January 1946. It continued to be used as a civil airport until it closed in 1984. Much of the area is now an industrial park.

### Manston, on the Isle of Thanet
RAF Manston can be traced back to being a Royal Naval station in 1916. It went on to have an 80-year association with aviation. Manston has a number of notable firsts:

- Barnes Wallace tested his bouncing bomb to be used for the dam busters raid in 1943
- The first ever jet fighters were based at Manston
- It once had the longest and widest runway in all of southern England

During the Battle of Britain Manston was home to Nos 600 and 604 Squadrons. The RAF officially left the airfield in 1999. However before that the USAF used Manston as a command base for many of its fighter and fighter bomber squadrons during the Cold War. They had left by 1961. With the closure of Manston it took on the guise of Kent International Airport.

### Martlesham Heath, southwest of Woodbridge, Suffolk
This was originally opened in 1917, primarily as an experimental station to test out new aircraft. It was the most northerly airfield of 11 Group during the Battle of Britain and in 1943 it was turned over to the USAAF. They operated their 365th Fighter Group out of Martlesham Heath from October 1943. They completed their last mission on 7th May, 1945. The RAF wanted to hang on to the airfield and extended the main runway in 1955. Despite this, the airfield gradually wound down and it was closed in April 1963. It then became an industrial estate and part of the airfield is the headquarters of the Suffolk Constabulary.

Old hangars from RAF Martlesham Heath. [*Image courtesy of Oxymoron*]

### North Weald, near Epping Forest, Essex

This was always designed to be a fighter base and operated as such from 1916. It was significantly improved during the 1920s and into the 1930s. By 1939 it was a significant airfield, with long concrete runways and a number of hangars. During the Battle of Britain it was used by RAF Squadrons Nos 25, 56, 151, 249 and 257. Norwegians, and US pilots flying Spitfires also used the site. In 1949 RAF jet fighters operated from North Weald but the last squadron, No 111, left the airfield in 1958. Six years later the RAF abandoned the airfield and it was used for a time, until around 1979, by the army and the Royal Navy. It was then sold to Epping Forest District Council. Nowadays there are still some original hangars and a number of important historic aircraft are based there. The airfield is protected, as it is now listed and it is also home to the North Weald Airfield Museum and a memorial to the pilots who operated from there during the Second World War.

**Group Captain Vincent**
He had shot down a German aircraft during the First World War. By the time the Second World War broke out Group Captain Vincent was considered far too old to be flying a fighter aircraft. Regardless, he took off in response to a raid and shot down a modern German fighter. He is possibly the only RAF pilot ever to achieve aerial kills in both the First and the Second World Wars.

### Northolt, London borough of Hillingdon

This was originally developed during the First World War by the Royal Flying Corps. By 1917 around 50 aircraft were based here and it was used to train pilots. Effectively it was the Royal Flying Corps Military School Ruislip. It was during the Second World War that Northolt took on an active combat role. It was home to the RAF and Polish pilots. Some 30 airmen operating out of Northolt were killed during the Battle of Britain, but they managed to score 148 kills, 52 damaged and 25 probables.

After the Second World War the airfield became a temporary civilian base whilst Heathrow was being built. It was still busy in the early 1950s but when Heathrow opened in 1954 it effectively ceased to be a civilian airport and switched back to military use. The site continued to serve as a major RAF base but shot to fame in 1997 following the untimely death of Diana, Princess of Wales. It was at Northolt that the aircraft carrying her body back to Britain landed. A more notorious arrival flew into Northolt in 2000 in the shape of Ronnie Biggs, who had evaded British police since 1965. Today the future of Northolt is in question and it has been suggested that it could be used as a satellite for Heathrow.

### Rochford, near Southend, Essex

This is now London Southend Airport, but its history goes back to the First World War when it was used by both the Royal Naval Air Service and the Royal Flying Corps to protect London. In 1920 the airfield was closed down and was used as farmland. But it was taken back in 1939 to become RAF Rochford. It was ringed by pillboxes, many of which can still be seen. Fighter squadrons that were operating out of Hornchurch and North Weald used the site as a base and it was subject to several raids until the operations room was closed down in early 1944. In 1946 the airfield was closed and civilian aircraft were allowed to use it again in early January 1947.

As a civilian airport Southend has developed considerably in the post-war years, with notable hiccups when operators such as Laker went bankrupt.

**Nighttime record**
South African pilot Flight Lieutenant 'Sailor' Malan, of RAF Squadron No 74, was the first pilot of a single-engine fighter to shoot down an aircraft at night. This took place on 18th June, 1940. On 25th June he topped his record by shooting two down in one night.

### Stapleford Tawney, Epping Forest, Essex
This was originally known as Essex Aerodrome and used by civilian aircraft, with flights beginning in 1936. The RAF requisitioned the airfield and the site was intended as a satellite station for their North Weald airfield. During the Battle of Britain it was home to Nos 46 and 151 Squadrons. In 1943 it was converted to use by the army and in

**Amy Johnson**
One of the early pilots for Hillman's Airways that operated out of Essex Aerodrome in the 1930s was Amy Johnson. She was a pioneering English aviator. During the war she transported RAF aircraft around the country but on 5th January, 1941, flying an aircraft from Blackpool to Kidlington, she apparently baled out after her aircraft ran out of fuel and she drowned in the Thames Estuary. Her body was never recovered.

1946 by the Royal Engineers. In the 1950s it became a private aero club and is now a privately run pilot training centre.

## Tangmere, east of Chichester, West Sussex
Tangmere was used by the Royal Flying Corps during the First World War as a training base and the American air force also used it for that purpose. After the First World War it was mothballed until 1925 when it was used by Fleet Air Arm. In 1939 it was significantly enlarged and during the Battle of Britain it was used by a large number of different RAF squadrons. But when the Battle of Britain began, four Hurricane squadrons were based there. It was very badly hit on 16th August, 1940 when Stuka dive bombers, protected by German fighters, made straight for Tangmere and virtually levelled the place. Incredibly the station remained in service. In the post-war period it continued to be used by the RAF until the 1950s. As it closed on 16th October, 1970 a Spitfire flew over the airfield to mark the removal of the RAF ensign. Most of the area returned to farmland and houses are also planned for the site. The control tower can still be seen amongst farm buildings. It is home to the Tangmere Military Aviation Museum.

## Thorney Island, near Chichester, West Sussex
The RAF showed an interest in this site in the late 1930s. The airfield was built in 1938 and improved in 1942. It was used first by RAF Coastal Command but in July 1940 RAF No 59 Squadron moved to the airfield, although the squadron that was involved primarily in the Battle of Britain was 236 Squadron. The site was ideally located to hunt German shipping and U-boats and operations continued there until early June 1945. In the post-war period it was still important for flight training and for the Royal Observer Corps as a training camp. This continued into the 1960s and the site was then used for search and rescue missions, but the RAF officially left in 1976. It was then used to house Vietnamese refugees in 1980 and in 1984 the Royal Artillery took over the site. It is still largely used by the Royal Artillery to this day.

## Uxbridge, in the London borough of Hillingdon
Originally the site was going to be a German prisoner of war camp in the First World War, but instead it opened as a hospital in September

1915. The Royal Flying Corps began using it from around November 1917. The RAF began to develop it into a station just after the First World War and it became home to recruit training and, amongst others, the RAF School of Music. It was an important command centre during the Battle of Britain and remained a significant site throughout the course of the Second World War. In the post-war years it was an Olympic village (in 1948) and it continues to be used by the RAF as a significant base, with many of the original Second World War features preserved and open to the general public. Officially the station closed in March 2010, with plans to build large numbers of houses across the site. Nonetheless, the commitment remains to retain all of the historic features and to incorporate them into any future development plans.

### Westhampnett, near Chichester, West Sussex

This is now Goodwood motor racing circuit and the Chichester Goodwood Airport. It was opened in 1940 with four grass runways. During the Battle of Britain it was home to RAF Squadrons Nos 145 and 602. It temporarily closed in 1945 and then was used briefly by the Royal Navy until it finally closed down in 1946.

### West Malling, Kent

This was originally a private airfield and used for air shows in the 1930s. It was taken over by the RAF in June 1940, by which time it was no longer West Malling airfield, but Maidstone Airport. During the Battle of Britain 66 and 141 Squadrons operated from here. In the post-war years it was a victim of cutbacks but was used by night fighters in the 1950s and 1960s and by the US Navy in 1967. Most of the site is now known as Kings Hill, with homes, businesses, schools and a golf course.

> In 1973 the accommodation on the site was used to house 30,000 British passport holders who were of Asian descent. They had been expelled from Uganda by Idi Amin.

## 12 Group

### *Church Fenton, North Yorkshire*

Construction began on this airfield in 1936 and it opened on 1st April, 1937. The first arrivals were the Gloster Gladiators belonging to RAF No 71 Squadron. Primarily, in the opening stages of the war, it was an air base designed to protect the cities of Sheffield, Leeds and Bradford. It was home for a time to American pilots in the RAF, as well as Canadians and Poles. In the aftermath of the Second World War it continued to be used for fighter aircraft and then for flight training. Today the base is home to the Yorkshire Universities Air Squadron (UAS) and the Air Training Corps.

### *Coltishall, northeast of Norwich, Norfolk*

Work began on RAF Coltishall in 1939 and it was then called Scottow Aerodrome. It became a fighter base in May 1940 and was also used by the Fleet Air Arm and by the end of the war had become a Vulcan base in the 1950s. It saw all of the iconic British aircraft, including

RAF Coltishall Hangar, Photo taken on the 'last' day of RAF Coltishall! [*Image courtesy of DI Wyman*]

33

Mosquitos and Lightnings. Jaguars also arrived there in 1974. Coltishall has the distinction of having been the last of the Battle of Britain air bases still in operation, however in 2006 is was scheduled for closure, with the Jaguar squadrons leaving. Some civilian flying did continue for a short time. It was handed over for disposal in 2006. The site is now earmarked for various purposes, one of which is for it to be used to strip down jet aircraft. But part of the site now houses HM Prison Bure, which opened in November 2009.

### Digby, southeast of Lincoln, Lincolnshire
The first pilots to fly from Digby were Royal Naval pilots in training. At this stage it was known as Scopwick but the name was changed to Digby when in 1920 vital aircraft parts were sent to the North Wales base of RAF Shotwick by mistake. The RAF closed the airfield in 1922 but reopened it again in 1924 as a training school. It underwent significant changes in the late 1920s and into the 1930s. In 1937 it became an operational fighter station and its role was to protect Leicester, Lincoln and Nottingham. Some of the squadrons based at Digby were relocated to other satellite fields. It was used to give exhausted Battle of Britain pilots a much-needed break. By February 1941 Canadians were operating out of the airfield and in fact it was passed on to the Royal Canadian Air Force in September 1942. Its geographical location made it important and rotated throughout the period of the Second World War no fewer than 50 different squadrons based there, including the RAF, Canadians, Belgians, Czechs and Poles. They had also been flying a huge variety of different aircraft. It was also an important emergency landing ground for bombers that were unable to find their way home. On one fog-bound night in November 1944 54 B-17s belonging to the USAAF made a landing there. In the post-war years Digby was initially used as a training school and in 1953 the airfield became dormant pending building of new facilities for a signals unit. It is now used as a school by the RAF, the British Army and the Royal Navy.

### Duxford, south of Cambridge, Cambridgeshire
RAF Duxford came into existence in 1918 and was actually built by German prisoners of war. It is now, of course, home to the Imperial War Museum, but it still runs as an airfield for flying instruction and

civilian aircraft. It was used by a wide number of different RAF fighter squadrons during the war and was the home of the commander of 12 Group, Air Vice Marshal Trafford Leigh-Mallory. The USAAF used it from 1943 and it retained its value to the RAF until 1961. The government decided to dispose of the site in 1969. It was initially proposed that a prison or a sports centre be built there, but in the end the Imperial War Museum, the Duxford Aviation Society and Cambridge County Council came together to buy the runway and the airfield.

### Fowlmere, southwest of Cambridge, Cambridgeshire
The RAF and the United States Army Air Service began using the airfield in 1918. After the First World War, in 1923, much of the airfield was demolished, including the hangars. It was to become a satellite station for Duxford during the Second World War and used by RAF Squadron Nos 2, 19, 111, 133 (Eagle), 154, 310 (Czech), 411 (Canadian) and 655. It was then handed over the USAAF who significantly expanded the airfield. From April 1944 it was used by the 339th Fighter Group who remained at the site until late 1945. The RAF then used it briefly in the post-war period and sold it in 1957. The vast majority of the buildings and the runways were demolished and all that remains are a few of the huts.

### Kirton in Lindsey, north of Lincoln, Lincolnshire
This airfield was used from December 1916 until June 1919, initially by 33 Squadron. It was closed after the First World War and not reopened until May 1940. Several fighter squadrons used the airfield to rest for short periods of time during the Battle of Britain. It became home to Squadron No 71, which was mainly manned by Americans. They arrived in November 1940 and remained there until April 1941, moving to Martlesham Heath. The USAAF began using it in 1942, notably the 94th Fighter Squadron, who operated there from June to October 1942. It was also used by the 91st Fighter Squadron for training purposes. They arrived in October 1942 and then made for French Morocco in the December. The RAF began using it again in May 1943 as a training centre. The airfield closed and went into mothballs between 1957 and 1960 but reopened for training between 1960 and the end of 1965. It then was used by the Royal Artillery and

renamed Rapier Barracks. It is now used as an air control radar centre.

### Leconfield, near Beverley in the East Riding

The airfield was opened at the end of 1936 to be used by Bomber Command. Fighter Command took it over in October 1939. In the post-war period it was used by RAF bombers and then Lightnings. Today it is the home of the Defence School of Transport (DST) and called Normandy Barracks.

### Tern Hill, near Market Drayton, Shropshire

The airfield was opened in 1916 and then closed in 1922. It was reopened in 1935 as an RAF base. It was always a relatively small airfield and was primarily used for training and for resting exhausted units. It was also used as a base for RAF fighters intending to protect the North Midlands and Liverpool. In the post-war times the airfield was used for gliding, training and for education. It was then used as an army base. It is still designated a military airfield and mainly used by helicopters.

### Wittering, near Peterborough, Cambridgeshire

This was originally named Stamford Airfield, but as RAF Wittering it opened in 1924. Initially it operated as a flying school, but in 1935 it became a fighter base. Wittering became the most important fighter airfield for the southern part of the East Midlands. In the post-war period it was used by British bombers and it was assigned to Strike Command in 1968. The last of the bombers left in 1976. The base, from 1968 to 2010, was home to Hawker Harriers and from 1970 to 1983 the RAF Regiment. It is now home to the Royal Engineers.

## 13 Group

### Acklington, Northumberland

RAF Acklington was opened during the First World War and was closed in the 1970s. It is now the site of HMP Acklington. Royal Flying Corps aircraft first used the airfield in 1916, at which time it was known as Southfield. The aircraft belonged to 36 Squadron. In the

Second World War, Hurricanes belonging to RAF No 43 Squadron carried out coastal patrol sweeps from the airfield.

In June 1940 43 Squadron shifted south and during the Battle of Britain, on 14th August, 1940, they shot down 15 German aircraft in one engagement over the North Sea. In the post-war years the site was used for armament training but in 1956 helicopters belonging to search and rescue operated from the base. The site was earmarked for the construction of a prison in 1969 and this led to the removal of the runways in 1974 and the helicopters leaving in October 1975.

The commander of 43 Squadron was the then Flight Lieutenant Peter Townsend, who later became more well known for his association with Princess Margaret. Three Hurricanes from the squadron are believed to have shot down the very first German aircraft over England in 1940.

### Castletown, near Caithness, Scotland
This airfield had a relatively short life, opening in 1940 and closing in 1945. Primarily the aircraft based there were to defend the important naval base at Scapa Flow. Castletown opened as an airfield at the end of May 1940 and was to be used as a satellite station for RAF Wick. Just a week later, however, it was re-designated as an operational station and Hurricanes belonging to RAF No 504 Squadron flew in on 9th June. After the Battle of Britain the airfield was host to 124 Squadron in 1941. They provided cover for convoys and launched coastal patrols. In 1943, 282 Squadron was based there and engaged in air sea rescue and 278 Squadron with the same purpose in 1944. The last aircraft left the station in 1945, by which time operations at Castletown had wound down.

### Catterick, North Yorkshire
The Royal Flying Corps used this airfield from 1914. In the interwar years it was used by the British Army, but it was officially handed back to the RAF in 1939. There was also RAF Scorton, which operated as a satellite station for Catterick. From 1946 it was the home of the

RAF Regiment, but in 1994 it was handed over to the army. It is now called Marne Barracks and is part of the much larger garrison at Catterick.

### Drem, East Lothian, Scotland

Originally this airfield was set up in 1916 and called West Fenton Aerodrome. It was used by No 77 Home Defence Squadron until 1917 then it was used as a training depot and, for a short time in 1918, the American 41st Aero Squadron was based at Drem. The Americans called the airfield 'Gullane' and from November 1918 it was known by this name. In the interwar years it was hardly used, but in 1939 the RAF took an interest in it again, renaming it Drem, resurfacing the airstrip and turning it into a training school. The operational aircraft based there were responsible for defending Edinburgh and the Firth of Forth. The primary unit at the time was RAF No 602 Squadron, flying Spitfires.

The airfield was bombed by the Germans in August 1942 and although they managed to damage part of the airfield all they managed to kill was a cow. The Royal Navy were active on the airfield between 1942 and 1946 and in fact it came under Admiralty control

RAF Drem: Park Hills. Surviving buildings with blast walls from the WWII fighter base that occupied a lot of land around Fenton. The buildings are used for cattle shelters now. [*Image courtesy of Richard Webb*]

The Spitfires out of Drem were involved in repelling the first German aerial attack on Britain in the Second World War. This took place on 16th October, 1939. Working with 603 Squadron two German aircraft were shot down.

in 1945, when it was known as HMS *Nighthawk*. Drem saw three Ju 52 transports fly in on 11th May, 1945. They were painted white and onboard were the German officers ready to negotiate the surrender of the occupational forces in Norway. The Royal Navy returned Drem to the RAF in March 1946 and soon afterwards the airfield was decommissioned and the land returned to agriculture. Some buildings still remain and there is a permanent museum on the site.

### Dyce, near Aberdeen, Scotland
This is now the site of Aberdeen Airport, which handles over three million passengers a year. This is far removed from the way in which the airfield began its life. It was opened in 1934 and the aircraft belonging to 13 Group based there were initially tasked with protecting the Scottish coast from bombing raids by German aircraft from Norway. It was also used for anti-shipping operations by Coastal Command and for photoreconnaissance aircraft. The airfield was identified for civilian transport in 1947 and the British Airports Authority took it over in 1975.

### Grangemouth, northeast of Falkirk, Scotland
This airfield had a very short life as a civilian air training school between May and September 1939. It was requisitioned by the RAF and until March 1941 it was used by Nos 141, 263 and 602 Squadrons. The runway was extended in mid-1942. It retained its use for training until the RAF closed the site in 1955. Much of the site is now an oil refinery and another part a housing estate. A handful of hangars still survive and one of the runways is now a road.

### Kirkwall, in The Orkney Islands
This airfield was originally called RAF Grimsetter and opened in 1940. It was primarily designed so that aircraft operating from the airfield

could protect Scapa Flow. The Royal Navy took over the airfield in 1943, renaming it HMS *Robin*. It passed into civilian hands in 1948 and is now the main airport on Orkney and provides links not only to the Scottish mainland but also to the Shetlands.

### Newcastle, Tyne and Wear
The site at Kenton Bar was 13 Group's Fighter Command headquarters during the Second World War. The location still exists and it was originally believed that it could be turned into a northern home for the Imperial War Museum. Kenton Bar was an underground operations centre, which became operational in March 1940. Primarily they were involved in protecting the West Midlands, Liverpool and Manchester. The bunker itself was last used in around 2000 by sea cadets. Much of the surrounding area is now a housing estate.

### Sumburg, Shetlands
Sumburg Airport, as it is now known, is the main airport on the Shetlands. The original RAF station had two runways and it was primarily used by RAF No 404 Squadron and their Beaufighters, who launched attacks against German shipping in the North Sea and off the Norwegian coast. The airfield had originally opened in 1936 and was used as a civilian airport and it returned to this purpose 10 years later.

### Turnhouse, near Edinburgh, Scotland
This airfield is now Edinburgh's main air terminal. It is the busiest in Scotland and handles 9.4 million passengers each year. Its history goes

Former RAF Turnhouse. The big hangar, viewed from Turnhouse Road. [*Image courtesy of Thomas Nugent*]

back to 1915, when it was known as Turnhouse Aerodrome. It was the most northerly airfield used by the Royal Flying Corps during the First World War. It was used by RAF Nos 3, 65 and 141 Squadrons during the Second World War and, in order to achieve this, the runway was significantly improved from that of a grass airstrip. In the late 1940s the airfield was turned over to civilian use and in 1947 flights began between Edinburgh and London. This paved the way for gradual expansion over the years, including the construction of an air traffic control tower in 2005, at a cost of £10m.

### Usworth, Sunderland, County Durham

This is another airfield that became a civilian airport, although it did not work commercially and now the site is being used to produce Nissan cars. The civilian airport closed in 1984, but it had opened in 1916 and was used by the Royal Flying Corps. In the interwar years it was largely inactive, although in the 1930s it was used to train the Auxiliary Air Force.

In September 1939 the airfield received a significant facelift, with new runways, dispersal pens and the construction of additional buildings. For a time the airfield was not used but it reopened towards the end of March 1940. In moved 607 Squadron, and in the May Spitfires belonging to 64 Squadron stayed for a brief period of time. A gliding school was formed there in 1944 and the RAF maintained an interest in the site until 1952, when it was sold to Sunderland Corporation. It became a flying club and the plan was to turn it into Sunderland Airport.

Empire Air Day on 24th May, 1934 saw over 6,000 people watch a flying display from the airfield. At the time there were just 14 aircraft in use. The popularity of the air show grew throughout the remainder of the 1930s.

### Wick, north of Caithness, Scotland

Originally this was a civilian airport that served the north-eastern part of Scotland. It ran as a grass airfield from 1933 to 1939. The RAF requisitioned it and it was used by Coastal Command, with a satellite airfield at RAF Skitten. In June 1940, for example, 269 Squadron was making upwards of 150 patrols a month and in the following month they made six attacks on German U-boats. The airfield was raided in late October 1940. In the post-war period it returned to civilian hands and today provides flights to Aberdeen and Edinburgh.

# Chapter Two

# English Airfields

SEPARATING the bulk of the airfields in England from those that were used during the pivotal battle of Britain is not to diminish their importance. The list of sites is extensive and many of the airfields can fall into the following categories:

- Sites that were known to or were in use by the Royal Flying Corps and later the Royal Air Force during the First World War
- Sites that were in continual use since the First World War or before, particularly for RAF Volunteer Reserve pilot training
- Airfields that had already been earmarked or were operational as civilian airfields
- Sites that had either been set up or had become successful and popular private flying clubs
- Areas of land close to existing airfields that could be used as satellite fields
- Sites that were not suitable for long-term development, but which were vital as either emergency or relief landing grounds
- Temporary sites that were requisitioned in the latter stages of the war to be used in support of land forces launching major offensives against German-held Europe

### Abbots Bromley, north of Uttoxeter

Abbots Bromley served as a satellite station for RAF Burnaston at Derby and it was also known as Stone. It was used by the RAF between June 1940 and the end of March 1949. It is still used as a private airfield today. Most of the airfield is now farmland, although there is a former guard room near the old entrance.

Old Control Tower at RAF Abingdon. RAF Abingdon was closed by the Air Force and became a base for Army units. Some small-scale flying and gliding still goes on here and it is open for emergency landings, but nothing that requires this building any more. [*Image courtesy of Des Blenkinsopp*]

### *RAF Abingdon, northwest of Abingdon*

RAF Abingdon is now used by the Royal Logistical Corps and called Dalton Barracks. It was originally opened in 1932 and used by Bomber Command. Shortly after the war RAF Transport Command took it over and it also became a parachute training school. It saw extensive activity throughout the 1950s and 1960s and was used as a maintenance field from 1975. Briefly, it was home to the Thames Valley Police Air Support Unit. RAF involvement ceased in 1992 and in addition to the British Army use it is also used for gliding courses.

### *Acaster Malbis, south of York*

The airfield originally opened as a satellite for RAF Church Fenton. For three months RAF Squadron No 601 operated from the airfield in the beginning of 1942. From April 1942 to January 1943 it was used for pilot training and it then underwent significant improvements to turn it into an airfield suitable for bombers. However the airfield proved to be unsuitable and no squadrons were assigned there. A bomber training unit moved in towards the end of 1944. It closed to flying at the beginning of 1946 and was then used for a time as a bomb store. The control tower still exists in a derelict state but very little else of the airfield remains and the runways have been removed.

### Akeman Street, northeast of Minster Lovell
Work began on the airfield in 1939 and it was intended for use as a satellite for Brize Norton. It actually opened in July 1940 and it was primarily used as a training school between the periods 1942 to 1945. After the bombing of Brize Norton in August 1940, additional training was carried out at Akeman Street. The flight training ended in August 1945 and the airfield was formally closed at the beginning of February 1947. Very little remains of the airfield today, except one of the larger hangars.

### Alton Barnes, near Devizes
The airfield was used for flight training between 1935 and 1945. Five of the airmen lost their lives on two separate dates in 1941, and in September 1999 a memorial was dedicated to them.

Two aircraft collided on 18th June, 1941. The accident claimed the life of Pilot Officer Holmes, who had only just been told that he had been awarded the Distinguished Flying Cross. Two other men, Pilot Officer Gibbons and Sergeant Bate were also killed and the only survivor was Flying Officer Price, who had been in the same aircraft as Holmes and had been his best man two years before.

### Ansty, northeast of Coventry
The site is now occupied by a Rolls Royce aero plant. Between November 1939 and July 1940 it operated as a school for observers and navigators. It was maintained throughout the rest of the war and for a short time at the beginning of the 1950s it was used for flight training. For a year before the outbreak of the war it was a civilian air navigation school. It had also operated for elementary and reserve flight training. It is believed that the airfield closed in 1953.

### Anthorn, west of Carlisle

This airfield had various names, including Cardurnock, Solway House and HMS *Nuthatch*. It is likely that the site began life as a relief airfield or a Royal Navy air station towards the end of the First World War. We know that the military retained an interest with the site until late 1959. The Royal Navy was certainly involved with the running of the base from December 1942, but it was not formally commissioned until September 1944. The site today is a transmitter station and there is also a village on the site, which was previously former Royal Navy housing.

### Appledram (Apuldram), south of Chichester

This airfield would appear to have had a very short life, opening in June 1943 and being derequisitioned in November 1944. The airfield was used by the RAF's 11th Fighter Group as an advanced landing ground. It is not surprising that there is very little left of the site, as the accommodation was tents and there was only one hangar. The land was quickly turned back to agriculture when the airfield closed.

### Ashbourne, south of Ashbourne

The construction of this site began towards the end of 1941 and when it was completed at the beginning of 1942 the intention had been to use it as a satellite station for RAF Seighford in Staffordshire. Instead it was used as a training field and a wide variety of aircraft visited the airfield. In 1943 the airfield was transferred to Fighter Command, where they were involved in marking drop zones for paratroopers on D-Day. In the post-war period it was used to store bombs and ammunition, but the airfield closed in 1954. The site is now occupied by a camping and caravan site, but many of the original buildings still remain, including Nissen huts as well as the runways.

### Aston Down, southeast of Stroud

The Australian Flying Corps used the airfield during the First World War and at that stage it was known as Minchinhampton Aerodrome. It received its name Aston Down in 1938 and underwent significant upgrades in the early years of the Second World War. It then became an operational training unit base and was also a ferry base for aircraft. A gliding club moved into the site in 1967 and they bought it in 1981. There are hangars that were still being used by the military until 2002.

### Babdown Farm, west of Tetbury

The airfield was originally planned out in 1939 and the RAF began night flights out of the airfield in July 1940. The RAF temporarily left the airfield in February 1942 so that improvements could be made and it was reopened in the August, again with night flying, along with training. Spitfires also flew from the airfield in 1943 and later the very bad winter of 1944 caused the partial closure of the airfield. The last aircraft left in June 1945. It was used for storage until the beginning of 1948 when it was officially closed. The site has now been cleared and very little remains of the airfield.

### Baginton, south of Coventry

It was originally planned that the site would be a civilian airport serving Coventry. There was already an aircraft factory on the site that built a variety of aircraft from 1937 until the factory closed in 1965. The RAF moved in during September 1939 and one of the early arrivals was the 308th Polish Squadron, with their Hurricanes, who operated from the base between September 1940 and August 1941. Other squadrons that operated from the base included Nos 41, 79, 135, 403, 457 and 605. There was an attempt to use the airfield for civilian flights in the post-war period but the airfield itself closed in 2009, although it is still home to the Midland Air Museum.

### Bardney, east of Lincoln

Bardney opened in April 1943 to become home to the RAF No 9 Squadron, with their Lancasters. They had been operating from Waddington, and Bardley served as a satellite station. They were to operate from the airfield until July 1945, during which time they lost 85 aircraft. RAF 227 Squadron was also briefly at Bardney in November 1944, as was 189 Squadron in the following month. By 1945 the airfield was being used to store vehicles by the British Army. The airfield had a new lease of life from 1959 to 1963, when it was chosen as a site for Thor missiles. The airfield closed in 1963, however several of the buildings still exist and there is a memorial to 9 Squadron that can be seen near the site of the old airfield.

Memorial on Bardney Village Green

IX Squadron RAF
In memory of all ranks
killed or missing 1939-1945

The squadron flew from Honington, Suffolk 1939-1942
Waddington 1942-1943, & from Bardney 1943-1945
*[Image courtesy of Richard Croft]*

## Barford St John, southeast of Banbury

The airfield was originally opened for flight training and had three grass runways. It only operated in this way from June 1941 to the end of the year. It then underwent significant improvements so that it could be used by Bomber Command. It reopened in December 1942 and until March 1946 was effectively a satellite station for Upper Heyford. In 1946 the airfield closed down but in 1951 the USAF opened a transmitter centre on the site. Many of the original Second World War buildings have been pulled down and replaced with later military buildings. Effectively it is now a satellite for RAF Croughton, the USAF's main communication base in Northamptonshire.

## Barnsley Park, northeast of Cirencester

The airfield opened in June 1941 and remained operational until September 1945. It was certainly used as a satellite landing ground in 1944 although it is not entirely clear when the airfield was closed down. There are still signs of some of the buildings on the site.

## Barrow, Walney Island, to the northwest of Barrow-in-Furness

Barrow, or Walney Island, has a very important place in aviation history, despite its isolated location. Between 1910 and 1920 the site was considered to be the most important British airship production factory. In fact during the First World War it was also used as an airship station and, later, three runways were constructed for use by the RAF. From 1942 it was used primarily for training and over the course of the next four to five years some 5,000 RAF crewmen were trained there. The airfield officially closed in the summer of 1946, but it was not sold off until 1959 when Vickers (now BAE Systems) bought the site. Since 1964 a gliding club has operated from the airfield. It is still an active airfield today.

## Barton, west of Manchester

Barton can claim fame as being Manchester's first airport and it is known as City Airport Manchester, or Barton Aerodrome. It was actually Britain's first purpose-built city airport. It still operates as an airfield and is home to light aircraft, and helicopters. Construction began in the autumn of 1928 and by January 1930 the airfield and a large hangar had been built and the first charter flights took place. It continued to be used for civilian flights until 1938 when many of the scheduled flights were transferred to Ringway Airport. The RAF requisitioned the airfield to repair and overhaul aircraft during the Second World War. They relinquished control by 1946 and it then became home of the Lancashire Aero Club. There was still some RAF

Barton retained the only wartime scheduled air service, running from Britain to the Republic of Ireland, during the period 1940 to 1942. In 1996 the last ever flying de Havilland Mosquito crashed over Barton during an air show.

involvement at the site until 1953, as primary training for the RAF was carried out here.

### Barton-in-the-Clay (Barton-le-Clay), north of Luton

In the late 1930s two private aircraft manufacturers began constructing on the site and a third joined them in 1937. A flying school was established there in January 1938. In July 1940 an elementary flying training school was set up at Luton and Barton-in-the-Clay was as a relief training field. Luton also became home to No 5 ferry pool of the Air Transport Auxiliary. This all-female unit also used the airfield as a training ground. This unit remained on the airfield until it was disbanded in November 1945. Just after the Second World War the airfield was returned to civilian use and much of it became farmland again. The buildings were turned over to industry.

### Battlestead Hill, west of Burton upon Trent

This airfield opened in around April 1941, finally closing in April 1946. Some of the site is now covered with housing whilst the remainder is farmland. It was used as a relief landing ground during the Second World War by RAF Penkridge.

### Beccles, east of Beccles

Also known as Ellough Airfield, or Beccles Airport, this site still operates as an airfield serving the oil and gas industry in the North Sea and some private aircraft. It was originally built to be used by the USAAF and construction was finished in August 1942. American bomber groups that were stationed at RAF Halesworth and Metfield bases intended to use the site. Due to its late completion the USAAF did not need the airfield so it was briefly used by Bomber Command and then by Coastal Command from around August 1944. It was also used by Fleet Air Arm and called HMS *Hornbill II*. An RAF Air Sea Rescue unit also operated from this airfield. The control tower was pulled down in 2009 and it was largely left to fall into disrepair until 1965. Much of the runway has been broken up and some of the ground has light industrial units on it.

### Bellasize, west of Hull

The airfield originally opened as a grass airfield base in April 1916. Aircraft based there were responsible for protecting the Humber

A Spitfire, one of the most iconic planes of the Second World War. [*Image courtesy of Gary Blakeley*]

estuary, which came under attack from Zeppelins. The station itself closed in June 1919 but 20 years later it was reopened and became a flying school and a relief landing ground. Aircraft operated on the airfield until 1945, at which point it was closed and there is very little left to be seen any more.

### Benson, southeast of Abingdon

This airfield is still a home to the RAF, having opened on 1st April, 1939. It would see a variety of different squadrons based there over the course of the Second World War, including RAF Squadrons Nos 103 and 150. It was also used by Wellington bombers, photo-reconnaissance aircraft, Mosquitos and Spitfires. The station was significantly upgraded in the early 1960s and is now home to support helicopters. There was some speculation that Benson would close down, but this does not now appear to be the case.

## Bentwaters, east of Wickham Market

Bentwaters was closed down in the 1990s and is now known as Bentwaters Park and is home to the Bentwaters Cold War Museum. Before January 1943 the airfield was known as Butley. It officially opened in April 1944 and was originally due to be used by Bomber Command. In fact it was used by Fighter Command and several squadrons were based there, including Nos 64, 118, 126, 129, 165 and 234. The USAAF began flying out of Bentwaters in early May 1945. It was officially closed down at the end of August 1949, but it was transferred to the USAF in March 1951. It would be used throughout the Cold War and was initially home to elements of the 7506th Air Support Group and later the 81st Tactical Fighter Wing. American presence continued until 1993 when it was handed back to British control.

## Berrow, west of Tewksbury

The airfield was certainly used between May 1941 and May 1945. It is still possible to see the airfield, as it is used as a private flying strip. The airfield is also known as Pendock Moor and during the Second World War it was used as a relief landing ground for other RAF airfields in the Hereford and Worcestershire areas.

## Bicester, north of Bicester

This is now known as Bicester Aerodrome and there are still many original buildings from the Second World War period in existence. The airfield dates back to 1911 when the first aircraft was landed in the field here. The Royal Flying Corps adopted the site in 1917 and it was used by bombers and fighters until 1919. The airfield closed in 1920 but work began on it again in 1925. It was used throughout the 1930s, mainly by bombers. More squadrons used the airfield during the Second World War, including RAF Squadron Nos 135, 308, 403, 457 and 605. Flying ceased from Bicester in 1944 and in the early 1950s it was used to salvage and repair aircraft. By 1976 the RAF had stopped using the base. It had a brief use by the USAF in the 1980s, but mainly for storage. The Americans returned in 1990 and again in 1991. The Ministry of Defence still owns some of the site and the British Army trains on the land.

### Bibury, northeast of Cirencester

Originally designed as a relief landing ground for RAF South Cerney, it was used during the Battle of Britain, notably by the Hurricanes of 87 Squadron and the Spitfires of 92 Squadron. The RAF stopped using the airfield at some point in 1944 and it was closed in 1945. Some of the buildings are still standing.

### Binbrook, northeast of Market Rasen

The airfield was closed down in the late-1980s, but many of the buildings are still used as part of an industrial estate. It was originally opened as a bomber station in June 1940. In 1942 it closed so that improvements could be made, allowing it to reopen in 1943. It then became home to the Royal Australian Air Force's 406 Squadron personnel. In the post-war years it saw Canberras, Meteors and Lightnings all based at the airfield. The last unit to remain was RAF No 11 Squadron, when they finally swapped their Lightnings for Tornados.

### Bircham Newton, south of Docking

Bircham Newton opened in 1916 to train fighter pilots with the Royal Flying Corps. In June 1918, 166 Squadron was created at Bircham Newton and provided with long-range bombers. It was planned that they would launch raids on Berlin. This is seen by many as being the birth of RAF Bomber Command. Although they did not launch any raids against Berlin, Bircham Newton was to go on to become a heavy bomber base in 1923. The airfield was substantially rebuilt in 1936 when Coastal Command took it over. From here they carried out air sea rescue operations, along with attacking German shipping and laying mines. After the war it was used for flight training and in October 1946 by Transport Command. Flying continued until December 1962. Bircham Newton briefly reopened in 1965, before it was finally closed. The site is now a construction college and other parts have been turned over to agriculture, although many of the original buildings still remain.

### Bircotes, northwest of Bawtry

The airfield opened towards the end of 1941 and was located alongside a Bomber Command headquarters based in Bawtry Hall.

The airfield was used to train bomber crews. Training took place between November 1941 and January 1943 and it was then decided to upgrade the airfield to make it a satellite station for RAF Finningley. There was further training until the summer of 1944 and it was then used to store equipment until 1948. When the airfield closed it was then turned over to agriculture, although some of the buildings and runways still exist.

### Bitteswell, southwest of Lutterworth

This was originally a grass runway used briefly by Polish pilots undergoing training in the latter half of 1941. It was then closed so that concrete runways and additional infrastructure could be built. The site was close by the Armstrong Whitworth factory, so it could also be used to test fly and distribute aircraft coming out of the factory. Bitteswell operated as a satellite airfield to RAF Bruntingthorpe from mid-1943 to the end of 1944. It then became a satellite for Bramcote until July 1945. After that it became home to transport units and then for the disposal of equipment. Between 1943 and 1983 it was used extensively by the Armstrong Whitworth Company. It was used to assemble and test a wide variety of aircraft. It was bought by a private collector of aircraft in the 1980s and the rest of the airfield was then closed up and has since become an industrial estate.

### Blackbushe, southeast of Reading

This airfield is now known as Blackbushe Airport. It was very briefly considered as a potential airport to serve London, but in the end it lost out to Heathrow. It was originally opened as RAF Hartford Bridge and was not renamed until November 1944. By this time it was being used by Transport Command, who also used it during the Berlin Airlift. The airfield was temporarily closed between 1946 and 1947 but before that it had actually seen many famous faces during the Second World War, including Field Marshal Montgomery, George VI and the Queen Mother and the general and future president of the United States, Dwight D Eisenhower. During the war it had been used by a wide variety of RAF Squadrons, flying Spitfires, Mustangs and Mosquitos. In its current use it saw the US Navy using the airfield in the early 1950s and it went into private ownership in 1962.

### Blakehill Farm, southwest of Cricklade
Blakehill Farm was opened up in 1944 and used by Transport Command. By 1948 it had become a satellite for RAF South Cerney but in 1952 it was returned to farmland. The site is now owned by the Wiltshire Wildlife Trust.

### Blidworth, southeast of Mansfield
The airfield was used for five years from 1940. Very little is documented about this airfield beyond the fact that it was grass and used as a relief landing ground. Aircraft apparently used to be hidden in the nearby woodland. After the war, the site was returned to agriculture.

### Blyton, northeast of Gainsborough
The airfield was built in 1942 and remained open until around 1954. It was originally home to a training unit, for various nationalities including Poles. The site was large and had accommodation for over 2,000 people.

During the time that Blyton was home to 1662 Heavy Conversion Unit, over 50 aircraft crashed in farmland around the airfield.

RAF 199 Squadron operated from Blyton and was engaged in the bombing of Germany in December 1942. By the following year the runways were in a poor state and, as the war continued the RAF ceased using it to fly from and allowed it to become run down. The USAF were handed the base as a potential airfield in the 1950s but it is apparent that they did not take up the offer. Much of the runways were removed and part of the airfield is now known as Blyton Park, home to motorsport.

### Bognor, northwest of Bognor Regis
The airfield opened in June 1943 and remained operational until November 1944. It is probable that the airfield was originally designed to be used by aircraft operating out of Tangmere and Ford. The runway still exists and this is probably due to the fact that for some

time after the war a private business used it as an airstrip until it closed in 1994.

### Bolt Head, southwest of Salcombe

This was a small, grass airfield that was open between 1941 and 1945. RAF Exeter used the site as a satellite airfield, but it was also home to a wide variety of squadrons between 1940 and 1944, flying primarily Spitfires, Typhoons and Lysanders. There is a handwritten memorial to those who died flying out of RAF Bolt Head in the Malborough Parish Church. It contains 17 names, most of who were killed in 1944.

### Booker, southwest of High Wycombe

This is now Wycombe Air Park, which is used by flying clubs and gliders. The future of the aerodrome is in question, as it has been suggested that it will be turned into a sports venue. The airfield opened for flight training in 1941 having been a civilian flying school before the war. The wartime flying school used Tiger Moths and Miles Magisters. By May 1942 it was also being used to train glider pilots. The site was again used by private fliers in the post-war period, but the RAF still retained a presence there until 1963. It became privately run in 1965.

### Boulmer, northeast of Alnwick

Boulmer is home to the School of Aerospace Battle Management, the Aerospace Surveillance and Control System Force Command and 202 Squadron Search and Rescue. The airfield began life in a fairly modest way, as a diversion field for RAF Acklington. By March 1943 it was being used as a proper satellite airfield and then by the end of the year it had become a training school. From around 1950 it became an integral part of the air defences and this trend continued until the current day. It is expected that the site will avoid cost-cutting and will remain open.

### Bourn, west of Cambridge

Bourn opened as a satellite airfield for RAF Oakington in 1940 and was then primarily used for training. It came under its first attack in April 1941. The airfield could consider itself to be fully operational by February 1942 and it was now home to the Wellingtons of RAF 101 Squadron. The airfield still retained its training role, seeing a wide variety of different aircraft. The squadrons operating from Bourn launched their last operation on 4th April, 1945.

Former RAF Booker from the air. [*Image courtesy of Thomas Nugent*]

Bourn had effectively been mothballed by 1947. From 1948 to 1961 sections of land were sold off. Part of the runway, however, is still used to this day by light aircraft and the runways host Bourn Market each bank holiday.

RAF 97 Squadron was operating out of Bourn when they were launched against Berlin on the night of 16th to 17th December, 1943. Twenty-one Lancasters were involved in the operation; one was shot down over Berlin and eight of the others crash-landed either in woods or fields around Bourn on their return.

## Bradwell Bay, east of Chelmsford

There was a small airfield here in the early 1930s but the RAF took it over in 1939, primarily as a relief airfield. In February 1941 a pair of concrete runways, a dozen hangars and fighter pens, along with Nissen huts, were constructed. It was capable of housing 2,000 personnel. The Royal Canadian Air Force's 418 Squadron flew their Bostons out of Bradwell Bay and later Mosquitos of RAF No 219 Squadron and Spitfires of 124 Squadron.

Most of the airfield is still intact. Some of the site is now a power station, the control tower is a house and farmers use some of the old hangars for storage.

Bradwell Bay was one of only a handful of RAF airfields that had fog dispersal equipment. This consisted of burning drums of petrol, which aimed to raise the air temperature and disperse the fog.

## Bramcote, southeast of Nuneaton

This is now an army base, known as Gamecock Barracks. It was also at one stage run by the Royal Navy and known as HMS *Gamecock*. It was originally opened to help train Wellington crews in the early part of the Second World War. It also saw the creation of four Polish squadrons in 1940. In the period April 1943 to October 1945 it was used to train pilots of Transport Command. The RAF left in November 1946 and handed it over to the Royal Navy. They began flying aircraft out of it in August 1947 and continued through to October 1955. By 1959 the army had control of the base and used it as a training school. The site is now used by the Royal Corps of Signals. The old control tower is used as the Officers' Mess.

### Braunstone, southwest of Leicester

The original airfield operated as the municipal airport for Leicester from 1935. It remained open until March 1946. It is almost impossible to see what remains of the airfield as it is now covered by an industrial estate. The airfield was primarily used as a satellite for RAF Desford and for training purposes. When the airfield was taken out of service in late-1947 Leicester realised that it was too small to develop a commercial airport on the site. Initially it was used as a playing field and a golf course before it was subsequently taken over primarily by an industrial estate.

### Bray, south of Maidenhead

This was also known as Bray Court, and was used as an emergency landing field for flight training. It is believed that the airfield originally opened in June 1929 and closed at some point in 1945. It is now surrounded on two sides by housing. Very little is visible of the airfield today, even from the air.

### Brayton Park, southwest of Wigton

This airfield opened in May 1942 and remained in service until the end of January 1946. It was used primarily to store aircraft, including Spitfires, Halifaxes and Flying Fortresses. There were also numbers of Wellington bombers and there is evidence to suggest that the airfield was linked to RAF Kirkbride. Some of the original buildings still remain, including a hangar and the building that would have been the original guard room.

### Breighton, northeast of Selby

Breighton is still an operating airfield and home to an aircraft museum. There is also air shows held there each summer. The airfield was opened in 1942 and used by the Royal Australian Air Force's No 460 Squadron. It was from here that the squadron launched its first air raid against Emden in mid-March 1942. The RAF left the airfield in 1947 but it was then used as a missile site, with launch pads being built between 1959 and 1963. The RAF relinquished control of the airfield in 1965. For a time the site was used for light industry and a flying club began using the airfield in the early 1980s.

### Brenzett, south of Ashford
This airfield is built on flat marshland and opened in September 1943. The accommodation for personnel was tents but there were five hangars. It is believed that the first squadron to use the airfield was RAF No 122 Squadron, with their Spitfires. In July 1944 elements of the No 133 Wing of the RAF were based at Brenzett, consisting of RAF Squadron No 129, 306 (Polish) and 315 (Polish), all flying Mustang aircraft. They were engaged in trying to deal with the V-1 threat. These squadrons left the airfield in October 1944 and the airfield closed in the December. For a time it was used as farmland but then in 1972, using some of the original buildings, the Brenzett Aeronautical Museum opened, mainly in buildings that had been used to house members of the Women's Land Army.

### Bridleway Gate, north of Shrewsbury
This airfield was opened in October 1940 as a satellite field for RAF Shawbury. It is believed that it closed towards the end of October 1945. There is very little left to be seen of this airfield, as it has been returned to agricultural use, although there are some small, concrete areas still in existence. It is thought to have been used until mid-1944, by which time it had been relegated to a storage area.

### Brize Norton, southwest of Witney
Brize Norton is still a major RAF base and it underwent recent redevelopment so that it could be used as the main embarkation point for British troops heading abroad. The air base was opened in the late 1930s and used for training. The airfield was used for training until mid-1942 when it began its association with gliders and paratroop operations. In fact it was used as a major base during D-Day and British paratroopers left Brize Norton to be dropped by parachute or

by glider around Caen. This role was repeated during the Arnhem landings during Operation Market Garden. Towards the end of 1945 Transport Command took over the base, but in April 1951 the USAF took the airfield over and there was extensive expansion. The Americans stationed bombers at Brize Norton until the last one left in April 1965. The RAF then took back control and it became a centre for RAF Transport aircraft. Brize Norton was important as many of the personnel and aircraft were used during the Falklands conflict of 1982. The air base has remained vital to transport British troops abroad. The airfield is used 24-hours a day and is now home to the RAF Air-to-Air Refuelling Fleet, as well as the strategic Air Transport Fleets.

RAF Brize Norton from the air. The largest RAF base as seen from a Gatwick bound flight from Glasgow. [*Image courtesy of Thomas Nugent*]

### Broadwell, southeast of Burford

This airfield had a relatively short life, being opened towards the end of 1943 and closing in March 1947. It was primarily used by RAF Transport Command. RAF Squadron Nos 512 and 575 operated Dakotas out of the airfield during D-Day. The former was also involved in Operation Market Garden, dropping British paratroopers around Arnhem. It is amazing that RAF Broadwell is so close to RAF Brize Norton, yet it is virtually unknown and now almost completely derelict. The control tower can still be seen and there are sections of the runways still visible.

### Brockworth, southeast of Gloucester

Brockworth is often referred to as Hucclecote, partly due to its location and the fact that this is what it was originally called when it was used by the Royal Flying Corps during the First World War. The site remained open until 1960, but it is now largely covered with a business and retail park. The site is closely associated with the Gloster Aircraft Company. They bought Hucclecote airfield in 1928. Effectively it was used as an aircraft acceptance park and its association with aircraft ended in the 1960s with the closure of the factory and other facilities.

### Brooklands, northeast of Byfleet

Brooklands is an incredibly important airfield historically. This is not because aircraft necessarily operated from there during key moments in the Second World War, but for the fact that it was the major site that saw the building of iconic aircraft. Vickers-Armstrong and Hawker were both based at Brooklands. Vickers built over 2,500 Wellington bombers there and they also carried out all of the tests on prototypes and new models. In fact a Wellington salvaged from Loch Ness in the

> The most significant and longstanding resident at Brooklands was Barnes Wallace. He worked there for around 40 years, during which time he not only designed the Wellington bomber but also the famous bouncing bomb that was used against German dams to such great success in 1943.

1980s went back to Brooklands to be restored. Meanwhile, Hawker was building Hurricanes at Brooklands and over 3,000 of them came out of the factory.

The airfield closed in early 1970 and the site is now a museum and a business and industrial park.

### Brough, west of Hull

This was originally a flying club and belonged to the Blackburn Aircraft Company. It was used for flight training. Today it is known as BAE Brough and was originally opened in 1916, but it is still an active airfield. At various times it has been home to a maintenance unit and was also used by the Hull University Air Squadron for 20 years from 1950.

### Broxbourne, southwest of Harlow

During the Second World War Broxbourne was used for flight training and aircraft repairs. It was also home to the Herts & Essex Aviation Ltd and their aero club.

### Bruntingthorpe, northeast of Lutterworth

The airfield opened in late 1942 as a training centre for Wellington crews. It also saw some test flights in 1945 of the new Meteor jet fighters. The airfield was mothballed between 1945 and the beginning of 1957 when it then became a satellite station used by the USAF. They built an additional runway and in January 1959 B-47s moved in. The Americans left in 1962. The site is now home to the Lightning Preservation Group and air displays are run from the airfield. Several of the original buildings still remain, including the watch office.

### Brunton, northeast of Alnwick

This airfield originally opened in August 1942 and until it closed in May 1945 it was used to train fighter pilots. It was most likely also used as a satellite field for RAF Milfield.

### Burn, south of York

The first squadron that used this airfield in 1942 was the Royal Canadian Air Force's 413 Squadron and their Wellingtons. In late 1943

Burn became a centre for air observation units and they remained there until the spring of 1944. At the same time RAF Squadron No 578 began using the airfield with their Halifaxes. The airfield closed in July 1945, just a few weeks after the squadron was disbanded. The Royal Army Service Corps used the site for a short time, but now the bulk of the airfield is farmland, although a gliding club uses part of the site.

### Burnaston, northwest of Burton upon Trent
This airfield began life as Burnaston Airport and was used by the Derby Aero Club and the RAF Volunteer Reserve. It became home to an elementary training school during the Second World War and was also home to glider pilots from 1942. The airfield was used after the war by Derby Airways and by the RAF Volunteer Reserve. It is believed that the airfield continued to be used into the 1960s, but the site is now completely covered with a Toyota vehicle factory.

### Burscough, north of Ormskirk
The airfield began life as a Royal Naval air station and was called HMS *Ringtail*. It was primarily used by Fleet Air Arm squadrons and large numbers of different squadrons were rotated through the base until May 1946, when the site was used as a storage depot. Some of the buildings were taken over by homeless people after the war. Subsequently, the structures were pulled down and replaced by council houses. What remained of the site was finally abandoned in 1957 and the rest of the site was given over to agriculture and to industry. It is believed that the control tower was probably demolished in 2004, although some of the other buildings still exist.

### Burtonwood, northwest of Warrington
Burtonwood was originally opened in the spring of 1940 and used to store aircraft. Later it was used for repair of American aircraft being used by the RAF. The Americans took over the base in June 1942 and again used it for repair until the end of 1945. It was one of the largest airfields in Britain and especially useful for handling the larger American aircraft. The RAF took back control of the airfield in July 1946 and it was used to store equipment. The Americans also used the airfield from 1948 to 1965. In 1967 it was temporarily used by the US

Army, but by this stage flying had ended and it was officially closed in the mid-1990s. Very little remains of the airfield and the old aircraft hangars were demolished in 2008.

### Bush Barn, southwest of Oxford
This was an emergency landing field that opened in September 1941 and remained open until 1945. It was also used as a satellite station for RAF Kemble. The airfield is also listed as having been used by the Royal Navy to store aircraft from Worthy Down from 1944.

### Caistor, northwest of Caistor
RAF Caistor opened in September 1940 and was largely a relief airfield. It was not in an exactly perfect location from a pilot's point of view and it only had grass runways. Flying ceased from the airfield in around 1944 and it was closed completely in 1945. It had a new lease of life in 1959 when missiles were based there, but these were removed in 1963. Very little remains of the site, as most of it is farmland.

### Calshot, south of Southampton
Calshot's history dates back to 1913 when it was used by the Naval Wing of the Royal Flying Corps. This eventually became the Royal

RAF USAF Burtonwood. These old aircraft hangars were once part of the RAF Burtonwood Airbase where the main runway now forms the base of the M62 motorway. [*Image courtesy of Paul Anderson*]

Naval Air Service. The RAF did not formally take it over until 1918 when the Royal Flying Corps and the Royal Naval Air Service were merged. Calshot was an important seaplane and flying boat station, but it was also a major Marine Craft training and maintenance centre. Many of the members of the RAF Air Sea Rescue and Marine Craft Section were trained at Calshot.

In the immediate post-war years Sunderlands operated out of Calshot and they flew over 1,000 missions during the Berlin blockade. The base itself finally closed in 1961 and eventually became an activity centre, and a base for HM Coastguards and the RNLI.

One of the most famous individuals detached to Calshot was the so-called Aircraftsman Shaw. He is better known as T.E. Lawrence, or Lawrence of Arabia. He was involved in developing vessels that would be used by the RAF Air-Sea Rescue and Marine Craft Section.

### Calveley, northwest of Nantwich

The airfield opened in March 1942 and was used for pilot training until May 1943. It was then used for further training all the way through to May 1946. It seems that the airfield officially closed in October that year. The site is relatively well preserved, with several of the buildings derelict but reasonably intact. Most of the rest of the site is now an industrial estate and farmland.

### Cammeringham (Ingham), northwest of Lincoln

Although there were plans to build an airfield here in 1936, work did not get underway until 1940. It was used as a satellite field for RAF Hemswell. Polish Wellington squadrons were based there from June 1941. In 1943 Stirling bombers of RAF No 199 Squadron arrived and there were also Hurricanes housed there. The airfield got a name change from its original RAF Ingham to Cammeringham in late-1944. By the beginning of 1945 the airfield was in a poor state and its grass runways were almost unusable, so flying ceased. But it was still used for ground training and for Polish resettlement until the station was closed towards the end of 1946.

Ingham's name change came about because there was an Ingham in Norfolk and in Suffolk. Urgently needed spare parts had been sent to both of these locations by mistake.

The bulk of the airfield has now been removed, although the control tower still remains in a derelict state.

### Cardington, southeast of Bedford

This opened in 1915 as a centre for building airships. It was owned by the Short brothers and it became the Royal Airship Works in April 1919 and additional hangars and sheds were built. In October 1930 production ceased on airships and Cardington was reduced to a storage facility. Balloons returned in the mid-1930s with the building of barrage balloons and an attendant training unit. It retained its association with balloons until 1967, as it was home to the RAF Meteorological Research Balloon Training Unit. There was an attempt to bring back airships to the site in the 1980s when Airship Industries used it for test flights and assembly, but they went into receivership in September 1990.

Cardington Airsheds. [*Image courtesy of Matthias Pfeifer*]

### Cark, north of Preston

The airfield was home to target tugs between 1942 and the end of 1944. It was also used for flight training and then by the RAF Mountain Rescue Unit. It is now in civilian hands and is primarily used by the Northwest Parachute Centre.

### Carnaby, southwest of Bridlington

This was opened in March 1944 and had an extremely wide runway designed to enable damaged bombers to land with ease. In fact some 1,400 bombers landed there. It was also used as a fog dispersal centre, where up to 250,000 gallons of fuel were burned in one hour to reduce fog over the airfield. The airfield closed in 1946 and was briefly used as a missile site between 1959 and 1963. It is now an industrial park.

### Castle Bromwich, north of Castle Bromwich

This airfield was used by private aviation pioneers before the First World War. The Royal Flying Corps took over the base in 1914 and considerably improved the infrastructure. The RAF continued to use the site into the 1920s but by this time the airfield was also being used by civilian aircraft again. Business fairs were run on the site from 1920 until the end of the 1930s. It was decided to turn the site into a major aircraft factory at the outbreak of the Second World War and it was run by Vickers-Armstrong. They built Spitfires, Lancasters and other aircraft there. The airfield became a training station after the war and the factory closed down in 1945 to become a car manufacturing plant (later part of Jaguar and Dunlop). Many of the buildings were demolished in the early 1960s and a housing estate was built.

Castle Bromwich factory managed to produce 50 Spitfires a week and over the course of the war they built 12,000 of them.

### Castle Camps, southeast of Haverhill

Castle Camps opened in June 1940 as a satellite form RAF Debden and it would later become a satellite for RAF North Weald. A wide variety of different aircraft flew from the airfield, including Hurricanes, Spitfires, Mosquitos and Typhoons. The airfield itself

Former RAF Castle Camps from the air. The airfield closed in 1946. [*Image courtesy of Thomas Nugent*]

closed in January 1946. A handful of the buildings can still be seen but the majority of it is now farmland.

### Castle Combe, southeast of Castle Combe

This was never a perfect site for an airfield, despite upgrades, as the grass would often become waterlogged. It opened in May 1941 and was primarily used as a landing ground for RAF Hullavington in Wiltshire. The airfield closed in October 1948 but in 1950 it became Castle Combe Circuit, a centre for motorsport. It is still used for this purpose.

### Castle Donington, south of Castle Donington

This is now East Midlands Airport and, as a consequence, most of the wartime airfield has been obliterated, although there are tracks and smaller buildings here and there. Castle Donington was primarily a satellite station for RAF Wymeswold and saw RAF transport units and a gliding school based there. The RAF relinquished use of the site in 1964, although it had been officially decommissioned in 1946. East Midlands Airport opened up in April 1965.

### Catfoss, west of Hornsea

This was a grass airfield that opened in the early 1930s. There was considerable expansion in 1940 when Spitfires arrived. It then became a training centre for Coastal Command. Additional runways were built towards the end of 1942 and it was used to train Beaufighter crews and then as the Central Gunnery School. The station closed down towards the end of 1945. There was some talk about it becoming a civilian airport, but this did not come to fruition. Instead, missiles were based there between 1958 and 1963. It was formally closed once again shortly after this.

### Caxton Gibbet, east of St Neots

It is believed that this airfield opened in 1934, but by 1939 it was being used as a satellite field for RAF Bassingbourn. It was also used as a landing area for a training school that was based near Cambridge. The airfield closed in July 1945 and it would appear that the airfield itself is now farmland although there may be vestiges of buildings, including a hangar.

### Chailey, southeast of Haywards Heath

Chailey was built in 1943 on land known as Bower Farm. It was used as an advanced landing ground for the Normandy landings. There were three Polish-manned Spitfire squadrons operating from the airfield. It was in use until 1945 and it may also have been used to store fuel for a time.

### Charlton Horethorne, northeast of Yeovil

Originally this was called HMS *Heron II*, a training base under the command of the Royal Naval base of Yeovilton, just to the north of Yeovil. It was originally designed to be a satellite station for Fighter Command and it opened in July 1942, but was first used by the Royal Navy. It was formally transferred to the Royal Navy in December 1942 but by 1945 the RAF were using it for storage. It had also become a

> The Plough Inn was located at the edge of the runway and it was demolished, with the pub moving to an old army hut in 1943. The pub remained in the hut until 1955 when the new Plough Inn was built.

satellite training field for RAF Old Sarum. At some point in the late 1940s it was returned to farmland, although the control tower has now been converted into a house.

### Chattis Hill, south of Andover

We know that this airfield was used by the Royal Flying Corps from 1917. It was also used as a Spitfire test site during the Second World War. It certainly remained open until 1948. Interestingly, the First World War site and the Second World War site may be slightly different in terms of their location. The First World War site retains some scarred detailing in the landscape but the Second World War site is almost entirely obliterated under farmland.

### Chedburgh, southwest of Bury St Edmunds

Initially this was a satellite station for Stradishall. Between October 1942 and November 1943 RAF No 214 Squadron was based here, flying Stirlings mainly over Germany. In June 1943 RAF No 620 Squadron was created at Chedburgh and they remained there until the end of 1943, by which time the airfield had become primarily a training base until December 1944. RAF No 218 (Gold Coast) Squadron carried out daylight bombing raids in their Lancasters from here until the end of the war. They left in August 1945 and the following month saw Transport Command aircraft using the base until at least the end of 1946. It is believed that the airfield closed towards the end of 1952. A heavily converted control tower is still being used, although much of the rest of the airfield has disappeared.

### Chedworth, north of Cirencester

Although the airfield closed in 1945 there is a remarkable number of buildings and part of the runways still intact. The airfield probably opened in August 1942 and was used throughout the war as a training

Derelict huts on the disused Chedworth airfield. [*Image courtesy of Terry Jacombs*]

centre. It is also understood that some secret flights were flown from Chedworth in B-17s and B-24s. Some of these flights dropped propaganda leaflets and others were involved in radar jamming.

### Chetwynd, northwest of Newport
This is still an active airfield, which opened in September 1940. It was a satellite ground for RAF Shawbury. The RAF still use the site for helicopter training.

### Chickerell, northwest of Weymouth
In 1918 Chickerell was opened as a satellite field for RNAS Portland. It was also used by American pilots on anti-submarine training courses. For a brief period in the interwar years it was used for civilian flights but in 1936 it was identified as a probable satellite field for RAF Warmwell.

It was from Chickerell that the US pilot John F. McNamara made the first ever attack on a submarine by an American pilot.

It appears that the airfield was derequisitioned in 1959 and that the site is now occupied primarily by housing and industrial units.

## Chipping Norton, southeast of Chipping Norton

This airfield was linked to Middle Wallop as it was used as a relief training ground until the beginning of 1941. It was also used for advanced pilot training and it underwent a major overhaul during 1941 and 1942. The RAF stopped using the airfield in December 1945. It is possible to see some of the watchtower, some of the perimeter track, air raid shelters and the remains of a military hospital.

## Chipping Warden, northeast of Banbury

For most of its existence between July 1941 and June 1945 this was a satellite airfield for RAF Edgehill, RAF Gaydon and RAF Turweston. By 1946 it was being used to store gliders and in 1953 the airfield closed. The site is now used to store vehicles and the remainder is used for industry and farmland.

## Chivenor, west of Barnstaple

From 1995 the Royal Marines have used this as a major base, although it is still also used by the Royal Navy and the RAF. It began life as a civilian airfield in the 1930s and in February 1940 it was decided to build an airfield next to the civilian airfield. Coastal Command began using it in October 1940. In the period 1942 to 1945 its major use was for aircraft undertaking anti-submarine patrols. There was still aircraft at Chivenor in the late-1940s. The RAF continued to use the site throughout the 1950s, mainly for training. Reserve squadrons were held there from the late-1950s until the early 1970s. It was believed that Chivenor would probably close in the mid-1990s, but instead the Royal Marines took it over as their main base.

## Church Broughton, west of Derby

Church Broughton was a satellite field for RAF Lichfield between August 1942 and June 1945. The site was relatively intact until fairly recently, but it has now undergone a great deal of development with a business park located on much of the site. More of the airfield has disappeared under an improved A50.

## Church Lawford, southwest of Rugby

This was primarily used for flight training and No 2 Central Flying School used the airfield between June 1941 and April 1945. It was used by other training units at least until March 1948. In all probability it was closed in 1955, however the original watchtower still remains, as do several of the other buildings.

### Cleave, north of Bude
Mainly target-towing aircraft were operated from Cleave between 1942 and around the end of 1943. In fact the flights that operated here became RAF Squadron No 639 in December 1943 and remained at Cleave until the end of April 1945. Since the war the site has been redeveloped as GCHQ Bude. However some of the wartime concrete track and buildings still remain.

### Clifton, York
The site is now covered with a retail park and housing but it originally opened as an airfield for civilian use in 1936. The RAF requisitioned it in September 1939. An Army Cooperation Unit was based there between August 1940 and March 1943. There were concrete runways built by 1942, allowing it to be used as a repair base for bombers. In March 1943 Fleet Air Arm's 809 Squadron was based there for a month. Fighter Command squadrons were also based there until May 1945. The airfield was closed in 1946 and for a short time civilian aircraft used the airfield again, but demolition of the site accelerated in the 1980s and now nothing remains of the original airfield.

### Clyffe Pypard, south of Royal Wootton Bassett
Situated close to RAF Lyneham, this site was open between 1941 and 1947 and was used for elementary flight training. It would appear that the airfield was still being used into the 1960s. Until relatively recently a large number of the buildings were still in existence. Many of the buildings on the edge of the old airfield remain, although there is little sign of the airfield runway itself.

### Coleby Grange, south of Lincoln
This airfield opened in April 1940 and was originally home to RAF Squadron Nos 253 and 264. By the middle of 1941 it had become a satellite to Digby airfield and home to RAF Squadron Nos 402 and 409. It was also used by the Royal Canadian Air Force's No 410 Squadron. Briefly it was home to RAF Squadron No 307 (Polish) who

left the airfield in May 1945. It was then used for four years from 1959 as a site for missiles. It was finally closed in 1963 and the derelict control tower can still be seen.

### Collyweston, east of Tixover
Originally this was an airfield known as Easton-on-the-Hill and it was opened in 1917. It got its new name, Collyweston, in 1918. During the Second World War it was used by No 1426 Flight of the RAF, which was known as the RAF Waffe. They flew captured enemy aircraft and Collyweston, as a satellite of RAF Wittering, was one of their main bases. The site was later used to store munitions by the USAF and it was designated as an explosives storage area.

### Condover, south of Shrewsbury
When Condover opened in August 1942 it was to be a satellite field for RAF Atcham. When Atcham was completed it was then handed over to the USAAF. As a result, Condover became associated with RAF Shawbury and RAF Ternhill. It was to be used by the RAF for flight training and the station was certainly used until 1945, but not disposed of until 1960. Towards the end of the war and into the late 1940s it was used as a prisoner of war camp, with Germans still being held there in 1947. It is now a riding school and fairly recently the control tower was put up for sale.

### Coningsby, south of Lincoln
Still an active RAF station and home to Britain's front-line fighters, Coningsby is also home to the Battle of Britain memorial flight, which has been at the base since 1976. The base is also involved in evaluating aircraft and weapons. Originally Coningsby was opened up as an airfield for bombers. The first arrivals were RAF No 106 Squadron in February 1941 and No 97 Squadron moved in during March 1941. The airfield underwent major improvements towards the end of 1942 and then, perhaps the most famous Squadron 617, led by Guy Gibson, moved in, operating from the base between August 1943 and January 1944. In the early months of 1944 RAF Squadron Nos 61 and 619 operated from the base and then in April through to November 1946 No 83 Squadron was based at Coningsby. No 97 Squadron was also there until July 1946. The base was used for operational training until

RAF Coningsby (CY), Coningsby. BBMF practice runs. [*Image courtesy of Dave Hitchborne*]

March 1950 and in October of that year until May 1954 there were a number of squadrons based there, including Nos 40, 44, 57 and 149. The airfield was considerably improved again in the mid-1950s. The original Second World War control tower was pulled down in 2007.

### Coolham, southwest of Horsham
Coolham opened up as an advanced landing ground in April 1944 and only remained operational until mid-January 1945. Despite its short existence a number of squadrons operated from the airfield, including Nos 129, 222, 306, 315, 349 and 485. The site is now farmland and very little remains of the airfield.

### Cosford, southeast of Shifnal
This is now a major air museum and home to an annual air show. It is still used as a major RAF base, primarily for technical training. The airfield itself opened in 1938 and was used to train aircraft technicians and a major hospital was built on the site in 1940. It was also used as a return base for RAF personnel that had been prisoners of war. The hospital stayed open until 1977.

### Cottam, north of Driffield
Cottam was originally designed to be used by squadrons operating out of RAF Driffield. It was not ideal as it had grass runways but

concrete runways were put in during 1942. It was never really used as a proper airfield and only occasional aircraft landed there. Ultimately it was used to store bombs. Much of the airfield was demolished in the post-war years, although a handful of buildings and a portion of the runway still exist.

### Cowdray Park, west of Midhurst
Cowdray Park was an offshoot of RAF Lee-on-the-Solent. Before the war it was a private airfield but it was requisitioned in 1941 and primarily used by the Royal Navy to store out of date aircraft.

### Cranage, west of Northwich
A school of air navigation opened on this site in October 1940. One of the airfield's most important roles was to operate as the despatch point for Wellington bombers that were being manufactured at a nearby factory by Vickers-Armstrong. There was a gliding school on the airfield in 1945 and they probably used it until around 1947. The airfield was used for storage until 1958, when it closed.

### Cranfield, west of Newport Pagnell
This airfield now operates as Cranfield Airport and is relatively close to Milton Keynes. The land was acquired in 1935 and the airfield opened in 1937. Better runways were installed over the winter of 1939 to 1940. By 1941 it had become a night fighter training centre. In 1945 it became the site for the College of Aeronautics.

### Cranwell, northwest of Sleaford
Originally, this was a Royal Naval Air Service base that opened in 1916. It is now, of course, the RAF College Cranwell. It is also the headquarters of the Central Flying School. It was from Cranwell that the first ever British jet fighter took off in May 1941.

### Croft, south of Darlington
Croft is now used for the British Touring Car Championship and the British Superbike Championship and is called Croft Circuit. The base opened in 1941 and by 1943 it was a satellite field for RAF Middleton St George. Two Royal Canadian Air Force squadrons operated from the airfield (419 and 427) both with Wellington bombers. The station

itself closed in the summer of 1946. The last squadrons using the airfield were also Canadian, Nos 431 and 434.

### Crosby-on-Eden, northeast of Carlisle
This site now houses Carlisle Airport, which opened in 1960. Originally Hurricane pilots were trained here, from March 1941 through to August 1942. It was then used to train Beaufort and Beaufighter crewmembers and this remained its primary role until August 1944. The airfield was then used by RAF Transport Command until the middle of 1946. Civilian flights ran briefly in 1946 to 1947 until the airfield closed.

### Croughton, southeast of Croughton
This is the home of the 422nd Air Base Group of the USAF. The Americans took over the base in 1950 and they have maintained a presence there to the present day. Effectively it is a major communications centre. The airfield itself opened up in July 1940 and was originally called Brackley. It did not receive its name of RAF Croughton for another year. During the war it was primarily used by training units then belonging towards the end of the war to RAF No 7 Group.

Many of the glider pilots that trained at Croughton were involved in the Arnhem landings and many were killed, captured or wounded.

### Culdrose, on the Lizard Peninsular
The Royal Navy is still using this site, which is appropriate because it opened as a Royal Naval Air Station. It was also known as RNAS Culdrose or HMS *Seahawk*. During the course of the Second World War the squadrons based there were mainly involved in anti-submarine warfare and search and rescue. It is in a similar role, including airborne surveillance that the current base operates.

### Culham, south of Oxford
Opened as a Royal Naval Air Station in 1941, it was known as HMS *Hornbill*. Its role was to accept, check and then despatch aircraft for

Vulcan bomber at RNAS
Culdrose Air Day 2010.
[*Image courtesy of Rod
Allday*]

the Royal Navy. It was used in the post-war period by a photographic unit but it closed in September 1953, becoming a storage base until ownership was transferred to the Atomic Energy Authority in 1960. It is now the home of the Culham Science Centre.

## Culmhead, southwest of Taunton
This was built as an offshoot to RAF Exeter and opened in August 1941. It was initially home to Polish-manned Hurricanes and Spitfires. In 1942 it was home to Czechoslovakian squadrons. All through this period the airfield was actually known as RAF Church Stanton but it was renamed Culmhead in December 1943. By this time it had seen several other fighter squadrons, but in 1944 the Royal Navy took it over and was operating Supermarine Seafires from there. Gloster Meteors operated from Culmhead, mainly for training before being put into front line service. After this the airfield became a glider training school until it was closed in August 1946. It had some military use all the way through to 1999. The site is now an industrial estate

## Dalton, south of Thirsk
This was a satellite station for RAF Topcliffe. It was originally home to RAF Squadron No 102. The airfield was improved in 1942 and was

used by the Royal Canadian Air Force's bomber squadrons. It became a training centre in late-1944 but towards the end of 1945 the airfield was effectively closed and now remnants of the airfield can be seen amongst industrial units.

### Darley Moor, south of Ashbourne
Built as a satellite station for RAF Ashbourne, this site opened towards the end of 1942. It was used for training and flying ceased at some point in 1945. It was then used to store ammunition and was not disposed of until the late-1950s. It is now the Darley Moor motorcycle circuit and microlights also use the site.

### Davidstow Moor, west of Launceston
The airfield was primarily used by Coastal Command. They were engaged in air sea rescue duties and anti-submarine patrols. The main airfield was opened in 1942 and remained operational until December 1945. At this point it became Davidstow Circuit for motor racing. It was home to three Formula One races in the early 1950s. There is a Davidstow Airfield and Cornwall At War Museum near the site and the control tower is still in existence.

### Deanland, northwest of Hailsham
Several squadrons used this airfield as an advanced landing ground during the Normandy landings in 1944. It was only opened in 1943 and primarily used from April 1944 until January 1945. Squadrons that used the airfield included Nos 64, 91, 234, 302, 308, 317, 322, 345 and 611. The site is now used for private light aircraft and it was reactivated as an airfield in 1963.

### Defford, southeast of Worcester
The airfield was opened in September 1941 and used as a satellite station for RAF Pershore. By 1942 it was being used by the Telecommunications Flying Unit and at its high point in 1945 there were 100 aircraft and 2,500 staff at Defford. They tested a variety of radar systems. The unit remained there until 1953. Now the site itself is owned by West Mercia Constabulary.

## Denham, east of Gerrards Cross

During the First World War the site was used as a flight training school. The land was handed back to agriculture in the interwar years but it was looked at again in the 1920s as a potential airfield. Flying began again in 1934 and the site became a private airfield in 1938. It once again served as a training school during the Second World War. After a pause it once again became a private airfield and is now the centre for several flying schools.

## Denton, east of Northampton

This was used from 1940 as a satellite for RAF Sywell. It is reported that the airfield closed in 1945 and very little remains of the original site.

## Desborough, east of Market Harborough

The airfield opened in 1943 and was initially used by a training unit until June 1945. It was then used by transport aircraft through to 1947. It was closed in around 1953. A handful of buildings still remain although little can now be seen of the runways.

## Desford, west of Leicester

This was an emergency landing field during the First World War but it was out of use by 1918. In 1929 it became home to the Leicestershire Aero Club. In the late 1930s it was used by RAF Volunteer Reserves and it was extensively used for training purposes throughout the Second World War. Many Spitfires passed through Desford, as they were assembled there after being manufactured in Leicester factories.

The RAF had seriously cut back on staff and facilities by the middle of 1947, but reservists were still using the airfield and there was a gliding school based there until 1950. It was used again at the beginning of the 1950s to train National Service pilots, but the airfield formally closed in 1953. It was then radically redeveloped, but aircraft returned to Desford in the late-1990s in the form of aerobatic overhead displays. The airfield is now an industrial site for Caterpillar, which has a large factory there.

### Dishforth, southwest of Thirsk

This airfield opened in 1936 and was used to train recruits for Bomber Command. RAF No 78 Squadron operated from the base between September 1939 and April 1941. It was then used as a satellite field for RAF Topcliffe and then for transport aircraft. In the 1960s Leeds University Air Squadron used the field and in 1992 it was transferred to the Army Air Corps. It is now a major helicopter base and was the first base to receive Apache helicopters.

### Docking, southwest of Burnham Market

This was a satellite field for RAF Bircham Newton. It opened in July 1940 and was used by RAF Squadron No 235, with their Blenheims, until May 1941. A number of other squadrons used the site, including Nos 53, 206, 221, 235, 304 and 415. It was a Coastal Command Air Sea Rescue station from June 1943. From late 1943 to the end of 1944 RAF Squadron Nos 415 and 524 flew their Wellingtons on anti-shipping missions from the airfield. It was also briefly used by the Royal Navy towards the end of 1944. The airfield formally closed in 1958. There are still several buildings in existence, although there is not much sign of the runway since it was a grass field.

### Doncaster

Confusingly, there are four airfields associated with Doncaster. The first is the Royal Flying Corps Doncaster, which is now Doncaster Racecourse. This was opened between 1909 and the 1920s.

The second Doncaster airfield was also only a First World War site, opening in 1916 and closing in October 1919. This site is now entirely covered in housing and is literally within hundreds of yards of the Doncaster Racecourse site.

The third airfield was only open briefly in the early 1930s and was a civil airfield. It was also known as Armthorpe and very little appears to remain of this site.

The fourth airfield is now the home of the South Yorkshire Aircraft Museum, which is actually on the site of the longer-standing RAF Doncaster, which was open from May 1934 to the end of December 1992. This airfield was home to RAF No 616 Squadron. Not only were they involved in the Battle of Britain, but they were also the first squadron to get the Gloster Meteor jet fighter. The original RAF buildings now house the museum.

## Donna Nook, southeast of Grimsby
From the late-1920s the airfield was used as a landing ground for RAF North Cotes and as a bombing range. It also served as a decoy field for RAF North Cotes. During the Second World War elements of Coastal Command were based there. RAF Squadron No 206 operated from Donna Nook between August 1941 and July 1942. Although the airfield closed in 1945 it was later reopened as a NATO bombing range, but not before it had been a prisoner of war camp.

In 2002 RAF Donna Nook, owned by the Ministry of Defence, became the very first piece of land owned by them to become a National Nature Reserve.

## Down Ampney, southeast of Cirencester
Down Ampney is most closely associated with RAF Transport Command. Their squadrons 48 and 271 carried British airborne troops into Normandy and Arnhem and then across the Rhine. The airfield is closely linked with RAF Broadwell and RAF Blakehill Farm. It was operational between February 1944 and February 1947. Aerial views of the site show clearly the runways and perimeter track. The site is used for rallying and motorsports and for flying model aircraft today.

## Down Farm, northeast of Chipping Sodbury
Down Farm opened in April 1941 and remained operational until February 1946. It would appear that the airfield was used for flight training, although the site has now been returned to farmland.

## Downham Market, north of Downham Market
Some of this site is now an industrial estate, but much of the infrastructure actually remained until the 1970s, when it was broken up to help build part of the A10. The RAF had opened the site as a satellite airfield for RAF Marham in 1942. It closed in 1946 but was not sold off until 1957. During its short life it was home to RAF No 218 Squadron in 1942 and the following year to RAF No 623 Squadron. Later it was home to 571 Squadron and then 608 Squadron. One of the last squadrons based there was 635.

> During the Second World War some 170 aircraft were lost from Downham Market.

## Driffield, southwest of Bridlington

The RAF finally relinquished this site in 1996, since when it has been used by the army for driving instruction and is now part of the Normandy Barracks (Leconfield). This brought to an end a history that stretched back to July 1918. It was only used for two years and then abandoned until new construction work began in 1935. By 1936 it had been selected as a major bomber base and was home to RAF Squadron Nos 77 and 102. By 1941 it was being used by Fighter Command, with Hurricanes and Spitfires operating from the airfield. Bomber Command returned in the spring of 1941, however, and there were considerable improvements to the airfield in 1943. It was still being used by bombers and the last squadron to leave was the Royal Australian Air Force's No 466 Squadron. Post-war, it was extensively

Entrance to Driffield Camp. [*Image courtesy of J. Thomas*]

> On the second night of the Second World War three Whitleys of RAF 102 Squadron dropped tens of thousands of propaganda leaflets over Germany.

used by training schools but in 1955 it once again became a fighter airfield. In the late-1950s it was home to Thor missiles, which meant that there were considerable numbers of American servicemen on the base. The British Army took it over officially in 1977, but the site was still considered to be an RAF base until 1996.

### Dunholme Lodge, north of Lincoln
To begin with this was used as a satellite for RAF Scampton. It was rebuilt towards the end of 1942 as an airfield capable of taking bombers. The first squadron to arrive was No 44 (Rhodesia) Squadron, with their Lancasters. They remained at the base until September 1944. Also there at the same time was 619 Squadron and 170 Squadron. The airfield was used to store gliders and then, between 1959 and 1964, there was a missile unit based there. The airfield was closed in 1964 and very little now remains of the original site.

### Dunkeswell, northeast of Exeter
This airfield has associations with Fighter Command, Coastal Command, the USAAF, the United States Navy and RAF Transport Command. It only has a very short history, running from 1943 to 1949. It was originally intended to be used by Fighter Command, but in fact the USAAF's 479th Anti-Submarine Group used it for a month from August 1943. It was then used between September 1943 and July 1945 by the US Navy. They trained alongside the RAF. By August 1945 it had been handed over to Transport Command, who were engaged in sending aircraft to the Middle East. Maintenance units were based there from September 1946 to the end of 1948. The airfield closed in February 1949. There are still a number of buildings on the site, including the control tower and various other buildings now being used for light industry.

## Dunsfold, southeast of Godalming

This airfield was actually built by Canadian engineers and was used by the Royal Canadian Air Force between 1942 and 1944. Tomahawks and Mustangs belonging to RCAF Squadrons Nos 400, 414 and 430 all operated from the airfield. RAF B-25s also used the airfield, and towards the end of the war it was used as a base to accept prisoners of war returning home. In 1946 it was taken over by a private company that used refurbished Second World War aircraft but by 1950 the site was involved in the development of the new Hunter jet. The site was taken over by British Aerospace in 1977. The aerodrome was sold in 2002 and it is now a driving test track, a drive-in cinema and it is expected that over 2,500 houses will be built on the site in the near future.

On 2nd July, 1986 Jim Hawkins, British Aerospace's chief test pilot, was killed when his Hawk 200 crashed. The site itself is now better known as being the home to BBC's Top Gear.

## East Kirkby, southwest of Spilsby

This is the home of the Lincolnshire Aviation Heritage Centre. The airfield was designed to be used by bombers and was opened in August 1943. It was home to the Lancaster bombers of RAF No 57 Squadron and also present was RAF No 630 Squadron. It also saw the brief stay of 460 Squadron, who were there for three months before they were disbanded in November 1945. The airfield was briefly used for a four year period by the USAF between 1954 and 1958 but it was sold off in 1970. The site is well preserved and is privately run by two farming brothers.

## East Moor, north of York

East Moor had a short history, from 1942 until 1946; however it saw Wellingtons, Lancasters, Halifaxes, Mosquitos and Spitfires. The airfield was primarily assigned to the Royal Canadian Air Force and their squadrons 415, 429 and 432 all operated from there. The airfield closed in November 1946, at which point it returned to its use as farmland and many of the buildings were demolished.

### Eastchurch, on the Isle of Sheppey

The first pilots to land here were the early aviation pioneers in around 1909. The airfield became the Naval Flying School Eastchurch in November 1910. Eastchurch was still active in the interwar years and during the Second World War it was home to RAF No 266 Squadron. The airfield closed in 1946 and the site is now a prison.

### Eastleigh, northeast of Southampton

Back in 1932 the site was bought to become Southampton Municipal Airport. It became known as RAF Eastleigh, but in 1939 it was renamed HMS *Raven* when it was turned over for use by the Royal Navy. They used it mainly for training and it was handed back to civilian use in April 1946. The site is now occupied by Southampton Airport, the twentieth largest airport in Britain.

### Edgehill, northwest of Banbury

This is also known Shenington and is now a gliding club and farmland. The airfield opened in October 1941 and was used to test the first British jet aircraft, the Gloster Pioneer. It was later used for flight training. The airfield closed in June 1945. Some of the runways still exist and several of the buildings are still standing in a derelict state.

### Elmdon, west of Birmingham

This airfield is now better known as Birmingham International Airport, but it opened in 1939. Back in 1928 Birmingham City Council had identified the site for a municipal airport and there were in fact services to some domestic destinations in May 1939. It was requisitioned and used for flight training and by the Fleet Air Arm. It was also a delivery base for bombers. It reopened for civilian flying in July 1946.

### Elsham Wolds, northwest of Grimsby

The Royal Flying Corps used this site between 1916 and 1919. It reopened in July 1942 and was home to RAF Squadron No 103 until November 1945. At the end of 1943 RAF Squadron No 576 was also based there and from April to December 1945 so was RAF Squadron No 100. It was used by Transport Command in the post-war period, but it closed in 1947.

**Lancaster bomber**
The most famous Lancaster bomber, ED888M2, part of 103 Squadron, made its first operational mission on the night of 4th to 5th May, 1943. By the time the aircraft was retired in December 1944 it had flown 140 missions over Germany out of Elsham Wolds. Unfortunately the aircraft was not preserved and it was scrapped in January 1947.

*Elvington, southeast of York*
The Yorkshire Air Museum now occupies this former bomber airfield that was initially opened as a grass airfield at the beginning of the Second World War. It then received concrete runways in October 1942.

The Station Chapel, Yorkshire Air Museum. The foundation stone for the chapel was laid in August 1995 and the dedication service took place in October 1996, conducted by the Chaplain-in-Chief of the Royal Air Force. Furniture and fittings came mostly from the station church at former RAF Scampton and silver flower vases were presented by RAF Church Fenton. [*Image courtesy of David Dixon*]

It is most closely association with RAF Squadron No 77 who lost half of their men over the course of the war. In 1952 it was handed over to the USAF but they never made it operational and left in 1958. It was then used for test flying but the RAF still continued to use it for training until it was closed in 1992.

### Enstone, east of Chipping Norton
This was a satellite field for RAF Moreton-in-Marsh and opened in September 1942. It was primarily a flight training base and then in the post-war years was used for storage. It closed in 1947 and was sold off. It is now the home of the Oxfordshire Sport Flying Club.

### Eshott, south of Alnwick
Spitfire pilots were trained here from November 1942 until August 1944. The airfield is also known as Bockenfield Aerodrome. In the post-war period the airfield returned to civilian use, primarily for flying schools and many of the original facilities are still being used today.

### Fairford, southwest of Cirencester
This is of course the home of the annual Royal International Air Tattoo. Although it is an RAF station it is used extensively by the USAF. Fairford was built in 1944 and was primarily used as a base to ferry both British and American airborne units into Normandy. Fairford was chosen in the immediate post-war period as an ideal base for the USAF and formally, in 1950, it was transferred to them as a base for their strategic bombers. It underwent extensive improvements in the early 1950s. Fairford is also famed for its involvement in the testing and development of Concorde. Its involvement with their aircraft lasted between 1969 and 1977. Since then, the USAF has used the airfield to support operations in Iraq. In 2009 it was decided that the airfield would be closed and that US personnel would leave the station by September 2010. Effectively Fairford is now a standby airfield but ready to be used at any time.

### Fairlop, London Borough of Redbridge
Fairlop was a satellite station for RAF Hornchurch. It is now part of the area known as Fairlop Waters, which has a golf course and two

lakes. Concrete runways were first built towards the end of 1940 and Spitfires belonging to RAF No 603 Squadron took up residence in September 1941. It saw several squadrons based at the airfield, including Nos 64, 81, 122, 164, 182, 247, 313 and 411. By June 1944 it was part of the balloon barrage defence network around London. This role ended at the beginning of 1945 and the airfield officially closed in the summer of 1946. Since then the entire area has been transformed due to gravel pits.

### Fairoaks, west of Woking
A private airstrip opened on this site in the early 1930s, at which time it was known as Dolley's Farm. RAF involvement began in around 1936 and throughout the course of the war it was primarily used to train pilots. During this time hangars and other buildings were constructed on the site. It retained this role until around 1947; however the airfield was not sold off until 1967, as it had been used for a brief period in the post-war era as a flying school again. The airfield is once again private and home to many different light aircraft. It is also used by helicopters.

### Faldingworth, southwest of Market Rasen
Work began on this airfield in July 1942 and it was first used by crews switching over to Halifax and Lancaster bombers. The most famous unit to serve there was RAF No 300 Squadron. This was a Polish-manned Lancaster bomber unit. They took part in many of the major operations of the Second World War and their last tasks were to drop supplies to civilians in Rotterdam on 7th May, 1945 and to help fly back Allied prisoners of war from Germany. The airfield was chosen in the post-war period as a site for storing nuclear weapons in underground bunkers. It was still retained into the 1990s and not sold off to be used as farmland until 1998.

**Cinema**
The airfield is still very much intact and even the station cinema can still be seen.

## Farnborough, west of Farnborough

Home to the Farnborough Air Show, a spectacular event that last for seven days, the site is also home to the Farnborough Collection, which is a huge archive of air-related artefacts. In all probability Farnborough is the oldest airfield in Britain. It can trace its aviation connections back to 1905, when the British Army used the site as a balloon school. Around 1908 it was renamed HM Balloon Factory. Many aircraft that were used during the First World War were built at Farnborough, at the Royal Aircraft Factory.

During the Second World War its most important role was as the Royal Aircraft Factory once again. The factory later had involvement in the development of the Harrier Jump Jet and Concorde. The site is now a private business airfield but home to the Air Accidents Investigation Branch, the Farnborough Air Sciences Trust and other commercial institutions.

### Farnborough

Farnborough has a number of notable firsts: Cowboy Cody made the first powered flight in Britain from Farnborough in 1908; John Derry was the first to break the sound barrier here in 1948.

## Felixstowe, southwest of Felixstowe

Back in 1913 this was opened as a Royal Naval Air Service station for seaplanes. Aircraft flew out of here during the First World War, hunting German U-boats. In 1924 it became home to the Marine Aircraft Experimental Establishment. They tested a wide variety of flying boats and other seaplanes. By 1937 the airfield was now controlled by Fleet Air Arm and it played in important role in the war in the North Sea during the Second World War. The station finally closed in 1962.

## Feltham, southwest of Hounslow

This airfield was also known as Hanworth Park. During the First World War, aircraft were assembled and tested here. In the 1930s the site once again became an airfield and aircraft were also manufactured there until 1949. The site was sold in 1956 and it is now the Hanworth Air Park Leisure Centre and Library.

**Zeppelin**
In 1932 the German airship Graf Zeppelin landed at Hanworth airfield.

## Feltwell, southeast of Downham Market

During the Second World War the airfield was home to several RAF bomber squadrons. It had opened in the late-1930s. The airfield remained important in the post-war period as the RAF stationed missiles there and, between 1989 and 2003, the USAF based several units at the airfield. The USAF still use the site today.

## Fersfield, northwest of Diss

Originally this airfield was known as Winfarthing but it was renamed Fersfield and built as a satellite for RAF Knettishall. It was used by the USAAF and their B-17 bombers belonging to the 562nd Bomb Squadron. Their last mission was in late January 1945. The RAF used it to launch an attack on the Gestapo headquarters in Copenhagen in March 1945. The airfield was closed in February 1946 and it became a racing circuit. The race meetings subsequently moved to Snetterton Circuit and since then most of the airfield has been returned to farmland, although several of the original buildings still exist.

**Lieutenant Joseph P. Kennedy Jr.**
One of the men stationed with the USAAF at Fersfield was Lieutenant Joseph P. Kennedy Jr. He was the brother of John F. Kennedy, the future US President. His aircraft exploded over Blythburgh in Suffolk.

## Finmere, west of Milton Keynes

Opened as a satellite for RAF Bicester in 1942, this was used to train pilots and crews. In the latter stages of the war it was used to store ammunition, but the base was closed in the summer of 1945. Although the area is very overgrown several of the buildings still exist.

RAF Finmere Control Tower. [*Image courtesy of Chris Lowe*]

### Finningley, southeast of Doncaster
Originally this was opened as a temporary measure in 1915, but its association with aviation would continue all the way through to 1996, although even then it would have a new lease of life as Robin Hood Airport, Doncaster Sheffield, which opened in 2005. The airfield now handles over 800,000 passengers a year. In the Second World War the airfield was used by several different squadrons and by training units. It temporarily closed for improvements, reopening in 1944, at which stage an instructor school had been set up there. The airfield was used by RAF fighters through to 1954 and then by bombers from 1957 until 1969.

### Firbeck, southwest of Doncaster
There was an air club based at Firbeck Hall in the mid-1930s and it was requisitioned by the RAF and became home to RAF No 613 Squadron in November 1940. It was used as a relief landing ground for various training units. Later it was used as a gliding school and the decision was made to retain it in the post-war period, but in the event it was closed in 1948.

### Fiskerton, northeast of Lincoln
The airfield opened in late-1942 and became home for RAF No 49 Squadron and their Lancasters. Later it was home to RAF Squadron

Nos 150, 576 and 625. In the post-war period it was used by the Royal Observer Corps, although it had been closed to flying towards the end of 1945. There is a memorial to the men of Nos 49 and 576 Squadrons near the former airfield.

### Foulsham, east of Fakenham
The airfield became operational in June 1942. Mitchell bombers belonging to RAF Squadron Nos 98 and 180 were the first arrivals. Later RAF Squadron No 514, flying Lancaster bombers, was formed here. Also on the site was RAF Squadron No 192 and, later, 462 Squadron. It closed in 1945 and much of the site is now a chicken farm, although it is understood that the Ministry of Defence hung onto the site until the 1980s.

### Friston, west of Eastbourne
The airfield was only open between 1940 and 1946. It was used by Fighter Command and it was also strategically placed so that it could be used by damaged bombers returning from missions in Europe. It was later used during the Normandy landings and for trying to intercept flying bombs. The airfield is now part of the Seven Sisters Country Park.

### Frost Hill Farm, northeast of Whitchurch
Primarily this was used as a satellite field for RAF Odiham and for flight training, opening in late 1940. It was later used in the post-war period for helicopter training, operating out of RAF Middle Wallop, but it is now farmland.

### Full Sutton, east of York
This airfield opened relatively late, in the summer of 1944. It was home to the Halifax bombers of RAF No 77 Squadron. In late 1945 No 231 Squadron was created here and they probably remained until the spring of 1946. The airfield was largely unused until 1959 when it became a missile site until 1963. The site is now a prison, an industrial estate, and farmland, although some flying still goes on at the former airfield.

### Funtington, northeast of Chichester
This was a relatively short-lived airfield, opening in September 1943 and closing in December 1944. Nonetheless it saw over 25 different

squadrons using the airfield. It was mainly used as a forward base during the Normandy landings and would have seen aircraft come and go very quickly. Most of the site is now a pig farm.

### Gamston, south of Retford
This was opened as a satellite for RAF Rossington in December 1943. It ultimately became a bomber base. The airfield was used as a repatriation centre shortly after the war and then opened once again in 1953 as an airfield, finally closing in 1957. It was used for sports car racing and then in 1993 it became Retford Airport. Consequently the airfield has a number of original features, as well as more modern buildings. The old control tower is now a house.

### Gatwick, London Gatwick Airport
Gatwick is, of course, a major international airport, with around 50 aircraft movements per hour. By 2011 over 33 million passengers were using the airport every year. The site, in terms of aviation, dates back to the late 1920s when Hunts Green Farm was being used as an aerodrome. In August 1930 it acquired its name Gatwick and the Surrey Aero Club took up residence. Later there was a flying school on the site and in the mid-1930s commercial flights from Gatwick were approved.

By 1936 flights had begun from the airfield but in September 1939 the Air Ministry requisitioned the site. It was primarily used to repair and maintain aircraft, but it was also used by night fighters. The RAF rapidly decommissioned the site and there was a time in the late 1940s when the derequisitioning was vital because Stansted could easily have become London's second airport. By 1950 Gatwick's future had been assured. There was still some military attachment at Gatwick into the late 1950s, with some military aircraft being serviced there.

### Gaydon, south of Royal Leamington Spa
Opened in the late summer of 1942, this was a satellite to RAF Chipping Warden. During the war it was primarily used by Wellington bombers, mostly for training but also for some bombing missions and air-sea rescue. The airfield closed in August 1946 and then underwent a period of reconstruction in the mid-1950s. It then became Britain's first V-bomber station. Ultimately it became a

navigation school and then the headquarters of the Central Flying School. The airfield was closed towards the end of 1974. By the late 1970s it was being used to test vehicles. A Heritage Motor Centre has been built on the site and the bulk of the airfield is now owned by Jaguar Land Rover.

### Gransden Lodge, west of Cambridge
This was a bomber airfield that opened in April 1942. Towards the end of 1945 Transport Command took it over and continued to use it until February 1946. It was formally closed in 1955. During the Second World War it was home to a number of RAF Squadrons flying Liberators, Lancasters, Mosquitos, Wellingtons, Spitfires and Halifaxes. The Cambridge Gliding Centre now occupies the site, having moved from Duxford in 1991.

### Grantham, southeast of Grantham
This is variously known as Royal Flying Corps Station Grantham and RAF Spitalgate. It opened in 1915 and it was not until 1942 that it became RAF Spitalgate. Its most significant event during the Second World War was being the staging post for the Polish paratroopers that were belatedly dropped near Arnhem in 1944 during Operation Market Garden. Post-war it was used for recruitment and training and in 1976 it became a Territorial Army barracks.

### Graveley, northeast of St Neots
Graveley was ready for use by 1942 and was initially home to Wellingtons and Lysanders. Ultimately it was used by a Pathfinder unit, who flew Halifaxes against targets in Europe. Later Lancasters and Mosquitos would also fly from this airfield. The airfield was mothballed in September 1945, but the RAF hung on to it for another 12 years. It finally closed in 1968 and was returned to agriculture. The tower has since been converted into a house.

**Graveley**
The 1967 film *The Robbery* featured Graveley's control tower. This was a dramatisation of the great train robbery that starred Stanley Baker.

## Great Massingham, northeast of King's Lynn

Built as a satellite station for RAF West Raynham, this site was home to RAF Squadron Nos 18, 90 and 107. Later it accommodated 98 Squadron and 342 (French) Squadron. It underwent improvements that closed it for just over a year from May 1944 and was then used by a training unit and RAF No 169 Squadron. By August 1945 it was being used for storage. The airfield was sold off in 1958. The runway still exists but most of the other buildings are now gone.

## Great Orton, west of Carlisle

The locals called this airfield Wiggonby and it opened in June 1943. It was to be primarily used to train pilots and crewmen. Consequently it saw Hurricanes and also Air-Sea Rescue squadrons using Warwicks. The airfield was formally closed in August 1952. In the 1990s a wind farm was set up there.

**Foot and mouth disease**
In 2001 this airfield was used to create burial pits for millions of farm animals during the foot and mouth outbreak.

## Grimsby, south of Grimsby

Opened in November 1941, this was home to RAF Squadron Nos 100, 142 and 550. For some time after the war it was used for storage and part of the site is now covered by a bypass, whilst the rest of it is farmland. Some of the perimeter track remains, as does one of the hangars.

## Haddenham, west of Aylesbury

We know that there was a propeller factory here in 1939, but RAF Haddenham, or Thame, would become more closely associated with glider training. It remained here from the beginning of 1941 to August 1942. A pilot training school was also here until June 1945 and in the post-war period a private company bought the airfield mainly to convert aircraft to civilian use. The company remained on site until the 1990s. The site is now still used by gliders and is also a private airfield, whilst other parts are used by industry and for agriculture.

## Haldon, west of Dawlish

This was originally a civilian airfield that was opened in 1929. It was requisitioned 10 years later and used by the Fleet Air Arm from 1941. It does not seem to have been used a great deal from May 1943, although from 1946 it was used as a gliding school. There were attempts to turn it into an airfield once again in the post-war period, but much of the site is now part of the Teignmouth golf course.

## Halfpenny Green, southwest of Wolverhampton

Originally this airfield was called RAF Bobbington, but now it is more commonly known as either Wolverhampton Airport or Wolverhampton Halfpenny Green Airport. It opened at the beginning of 1941 and was used for training air observers and navigators. Between 1946 and 1951 it was effectively mothballed but it reopened again as an air navigation school during the Korean War at the beginning of the 1950s. The airfield was sold into private hands in 1960 and has been developed as a commercial airport capable of handling half a million passengers a year.

## Halton, southeast of Aylesbury

Halton has a long history with the RAF and is still used today as a training base. Military use of the area began as early as 1913 when the Royal Flying Corps used part of the area for training. Halton would go on to be a vital training base for aircraft mechanics during the First World War. In the immediate aftermath of the war the estate was bought to become an officer cadet college. This tradition continued during the Second World War and into the post-war period. In addition to the training during the Second World War at least two squadrons, 112 and 402, both of the Royal Canadian Air Force, were based at Halton.

## Hamble, southeast of Southampton

Hamble was not just one airfield, but two. The Hamble seaplane base was open between 1915 and the 1930s. With a slight shift of position there was a seaplane base there between 1936 and September 1939. The landplane base was open between 1913 and the mid-1920s. It is now covered with industry and housing and was known as Hamble South. During the Second World War the area was primarily used to

Control tower buildings at Wolverhampton Halfpenny Green Airport, Staffordshire. [*Image courtesy of Roger Kidd*]

repair and overhaul Spitfires. Flight training took place in the post-war period and the airfield effectively closed in around 1985.

### Hampstead Norris (also known as Hampstead Norreys), northeast of Newbury

A large number of Wellington bombers and Tiger Moths used this airfield from June 1940. In the latter part of the war it was used to train glider pilots. The airfield had an important role, as it was used as a base to ferry Wellingtons to North Africa. They would fly via Gibraltar and Malta. By 1945 the airfield had become a satellite field for RAF Harwell. It was then used to store ammunition and the airfield was closed in 1946. Very little of the site now remains.

### Hamworthy, west of Poole

Based in Poole Harbour, this was a seaplane base used by RAF Coastal Command. It saw Sunderland flying boats of 461 Squadron of the Royal Australian Air Force and Catalinas of 210 Squadron of the RAF. It is also known as RAF Poole and by the Royal Navy as HMS *Turtle*. The base closed towards the end of March 1948.

### Hardwick Park, northwest of Mansfield

Little remains of this airfield, which is now on National Trust property within the Hardwick Hall estate. The airfield opened in September 1941 and only remained operational for two years. The site, however, was very important because Hardwick Hall was the main headquarters of British parachute troops. In December 1941 the search began for likely volunteers to join the new parachute battalions. Many of the men that would make parachute jumps into Normandy, Holland and across the Rhine passed through this base.

### Harlaxton, south of Grantham

There were three grass runways here from November 1916, because the Royal Flying Corps used the site. The airfield went into mothballs in the interwar period, but it was then chosen as a potential site to protect the East Midlands. It reopened as effectively a training base and satellite field for RAF Spitalgate. In the immediate vicinity the local manor was used as not only the station Officers' Mess, but also as the headquarters of the British 1st Airborne Division in the run up to the Normandy landings. The RAF continued their association with the site in the post-war period, but the grass runways were of no use to jet aircraft and the station closed in 1957. Most of the site is now farmland but there are a handful of smaller buildings still in place.

### Harrowbeer, west of Yelverton

The original site was considered as a civilian airport in the 1930s but the RAF opened it towards the end of 1941. Although they had intended to use it as a bomber base, it was in fact only suitable for fighters. There was considerable expansion of the base in 1942, with RAF squadrons, as well as Polish and Czech units, operating from the base. It was well placed for involvement in the liberation of France and as the operation developed Typhoon units based at Harrowbeer moved across to the continent, to be replaced by Spitfires. Ultimately Harrowbeer would become a satellite airfield for RAF Exeter. The site once again was considered to become Plymouth's airport in the post-war period but this never came to fruition. There are still some parts of the runway and other buildings still visible.

### Harwell, southwest of Didcot

Harwell is now the home of the Atomic Energy Research Establishment and the Rutherford Appleton Laboratory. The airfield was a pre-Second World War Bomber Command station, opening in 1937. From September 1939 to March 1944 Wellingtons were based

Doorway leading to the old admin block at Harwell. [*Image courtesy of Bill Nicholls*]

there and then from March 1944 through to the September it was home to aircraft that would tow British gliders into Normandy and Holland. During 1944 it was also used by the Special Operations Executive. It was still being used by the RAF until the end of 1945, and it then became the Atomic Energy Research Establishment in 1946.

### Hatfield, west of Hatfield

The University of Hertfordshire is now on this site. The main hangar is a sports centre. The site was originally an aircraft factory and RAF pilots were trained there. Aircraft were ferried from this site to their squadrons. In the post-war period it was still being used for flight testing and it formally closed for flying in 1993.

**Hatfield**
The town has several notable firsts: the de Havilland Mosquito flew its first flight from here in November 1940; and the pilot Amy Johnson was based here for nearly two years.

## Heathrow, Heathrow Airport

Back in 1929 the Great West Aerodrome, grass airfield, (also known as Harmondsworth Aerodrome or Heathrow Aerodrome) opened on this site. Heathrow is now the third busiest airport in the world. At one time it was in direct competition with RAF Northolt to become London's main airport. Development of the site to become a major airport did not begin until 1944. The idea was to use Heathrow for flights of military aircraft to the Far East. Before that, however, the RAF had begun using Great West Aerodrome to divert some of their aircraft. In 1943 the aircraft manufacturer Fairey bought up more parcels of land with the intention of moving their factory to Heathrow. Large numbers of bombers were based there in the run up to the Normandy landings but the new airfield was still actually under construction when the war ended. It was decided in the immediate post-war period that Heathrow was sufficiently developed to continue its transformation into London's major airport.

## Hemswell, west of Market Rasen

This was a Bomber Command base, closely associated with RAF Ingham. During the First World War it had been used as a night landing ground. A large number of different units used the airfield before and after the concrete runways were laid in July 1943. The station in the post-war years was a missile site and then a training school. Officially the base closed in 1974 but before that it was a temporary camp for Ugandan Asians that had been expelled from Uganda. Most of the original airfield buildings still exist.

## Henley-on-Thames, east of Henley-on-Thames

This was opened in July 1940, primarily as a relief landing ground. More importantly, it was used as a site for the final assembly and test flying of Supermarine Spitfires. The site was closely associated with

RAF White Waltham and RAF Woodley. The airfield closed in October 1945 but there is now very little remaining, apart from a pillbox.

### Henlow, southwest of Henlow
In the First World War aircraft were repaired on this site. In the 1920s it was an engineering school and Hurricanes were assembled here during the Second World War. In the post-war period it became a training college but even today it maintains its links with aviation and is now known as Henlow Camp and there is also an RAF signals museum on the site.

### Henstridge, southeast of Wincanton
This was a Royal Naval establishment named HMS *Dipper*. The Royal Navy posted several of their squadrons on the base between 1943 and 1946. After a period of being in mothballs between 1946 and 1949 the Royal Navy again began to use it and in the 1950s it was opened as a satellite to Yeovilton. It was then sold and is used today for civilian air traffic.

### Heston, east of West Drayton
This opened as a private airfield in the 1920s and was originally called Heston Air Park.

Even after the outbreak of the Second World War civilian flights still continued, notably to Lisbon in Portugal. Stationed at the site during the war were a secret photographic unit and many fighter squadrons, as well as aircraft belonging to the USAAF. Part of the site is now Heston Services on the M4. The last flight out of the airfield was in June 1978 and the rest of the site is now a golf course, housing and an industrial estate.

---

**Neville Chamberlain**

It was from Heston that the British Prime Minister, Neville Chamberlain, flew for talks with Adolf Hitler in September 1938.

---

### Hibaldstow, southwest of Brigg
RAF night fighters were the first tenants from May 1941. Later Beaufighters were also based here. The airfield was used for training

---

**The forgotten passenger**
Apparently, during the war Margaret Horton, a WAAF, was sitting on the tail of a Spitfire. This was common practice in order to stop the aircraft from overturning on the grass field. The pilot forgot she was there and took off. He soon realised there was a handling problem and luckily he managed to land without injuring the WAAF.

---

purposes throughout the rest of the war and it closed in August 1947 before being sold in the early 1960s.

### High Post, north of Salisbury
Spitfires were test flown from this site. Salisbury was one of the centres where workshops that manufactured the fuselages and installed the engines were based. The remains of the airfield are now to the rear of the High Post Inn. It is understood that the original airfield was opened by the Wiltshire School of Flying in around 1931.

### Hinstock, south of Market Drayton
This was opened as a satellite airfield in October 1941 but it was transferred into the control of the Royal Navy and renamed HMS Godwit in the summer of 1943. It was mainly used as a flying school until the beginning of 1946. The airfield closed in February 1947. The control tower has since been converted into a house.

### Hinton-in-the-Hedges, west of Brackley
Built as a satellite airfield for RAF Bicester, this opened in November 1940 and closed in the summer of 1945. It was mainly used by RAF bombers. Several of the perimeter defence buildings still exist. The site is now run by Banbury Gliding Club.

### Hixon, northwest of Stafford
This satellite field to RAF Lichfield opened in May 1942. It was home to aircrews training for night flying of Wellington bombers. In the spring of 1945 there were additional training units here, but it was

WW2 RAF Hospital, Hixon. [*Image courtesy of Mick Malpass*]

then used mainly for storage until it was closed in 1957. The existing control tower is now used as offices.

### Hoar Cross, southeast of Abbots Bromley
The airfield was used by 51MU, whose job it was to check over new aircraft and carry out any modifications before sending them on to their squadrons. As a result, large numbers of different aircraft flew in and out of Hoar Cross, including:

- Hurricanes
- Typhoons
- Liberators
- Mosquitos

The airfield was open between July 1941 and June 1945.

### Hockley Heath, south of Solihull

This airfield was also known as Box Trees. It opened in 1941 and before that it was a satellite to the training school at RAF Elmdon. Training courses continued throughout the course of the war and the last units to use the airfield left in September 1946. The base closed in 1948 and was returned to farmland.

### Hodnet, southwest of Market Drayton

Nearby Hodnet Hall was used as a hospital during both World Wars but RAF Hodnet opened in June 1941 and remained open until February 1945. Four maintenance units were based there during the course of the war.

### Holme-on-Spalding-Moor, southwest of Market Weighton

This was built as an RAF bomber base and received its first arrivals in the form of Wellingtons belonging to the Royal Australian Air Force Squadron No 458. They remained there from August 1941 to January 1942. More work was carried out on the airfield and it was then used by the RAAF's 460 Squadron and then RAF Squadron No 101. Later RAF Nos 76 and 512 Squadrons also used the airfield. The airfield was used to store bombs until 1951 when it was handed over for use by the USAF. They barely used the airfield and returned it to the RAF in 1957. Blackburn Aircraft used it as a test base between 1958 and 1983. The airfield was then closed but many of the original buildings survive and are now part of an industrial estate.

### Honeybourne, northwest of Chipping Campden

Some of the buildings have survived on this site and are now part of an industrial park. The airfield itself opened in 1941 and was used by a training unit until 1946. When it closed in 1948 much of the site was returned to agriculture, but it was not until the 1960s that the runways were removed.

### Honiley, west of Kenilworth

Night fighters took up residence here in 1941. The airfield was originally called Ramsey. A training unit was based here between August 1943 and March 1944 and it was then used by a signals unit and in the post-war period it was used by the Royal Navy Volunteer

Reserve. The airfield was mothballed in April 1957, closing 11 months later. The control tower was demolished at some point in the late-1960s.

### Hooton Park, northwest of Ellesmere Port

This airfield has a considerable span of history, as it was originally built as a training base for the Royal Flying Corps in 1917. In the interwar years it was still being used by the RAF, but also found a new lease of life as home to an aero club and as Liverpool's main airport. During the Second World War around 10,000 aircraft were either assembled or repaired on the site, but the RAF maintained a Coastal Command unit here, engaged in patrols over the Irish Sea. In the post-war period the factory remained and a gliding club and flying school opened on the site. It was still being used until 1957 by the RAF but in 1960 Vauxhall Motors bought the site. The original hangar is now owned by the Hooton Park Trust. In 2007, a kart circuit opened on the old airfield.

### Hornby Hall, east of Penrith

This was a satellite landing ground that opened in March 1941 and remained open until July 1945. No 22 Maintenance Unit was based here. In the immediate aftermath of the war it was used to house German prisoners of war.

### Horne, northeast of Smallfield

This airfield had a very short life and was an advanced landing ground that was only operational during 1944. There is a plaque near the site which commemorates the Spitfires of the RAF that operated from here between April 1944 and June 1944. These were the RAF Squadron Nos 130 (Punjab), 303 (Koscluszko) and 402 (City of Winnipeg). The airfield is now almost obliterated and returned to farmland.

### Hucknall, southwest of Hucknall

RAF Hucknall is now the home of the Merlin Flying Club, which opened in 1962. The site can trace its aviation history back to 1916. During the First World War it was used by a number of Royal Flying Corps and Royal Naval Air Service squadrons. It became RAF

**German escapee**
Oberleutnant Franz von Werra, an escaped German prisoner of war, tried to steal an aircraft from Hucknall in December 1940. He pretended to be a Dutch pilot. In the film *The One That Got Away*, von Werra was played by Hardy Krüger.

Hucknall in 1918 but it closed the following year. The RAF was back in 1928 and in the remaining interwar years it was used by several bomber squadrons. In 1939 it began a new life, primarily for training pilots. Between 1935 and 1971 Hucknall was used by Rolls Royce for flight testing. Rolls Royce left Hucknall in 2008.

## Hullavington, north of Chippenham
This was mainly a flight training school, but it was also home to the Empire Central Flying School. The airfield opened in 1937 and in the

Headquarters, Buckley Barracks, Hullavington. Formerly the Station Headquarters (SHQ) of RAF Hullavington. [*Image courtesy of Paul Shreeve*]

post-war years was a navigational school. The airfield closed in 1965. A large number of the original buildings still exist, including the control tower. The site is now used by the Royal Logistic Corps and has been renamed Buckley Barracks. The RAF still maintains an interest in the site and uses it for parachute training.

### Hunsdon, northeast of Harlow

This was a Hurricane base for RAF Squadron No 85 when it opened in May 1941. Later in the war it became closely associated with Mosquito squadrons. The airfield closed in 1945 and only a handful of buildings still survive. The last hangar was pulled down over a decade ago.

### Operation Jericho

It was from Hunsdon that Operation Jericho was launched in February 1944. It was a precision strike against the Amiens prison, where hundreds of members of the French resistance were being held by the Germans. Many of the prisoners were able to escape.

### Husbands Bosworth, southeast of Husbands Bosworth

Flying did not begin until the summer of 1944 at this airfield, by which time four hangars had been built along with three runways and other facilities. Essentially it was a satellite for RAF Market Harborough. Bombers flew out of the airfield, including Wellingtons and Lancasters. It is understood that the airfield was decommissioned in 1946 and two years later the site was used to house displaced Polish refugees. Many of them were still there 10 years later. In 1965 it became a gliding centre and in 1996 home to the East Midlands Air Support Unit.

### Hutton Cranswick, south of Driffield

This airfield opened in 1941 and only remained in operation for four years. In this short time there were three runways and eight hangars built. Fighter Command squadrons operated from the airfield. The control tower has been converted into a house and there are several other buildings related to the airfield still standing.

### Hutton-in-the-Forest, northeast of Penrith
This was an airfield that was protected by the local Home Guard and used as a satellite landing ground. It opened in around June 1941 and remained open until 1945. For a year afterwards it was used to store ammunition. All that now remains of the airfield is a building that was used to test machineguns, although at one stage Hurricanes, Mustangs and Blenheims were all maintained here.

### Inskip, southeast of Great Eccleston
Inskip was better known as HMS *Nightjar* and it opened in May 1943 and closed to flying in the summer of 1946. It was primarily used by the Fleet Air Arm and many squadrons operated from there. In the post-war period it became a military communications centre and was also used for training.

### Ipswich, southeast of Ipswich
It was proposed that a municipal airport be built for Ipswich on the site known as Ravens Wood in the 1920s. The airport was actually opened by Prince Edward in June 1930. The airfield was requisitioned during the Second World War and by March 1942 it was essentially a satellite airfield for Martlesham Heath. It saw Spitfires and Blenheims during this time. The RAF ceased operations in the late summer of 1945 and allowed civilian aviation to recommence in 1946.

Various attempts were made to turn it into a commercial airport but by the 1980s it was home to three flying schools, a maintenance company and there were parachute drops being made from the area. More attempts were made to develop the site and it returned to council hands in the late 1980s and scheduled for closure in 1993. The last aircraft to take off did so in January 1998. The facade of the original terminal building was retained in a subsequent housing redevelopment on the site.

### Kelmscott, northeast of Lechlade-on-Thames
This was a relief landing ground for RAF Brize Norton. It was extensively used for preparations for the Normandy landings. It was also used as a relief landing ground for RAF Watchfield. It is not entirely clear exactly when the base closed, but in the late 1950s a navigation beacon was set up in the area.

> **Arts and Crafts**
> Kelmscott Manor was rented by the writer and designer William
> Morris.

### Kelstern, northwest of Louth
RAF Kelstern was originally opened as a night landing field in 1917
for fighters hunting Zeppelins. The airfield closed in 1919 but
reopened in 1943. It was primarily home to RAF Squadron No 625,
who was there between 1943 and 1945. In October 1944 RAF Squadron
No 170 was also based at Kelstern and like 625 they flew Lancaster
bombers. The airfield closed in May 1945. The hangars were sold off
and the runways were broken up.

### Kemble, southwest of Cirencester
This is now known as Cotswold Airport. It is perhaps most famous
for the fact that it was the home to the Red Arrows from 1967 until
1983. Construction work actually began in 1936 and it was an
important maintenance centre during the Second World War. In the
immediate post-war period it was used by RAF Transport Command.
The USAF also used the site between 1983 and 1992 when it was used

Hawker Hurricane, Kemble Air Show, 2009. [*Image courtesy of Brian Robert
Marshall*]

by the British Army, with military flights ending in 1993. The army remained in control of the site until 1995. The Ministry of Defence first leased and then sold the site, with the idea that it would become an airport. It is now home to the British Aero Collection and is used for a film location for many TV programmes.

### Kiddington, southeast of Chipping Norton

This airfield is sometimes referred to as Glympton. Confusingly it was opened as a relief landing ground in 1940 for Kidlington. It was primarily used for training and in 1942 for glider training. The airfield closed in June 1945 and there is very little trace of the airfield today.

### Kidlington, northwest of Kidlington

This airfield opened as a flying school in the 1930s and is now known as Oxford Airport. Initially it was used by bombers belonging to RAF Squadron Nos 106 and 185. For the majority of the war, however, it was a training school and in 1942 was used for glider training. The RAF relinquished control of the airfield in 1951, although private flying had already recommenced by then. Ultimately it became Oxford Air Training School. Several of the original buildings are still in use today.

### Kingstown, northwest of Carlisle

This is alternatively known as RAF Carlisle, although it did not acquire this name until the 1950s. Originally, Carlisle Borough Council opened the site as a municipal airport. In the 1930s, due to its lack of

**Bold escapees**
Leutnant Heinz Schnabel and Oberleutnant Harry Wappler, escaped German prisoners of war who had been held at Shap, strolled onto RAF Kingstown and persuaded one of the ground crew to help them start up a training aircraft. They flew off and even landed at another RAF airfield to refuel. Still lacking sufficient fuel, they turned back from their intended destination of Holland and landed in a field near Great Yarmouth, where they were recaptured.

use, it was only really being used by a local flying club. It was bought by the Air Ministry and opened as RAF Kingstown in September 1938. Although the airfield was perfectly adequate for smaller aircraft, it was not ideal for bombers. As a consequence it was downgraded to a training school. It was closed in 1945, but opened again in the 1950s. It continued its association with the RAF until its final closure in 1996. It has since become an industrial estate.

### Kirkbride, north of Wigton

RAF Kirkbride opened in the early summer of 1939. Primarily it was used to store and maintain aircraft before they were passed on to their squadrons. It was therefore used by pilots to ferry the aircraft. There was also a maintenance unit on site that would retain an association with the site until 1960. The main Officers' Mess is now the White Heather Hotel. Today the site is open for private flying and retains many of the features of the original base.

### Kirmington, west of Immingham

This airfield was primarily home to Wellington and Lancaster bombers. The airfield actually opened for advanced flying training in March 1942. The longest standing RAF squadron to be based there was No 166, who arrived at the beginning of 1943 and remained there until November 1945. By the following year the airfield had been mothballed and the RAF relinquished their control of the site in 1953. After many twists and turns Kirmington finally became Humberside Airport.

---

**Kirmington losses**

During the Second World War, 166 Squadron lost 178 aircraft and 127 of these were Lancasters with the remainder being Wellingtons. There is a memorial plaque in Kirmington Parish Church for the squadron.

---

### Knowsley Park, west of St Helen's

This is now the site of Knowsley Safari Park. The airfield opened in May 1942 and closed in November 1944. It was primarily home to maintenance units. The site, originally owned by Lord Derby, had a long-standing association with the military. It was used as a muster point for troops during the First World War.

### Lakenheath, west of Thetford

Although Lakenheath is more associated with the USAAF and later the USAFE the airbase actually dates back to its use by the Royal Flying Corps for flight training in the First World War. It seems that the airfield was abandoned shortly after the armistice. In 1940, however, it was chosen as a decoy field for RAF Mildenhall. As a result, a runway was built along with hangars and other buildings. Towards the end of 1941 it became the home of RAF Squadron No 149. They would fly 350 missions from the airfield. There was additional building in 1943 and then RAF Squadron No 199 moved in, although 149 was still operating from there.

In the summer of 1944 Lakenheath underwent a massive upgrade; it was to become the home of the new B-29 Superfortresses. The work took over two years. As it was, the war was already over by the time it was ready and the RAF maintained the airfield until 1948, at which point it was transferred back to the Americans. Ultimately it became an important US bomber base and many squadrons have passed through Lakenheath over the years. It has also seen the 48th Fighter Wing who has also had a long association with the airfield. The Americans are still there, as are the 48th, the unit having spent 50 years in Norfolk.

### Langham, northwest of Holt

When the airfield opened in 1940 it was a satellite field for RAF Bircham Newton. By 1942 it had become an airfield in its own right, with new concrete runways. RAF Squadron Nos 521 and 524 operated from the base, as did the Royal Australian Air Force's 455 Squadron and the Royal New Zealand Air Force's 489 Squadron. The airfield was mothballed in 1947 and it was finally closed in 1961. In the following years it became a turkey farm with sheds placed along the runways.

### Langley, east of Slough

Behind the impressive Langley Hall is a large underground operations room. This was used by the RAF as a headquarters and was part of Bomber Command. Significantly, the site was also a major aircraft factory and many Hurricanes were built there. The Hawker factory opened in the late 1930s and remained open until 1958. The airfield was then bought by Ford and ultimately in 1997 the factory was demolished and is now office buildings, warehousing and housing.

### Larkhill, southwest of Netheravon
Although Larkhill is more closely associated with the British Army, the site can argue that it was the very first military airfield in Britain. The site had been developed by private pilots and Larkhill became an army airfield in 1910. Hangars were built and the company involved would later develop into British Aerospace. The men that were involved in flying the first aircraft here would later become the Royal Flying Corps No 3 Squadron, the very first to use aircraft in 1912. The airfield was closed in 1914 but the original hangar still exists. Since then it has retained its association with the British Army. The RAF does appear to have used the airfield in the early part of the Second World War, where it was home to a training unit. They would have used Salisbury Plain for their training.

### Larks Barrow, north of Whitchurch
This is a strange case because the site was identified as a relief landing ground in 1940 and then as an advanced landing ground in 1942. Plans to develop the site, however, were cancelled in 1943 and, apart from being used as a practice landing field, it does not appear that the site was ever used.

### Lasham, south of Basingstoke
This is the home of Lasham Gliding Society who effectively carried on the tradition of gliding from this site from the Army Gliding Club. The airfield was built in 1942 and in 1943 became a Fighter Command base. Several squadrons used the airfield, many of them for very short periods of time, but, nonetheless, the airfield saw Mosquitos, Typhoons and Spitfires, amongst others. The RAF relinquished their control of the airfield in 1948.

Leavesden Aerodrome. [*Image courtesy of Martin Addison*]

### Leavesden, south of Abbots Langley

This former aircraft factory is now a film studio and housing estate. There were two factories and assembly hangars on this site from around 1940. It remained open until 1946 and after the war it was used to service and repair aircraft and, for a time, the site was owned by Rolls Royce. The airfield itself closed in 1994; it had been used by civilian aircraft. Over the course of the war more than 2,000 aircraft had been built on the site.

### Leeming, southwest of Northallerton

Leeming is still an RAF base today, but it began operations in 1940. During the Second World War it saw Lancasters, Stirlings, Whitleys and other aircraft. It was used for night fighters in the post-war period and then as a training school. It has seen many squadrons pass through it over the 70 or so years of its existence.

### Leicester East, east of Leicester

This is the home of the Leicestershire Aero Club. The airfield opened in October 1943 and during the war RAF Squadron Nos 190 and 196 operated from the base with their Stirling bombers. The RAF stopped using it for flying in March 1945 and it was mothballed until its closure at the end of 1947. The airfield, due to its proximity to Stoughton, is often referred to as Stoughton Aerodrome.

### Lichfield, northeast of Lichfield

This airfield was open between 1940 and 1958. A maintenance unit operated from there between 1940 and 1946. Wellingtons and Ansons also flew operational missions from the airfield between the spring of 1941 and the summer of 1945. In the post-war period it was used as a flying school and for further maintenance, but it officially closed in April 1958. It would appear that the majority of the buildings were demolished in the 1980s, since which the site has been returned to farmland, although there is still some industry there.

### Lindholme, southeast of Hatfield

This is now the site of HMP Lindholme, which was established in the 1980s. The airfield was also known as Hatfield Woodhouse. It is reported that the airfield opened in June 1940 and shortly afterwards it became known as RAF Lindholme. RAF Squadron No 50 was initially based there but it was soon joined by the Royal Canadian Air Force's No 408 Squadron. Polish squadrons also served on this base and after some additional building work heavier bombers moved in towards the end of 1942. Units operating from Lindholme were involved in many combat missions over the course of the war and some 76 of their bombers were lost. The RAF retained its interest in the post-war period and Lindholme was home to a variety of different aircraft. There was also a radar base established there. Gliding enthusiasts also used the site and there was an Air Training Corps unit based there for some years.

### Linton-on-Ouse, southwest of Easingwold

Today, the airfield is used for training fast jet pilots. The airfield opened in May 1937, receiving its first squadrons in April 1938. Throughout the course of the war many bomber squadrons passed through this airfield, some for relatively short periods of time, but others were more long-term. Even in the post-war years it retained close associations with a variety of squadrons and saw many of the new generation of RAF jet aircraft.

> **By royal approval**
> Prince William took part in a training course at the Linton-on-Ouse base at the beginning of 2008.

### Lissett, southwest of Bridlington
The airfield originally had three runways and two hangars and opened in February 1943. It was to be a satellite field for RAF Catfoss. It was home to RAF Squadron No 158 that remained there until the summer of 1945. Today the site houses a wind farm but there is a memorial to the 851 members of RAF Squadron 158 that were killed or pronounced missing in action during the course of the Second World War.

### Little Rissington, southeast of Bourton-on-the-Water
The airfield was opened in 1938 but proper runways were not installed until 1942. It would be primarily used for flight training and for the storage of aircraft. In the post-war years it was the RAF Central Flying School and it was home to the Red Arrows. In the late 1970s it was used by the British Army and renamed Imjin Barracks. The USAF used the site between 1981 and 1993 and it was then decided that the airfield would be surplus to requirements. Several of the buildings became part of a business park. There was a change of heart in 2008 and it would appear that Little Rissington will continue to have military connections. It is still being used today for aircraft maintenance and flight training.

### Little Snoring, northeast of Fakenham
In the period 1943 to 1945 this airfield saw Mosquitos, Lancasters and Beaufighters all operating out of it. The last squadron, RAF No 141, left in September 1945. For a time, it was mothballed and then finally sold off in 1958. The site is now used by private aircraft.

### Little Staughton, northwest of St Neots
This was built for the RAF but allocated to the USAAF in May 1942. It was officially transferred to them a year later and was used for the repair of B-17s. It did not suit the Americans' purpose, mainly due to

its location and consequently the RAF took it back in March 1944. Lancasters and Mosquitos flew out of the airfield and the last sortie took place on the night of 2nd/3rd May, 1945. In the post-war years, the Americans extended the runway so that it could be used as an emergency airfield. The site is now used by private aircraft, whilst other parts have been returned to farmland and some industrial units.

### Little Sutton, northwest of Ellesmere Port
This airfield had a short existence and although the current site is farmland, housing is beginning to encroach. The airfield opened in 1941 and was a grass airstrip. It was used as a satellite field for RAF Sealand. It would appear that this site was primarily used for pilot training.

### Long Marston, southwest of Stratford-upon-Avon
A wide variety of leisure activities, including a flying school and a microlight club are based here now and it is also used as a venue for music festivals. The airfield opened in 1941 and from March 1943 it operated as a satellite station for RAF Honeybourne. The base also operated as a satellite for RAF Pershore for a year from July 1943. The RAF relinquished control of the base in 1954, at which point it was sold to its current owners.

### Long Newnton, east of Tetbury
This was opened in 1940 and was used as a landing ground for several other airfields in the local area. It is understood that the airfield closed in April 1947, however there are many relics left there, including the control tower, Nissen huts and taxi ways.

### Longtown, east of Gretna
This airfield was also known as Hallburn and opened in July 1941, closing in September 1946. The site now has several businesses based there, but some of the original buildings do remain. It was also a displaced persons camp in the 1940s and it would appear that they were predominantly Polish people living there.

### Loughborough, northwest of Loughborough
This was a grass airstrip that was known as Loughborough Meadows, where a private aircraft company used to test aircraft here from 1915.

Plans were afoot to develop a civilian airport at Bishops Meadow, but instead it was turned over to aircraft manufacture. The airfield itself was probably based on a horse racing track and was primarily used to repair aircraft. Loughborough Meadows, according to the Airfields of Britain Conservation Trust, ceased flying operations in the 1920s, whereas the second airfield was still being used into the 1960s.

### Ludford Magna, east of Market Rasen
RAF Squadron No 101 was the first to use this airfield in June 1943. The poor drainage at the airfield led it to become known as Mudford Magna. For a period of eight years from 1948 Polish refugees were housed here. In the 1950s it was a site for ballistic nuclear missiles. Part of the site was sold off in 1964 and the remainder in the following year. Most of the buildings were demolished although some of the perimeter track still survives.

One of the access roads to former RAF Ludford Magna. As with many disused airfields in Lincolnshire, the concrete roads and runways are used as hardstanding. [*Image courtesy of Kate Nicol*]

## Ludham, west of Potter Heigham

This opened as a satellite field for RAF Coltishall but it was extensively used by RAF fighter squadrons between November 1941, a month after its opening, and August 1943. Spitfires belonging to RAF Squadron Nos 19, 91, 152, 167, 602, 603, 610 and 611 were all stationed here. Typhoons belonging to 195 Squadron also operated from the airfield. After this time the USAAF were given the base but they never used it and in August 1944 through to the early months of 1945 it became HMS *Flycatcher* and was used by the Royal Navy. Spitfires returned in February 1945 and remained there until the July, notably RAF Squadron Nos 1, 91, 602 and 603. Ludham airfield is now a private airfield.

## Lulsgate Bottom, southwest of Bristol

This site is now better known as Bristol Airport, which handles some 5.7 million passengers a year. A flying club was established at Filton Aerodrome in 1927. They moved to Whitchurch two years later and this was recognised as being an ideal site for a civilian airport. Meanwhile, in September 1940, a relief landing ground was set up at Broadfield Down, near Lulsgate Bottom. It was declared fully operational in January 1942 and was used through to May 1946. For a time it was to become the home of a gliding club and have a motor racing circuit on it. It had always been assumed that Whitchurch would become Bristol's civilian airport, but housing estates were encroaching on the site and instead Lulsgate Bottom became Bristol Lulsgate Airport, which opened in 1957. Forty years later, it became Bristol International Airport.

## Luton, Luton Airport

This is the site of London Luton Airport. The original site was officially opened in 1938 and was used as a flight training school and by ferry pilots. This must have still been a grass runway during the war because the first concrete runway was not laid until 1960. During the war it was home to RAF Squadron No 264 and the site is also closely associated with the factory that produced Mosquito fighter bombers. The civilian use recommenced in 1952 and it has since gone on to be developed into a full international airport.

## Lyneham, southwest of Royal Wootton Bassett

RAF Lyneham has been home to air transport operations from the mid-1960s to the current day. It was decided in 2003 that Lyneham would close in 2012. In 2011, it was announced that the site would continue to be used, however flying operations ceased in September 2011.

Lyneham Court Manor House was demolished to make way for the airfield in 1939. It opened in May 1940 and was originally used by a maintenance unit. The runways were built and extended in the period 1940 to 1943. One of the important duties of the airfield was to provide transport to Gibraltar and to Malta. Flights also headed for India during the war. In the post-war period the base was used for the Berlin Airlift and numerous squadrons continued to use it. In more recent years the most notable aircraft was the Hercules. At present Lyneham's future is in the balance, although the most likely outcome is that the site will be used by the British Army.

## Madley, southwest of Hereford

Madley was primarily a radio signals training school and an airstrip was added in 1943. The airfield saw a variety of aircraft, including Hurricanes and Mustangs. The site closed down in the 1950s and it was returned to farmland. Today the site is Madley Communications Centre, owned by British Telecom.

**Rudolf Hess**

Rudolf Hess, Adolf Hitler's deputy, was held at Abergavenny and flown out of Madley to attend the Nuremburg trials in 1946.

## Manby, east of Louth

The RAF originally set this up to be used as a base to teach bomb disposal techniques. The airfield opened in 1938 and it was to retain its association with the RAF until 1974. Many of the original RAF houses were sold off and some of the roads around the area are named after RAF aircraft. Several of the buildings from the original airfield still exist today.

The southeastern corner of RAF Marham airfield. [*Image courtesy of Evelyn Simak*]

## Marham, west of Swaffham

This is still an important RAF base and one of the busiest. The airfield was opened in 1916 and was primarily used as a night time landing ground. At the end of the First World War Marham was closed, but the RAF took an interest in the site again in the mid-1930s and began redeveloping the site. The first squadron arrived in May 1937. During the course of the Second World War primarily bombers, including Wellingtons, Stirlings and Mosquitos all operated from the airfield. Marham once again closed to be upgraded with concrete runways and this work was completed towards the end of 1945. At that point Lancaster bombers began using the airfield. In the late-1940s several American bomber groups, using B-29s and B-50s, were based at Marham. By the late-1950s the RAF based some of their V-bombers on the site. One of the key roles of Marham was also to provide flight refuelling and some of its aircraft were based on the Ascension Islands during the campaign to liberate the Falklands in 1982. Marham is still as busy as it has ever been, with a succession of squadrons moving in and out of the station, punctuated by periods of deployment overseas.

## Market Harborough, northwest of Market Harborough

Gartree Prison now occupies part of the original site. The airfield was opened in 1943 and the site is currently being considered for a housing development. For the majority of the war it was used by training units and it closed in either late 1947 or the beginning of 1948.

### Marston Moor, northeast of Ingmanthorpe

This is a relatively well preserved, heavy bomber training school. Half a dozen of the hangars still exist and the control tower is used for offices. The airfield opened in 1941 but it was still apparently undergoing development in the post-war period. It was originally called Tockwith, but its name was changed to Marston Moor because of potential confusion with Topcliffe. The last aircraft left the airfield in November 1945, at which point it was closed for flying, but it was retained until at least 1949.

---

**Marston Moor stars**

Two notable individuals are associated with RAF Marston Moor; Group Captain Geoffrey Leonard Cheshire, VC OM DSO DFC, the famous bomber pilot, was the station commander here in 1943. The second person was Clark Gable, who was at the airfield before being posted to RAF Polebrook.

---

### Marwell Hall, northeast of Eastleigh

It would seem that Marwell Hall was used between 1941 and 1944, primarily to test aircraft. It was then used for training and for experimental aircraft. The airfield was actually located on the grounds of Marwell Hall. The building and land was owned by the managing director of Cunliffe Owen Aircraft. They modified aircraft at their factory at Eastleigh. Consequently there were around 20 hangars built amongst the trees and the airfield itself saw Spitfires, Blenheims and other aircraft. It would seem that this arrangement ceased in March 1944. The site is now a zoological park and the hangars are used as farmyard buildings.

### Matlaske, southeast of Holt

Originally this was a satellite field for RAF Coltishall, but it also had links to other airfields. In the first three years of the war the airfield saw Spitfires, Hurricanes and an Air-Sea Rescue unit. The 8th USAAF took it over as a fighter base but they only used it for a month in the spring of 1943. Meanwhile the RAF continued to use the base and

Typhoon and Spitfire squadrons were based here and, on occasion, USAAF aircraft. When the airfield was transferred over to the control of the 8th in August 1943 it was rebuilt, but it was only really used by the RAF, who continued operations there until October 1945. It would seem that the airfield then closed and most of the buildings were demolished in the late-1970s.

### Meir, southeast of Stoke on Trent
This site is now covered with housing and industry. The airfield was variously known as Blythe Bridge, or Longton. It was mainly used for flight training and then as a gliding school. The RAF's association with this base may have lasted into the 1970s.

### Melbourne, southwest of Pocklington
The squadron with the longest association with this airfield was RAF No 10 Squadron. Their Whitley bombers began using the airfield towards the end of 1940. It was then closed for redevelopment but they returned, now flying Halifax bombers. They continued using Melbourne until March 1945, losing 109 aircraft during this period. Transport Command took it over in May 1945 but within a year the RAF had stopped using it for flying and the airfield is now York Raceway.

### Melton Mowbray, south of Melton Mowbray
The airfield opened in 1942 and seems to have been primarily used by RAF Transport Command. It was certainly officially opened by August 1943 and many of the aircraft that used the airfield were being prepared for duties overseas. By late-1944 it was being used for the same purpose, but by a different unit. In November 1945 the airfield was closed and was maintained until 1958. Missiles were then based there and it is likely that the airfield closed around 1967.

### Mepal, west of Ely
A memorial to the New Zealanders of RAF No 75 Squadron can be seen at this airfield. They moved in during June 1943, initially flying Stirlings and later Lancasters. They flew a remarkable 8,017 sorties out of Mepal, which equated to 739 combat operations. This was the highest number of sorties in all of Bomber Command. In all they lost

193 aircraft from this base until they left in July 1945. It was then occupied briefly by a succession of other Lancaster squadrons: Nos 7, 44 and 49. The last flying took place in July 1946. Thirteen years later the airfield was reopened as a missile base and at some point in late 1963 it was sold off. Most of the airfield was cleared in the late-1980s.

### Merston, southeast of Chichester
Merston airfield was originally set up to act as a satellite for RAF Tangmere. Over the winter of 1943 to 1944 RAF Squadron No 124 was based there and later RAF Squadron Nos 181, 182 and 247 were amongst other squadrons to use the airfield. Aircraft operating out of Merston were involved in fighter sweeps along the Normandy beaches in June 1944. The site today is an industrial estate and farmland.

### Metheringham, southeast of Lincoln
RAF Metheringham Visitor Centre is in the former rations store and there is also a memorial garden and plinth that is dedicated to RAF

RAF Metheringham memorial to 106 Squadron, Royal Air Force, 1917–19, 1938–46. [*Image courtesy of Richard Croft*]

Squadron No 106, which operated from the airfield from November 1943 until they were disbanded in February 1946. The airfield itself opened in October 1943 and was designated as a bomber airfield. Towards the end of the war the Royal Australian Air Force's No 467 Squadron arrived to train alongside 106 Squadron, as they were to be deployed to the Far East. As it was, the war ended and the Australian unit was disbanded. By February 1946 the airfield was closed to flying and whilst it was retained for a while, it was returned to farmland in the early 1960s.

**Victoria Cross**
During the night of 26th to 27th April, 1944 Flight Engineer Sergeant Norman Jackson climbed out onto the wing of his Lancaster to put out an engine fire. He was badly burned in the attempt and then was blown off the wing. He managed to parachute to safety and became a prisoner of war. He was subsequently awarded the Victoria Cross.

### Methwold, northwest of Thetford
Most of this site is now a poultry farm and it is also used to prepare salads for supermarkets. It originally opened as a satellite station for RAF Feltwell. Initially it was a grass airfield, but it underwent a considerable upgrade in the late summer of 1943. At various times Methwold was home to RAF Squadron Nos 21, 37, 149, 207, 214 and 218 and it also saw the Royal Australian Air Force's Squadron No 464 and the Royal New Zealand Air Force's No 487. The flying finished in April 1946 but it was not sold off until the 1960s.

### Middleton St George, east of Darlington
This is now Teesside International Airport. It was opened at the beginning of 1941 and until the autumn of 1942 saw Whitley and Halifax bombers. Canadian units moved in during October 1942 and remained there until the end of May 1945. These Royal Canadian Air Force Squadrons 419 (Moose), 420 (Snowy Owl) and 428 (Ghost) launched many raids in Wellingtons, Halifaxes and Lancasters. Some 279 of their bombers were lost.

In July 1945 through to May 1947 Mosquitos were based at the airfield and after this, until 1956, the airfield was a training school. It underwent a rebuild in the 1950s and the RAF stationed Lightnings there between 1963 and 1964. The RAF closed the station in 1965 but it opened the following year as a civilian airport.

### Mildenhall, northwest of Mildenhall
Mildenhall is still being used as a refuelling base by the USAF. They have been involved with the airfield since 1950. Initially, when Mildenhall opened in 1934, it was the RAF's only bomber station. It was not until 1943 that it had concrete runways. Several bomber squadrons operated here from 1943 through to the end of the war. These included:

- 15
- 44
- 622

In all, around 250 aircraft were lost during the course of the war from this airfield. The RAF continued to use the airfield until 1950, with additional work taking place. Since then it has had periodic but considerable investment from the United States.

### Millfield, southeast of Coldstream
Millfield was used during the First World War, primarily as a refuelling site. It seems that operations lasted between 1917 and 1919. A newly improved Millfield opened during the Second World War and it was used by an operational training unit and then for developing new aircraft tactics and weapons. The site has also been subject to excavation, with sand and gravel being removed, so this has meant that the landing strips have disappeared. As part of the broader recognition of the heritage of the area, there is a memorial to those that served at Millfield between 1941 and 1946.

### Millom, northeast of Haverigg
There was once an aviation and military museum on this site, but this is now closed. It was there to highlight the use of the site as a gunnery and air observer school. The airfield opened at the beginning of 1941

and by 1942 it was also being used for advanced flight training. It was mothballed in 1946 but reopened briefly in 1953 and then through the early 1960s it was used by the British Army. The majority of the site is now HMP Haverigg.

### Montford Bridge, northwest of Shrewsbury
This station was operational between 1942 and 1945. It was a satellite field for RAF Rednal and building had begun around 1940. It was occupied by an operational training unit and saw Mustang and Spitfire aircraft. Towards the end of the war it was used as a centre by a maintenance unit to scrap aircraft. It seems that the airfield closed in December 1945, but many of the buildings still stand although some are in a dilapidated state.

### Moreton Valence, northwest of Stroud
This airfield was called RAF Haresfield when it opened at the beginning of the Second World War. It was then closed, upgraded and renamed. It was home to advanced flight training courses and from October 1943 through to July 1962 it was a flight test factory run by Gloster. The airfield itself closed in July 1962 and despite the fact that some of the airfield is now under the M5 motorway, many of the buildings remain and are used by industry whilst the rest of the site is farmland.

### Moreton-in-Marsh, northeast of Moreton-in-Marsh
At Moreton-in-Marsh there is the Wellington Aviation Museum and the airfield itself is now used for fire training. The airfield opened in November 1940 and was used through to 1948 although it was not disposed of until 1955. It was a flight training station and in the Moreton-in-Marsh cemetery there are dozens of British, New Zealand, Australian and Canadian servicemen who died whilst serving at the base. Outside the fire service college on the site there is a memorial to the men that launched many raids over Germany from here.

### Morpeth, southwest of Morpeth
This airfield is also known as Tranwell airfield. It was home to No 80 (French) Operational Training Unit. The airfield opened in January 1942 and was used as an air gunnery school until December 1944. It

is not documented when the airfield actually closed, but there are still several buildings, including an underground control room at the site, which is now a National Trust site.

## Mount Batten, south of Plymouth

In 1913 this area was used for seaplane trials and in 1917 Royal Naval Air Service station Cattewater was opened. When the RAF was formed in April 1918 it was renamed RAF Cattewater. During the 1920s it was rebuilt and it reopened in 1928 as RAF Mount Batten. It was still used as a seaplane base and also by the RAF Air-Sea Rescue and Marine Craft Unit. In the post-war period it became the Marine Craft Training School and in the 1960s it was the RAF Marine Branch main base. This branch closed in 1986 and the School of Survival moved in during 1992. A considerable amount of the infrastructure still remains, although many of the buildings were demolished towards the end of the late-1990s.

## Needs Oar Point, northeast of Lymington

Over the course of the winter of 1943 the RAF built the airfield to be ready for use by the next spring. It was said to be the busiest airfield in the whole of Britain during the run up and immediate aftermath of the Normandy landings in June 1944. Its use was extremely short-lived and within 11 weeks of the landings the airfield was no longer in use and was ready to be returned to agriculture. It was exclusively used by Typhoon squadrons, including RAF Squadron Nos 193, 197, 257 and 266. Many of these squadrons were literally on the airfield for a matter of weeks.

## Netheravon, north of Salisbury

Balloons were the first to use this airfield before the First World War. During the Second World War it was primarily used by RAF Squadron Nos 296 and 297. Netheravon is now, of course, home to the Army Parachute Association and it is still a major airfield that provides transport aircraft for the British Army.

## Netherthorpe, northwest of Worksop

Aerial photographs today of the base clearly witness that it is still in use and that its grass runways are plainly visible, as are many of the

The easternmost building on Netheravon Airfield. [*Image courtesy of Andrew Smith*]

**Netheravon**
This lays claim to being one of the airfields that has the longest unbroken association with flying in Britain, dating from 1912 all the way through to the present day. It was also involved in the very early Royal Flying Corps, Royal Air Force, Fleet Air Arm and the Army Air Corps.

buildings. It opened in 1935 and is home to the Sheffield Aero Club today. Information is sparse about this airfield but we know that RAF No 613 Squadron was there in 1940. There was an incident when one their Lysanders hit an army truck. Two RAF men tried to save the pilot, who subsequently died. The RAF servicemen were both awarded the George Medal for their gallantry.

### Newchurch, northwest of Dymchurch
This was another short-lived airfield that operated from mid-1943 to the end of 1944. It was mainly used by squadrons flying Hawker Tempest or Supermarine Spitfire aircraft. Their job was to intercept V-1 flying bombs. By April 1944 it had also become the home of 150 Wing who had three Tempest squadrons and managed to destroy 638 V-1s. The squadrons that were based there were RAF Squadron Nos 3, 19, 56, 132, 184 and 602, along with the Royal New Zealand Air Force's No 486 Squadron. After its closure the airfield was returned to farmland.

### Newmarket Heath, west of Newmarket
Aircraft began landing on Newmarket Heath during the First World War. In 1939 it was once again chosen primarily as a satellite field for RAF Mildenhall. It became home to RAF Squadron No 99 and their Wellingtons. Later it was also used by aircraft operating out of RAF Oakington. There were improvements made over the winter of 1941 to 1942 and while work was being carried out at Mildenhall, Newmarket Heath was extensively used. This was until mid-1943, at which point RAF Mepal was ready for use. Some 76 aircraft were lost from the squadrons operating from this airfield during the course of the war. The airfield was closed soon after VE Day, but a small part of it is still used for civilian flying.

### New Romney, north of New Romney
An airfield existed at New Romney during the First World War but this was closer to the coast than the airfield that was opened in July 1943 and remained operational until December 1944. This airfield was also known as Honeychild. RAF Squadron Nos 181, 182 and 247 all used the airfield. The site is now farmland once again.

### Newton, northeast of Radcliffe on Trent
This airfield had a 60-year history, running from July 1940. It was originally a civilian airfield but aircraft that had managed to survive the battle of France occupied the site in June 1940. It was then used as a training base and in the post-war period became the home of No 12 Group Fighter Command, who remained there until 1958. It was also the RAF School of Education, the RAF Police Training School, the headquarters of the Air Training Corps and at various times was home to university air squadrons. It is planned that the site will eventually be developed into a housing estate.

### North Cotes, northeast of Louth
Today, this is the home of North Cotes Flying Club. The army opened a camp here in 1914 and the first aircraft landed in August. The RAF began to use it as an air observer school but in 1939 it was transferred to Coastal Command. In the post-war period the RAF used it as a maintenance centre and there were also helicopters based there before

it became a missile site. The RAF relinquished control of the airfield in 1990.

### North Creake, south of Wells-next-to-Sea

The airfield was constructed from October 1942 and opened as a bomber base. RAF Squadron No 199 operated out of the airfield in May 1944 and later No 171 was created there. They flew missions from the airfield until 2nd May, 1945 and in all they lost 17 aircraft during their operations. In the post-war period the airfield was used to store aircraft but the RAF left in the autumn of 1947. The control tower is now a house, and caravans occupy some of the rest of the site.

### North Killingholme, northwest of Immingham

In 1914 this was called Lindsey but by 1943, when it opened, it was now called North Killingholme. It did not become fully operational until the beginning of 1944 when RAF Squadron No 550 arrived from RAF Waltham. They were to lose 62 of their Lancasters in 190 combat missions whilst there. They remained operational there until October 1945, at which point the station closed and it was to be returned to farmland and part of the site is an industrial estate.

---

#### Normandy landings

RAF Squadron No 550 was the first squadron to launch operations in support of the Normandy landings when they made attacks on 5th June, 1944.

---

### North Luffenham, south of Empingham

The airfield was two years short of 60 years' association with the RAF when it closed in 1998. At this point it was taken over by the army and renamed St Georges Barracks. During the Second World War it was originally designed to be a training base but in fact was used as a heavy bomber station. In the post-war period the Royal Canadian Air Force were based here from 1951 to 1955. It was then used once again by the RAF and in the early 1960s as a home for ballistic missiles. It retained its association with the RAF, serving variously as a medical training centre and a language school.

The gates to the airfield, along with the station badge, can be seen at the recreation ground in North Luffenham village.

### Northleach, southwest of Stow-on-the-Wold
This was an emergency landing ground, but in July 1942 it became a glider training school. It was linked to RAF Stoke Orchard near Cheltenham. Members of the RAF Regiment were also trained here. One of the major problems with the airfield was that it became waterlogged, which reduced its value. Plans to upgrade it never came to fruition and it is understood that it was last used for flying in October 1944. The airfield was soon decommissioned and the RAF left it in May 1946, for it to become farmland once again.

### Nuneaton, north of Nuneaton
This is now the home of the Motor Industry Research Association, who still uses the control tower. It was opened at the beginning of 1943 to be used as a satellite station for RAF Bramcote. RAF Transport Command, along with an operational training unit, used the airfield between June 1943 and November 1945. For a brief period before the Normandy landings the US Army also made use of the airfield. RAF Nuneaton was mothballed between the end of 1945 and the end of 1948, from which point it has been used by MIRA.

### Oakington, northwest of Cambridge
This site was the Home Office's Immigration Reception Centre but plans are already underway to build 9,500 homes on the site. The airfield opened in 1939 and was first used in July 1940 by RAF Squadron No 218, known as the Gold Coast Squadron. Oakington went on to become a base for Stirling bombers and then home to a photographic reconnaissance unit. In the post-war period the RAF used the site mainly for training before it became an army barracks.

### Oakley, northeast of Oxford
Oakley opened in May 1942 as a satellite field for RAF Bicester. It would then also become a satellite for RAF Westcott. It was used primarily for training bomber crews. In May 1945 the first batch of British prisoners of war began arriving there. This process continued and over 15,000 men were brought home during what was known as

Operation Exodus. The station closed in August 1945. Part of the site is now an industrial estate and it has been used on occasion for films and television programmes. Several of the original buildings still survive, including some of the hangars.

### Oatlands Hill, west of Amesbury
This airfield has now all-but disappeared beneath farmland. It opened in June 1941 and closed in May 1946. It was a satellite station for RAF Old Sarum. To begin with it was used to train pilots but an operational unit moved in during 1944, along with elements of the US 9th Air Force. Canadian units were present in the spring of 1945. Today the airfield is a dairy farm and one of the original hangars existed until relatively recently.

### Odiham, southeast of Basingstoke
Today Odiham is a helicopter base but the first aircraft to use it were Army Cooperation machines in 1925. It was decided to make the grass runway more permanent and it was officially opened in 1937.

The airfield would see British, Belgian, Canadian and Free French pilots and in fact in 1945 it became an official Royal Canadian Air Force base. After this Fighter Command used it and by 1960 it had become part of RAF Transport Command. This was a role that it has continued to perform to the present day.

Entrance to the airbase, Royal Air Force Odiham. [*Image courtesy of Sebastian Ballard*]

> **German admiration**
> The Chief of Staff of the Luftwaffe, General Erhard Milch, actually opened RAF Odiham. He must have been suitably impressed; not only did he forbid the Luftwaffe from bombing the airfield (it never was bombed during the war) but he intended to use it as his headquarters in the event of a German victory.

## Okehampton, north of Okehampton

This is sometimes referred to as Folly Gate. It was used by aircraft belonging to Army Cooperation squadrons between 1928 and 1939. It continued in this role until 1942 and then was used to store aircraft. It was also used during the run up to the Normandy landings. The airfield was closed in July 1945 but it was still used by Army Cooperation aircraft for some time. Shortly afterwards it was returned to farmland.

## Old Sarum, north of Salisbury

Microlight aircraft still fly from this airfield and it is still a remarkably intact First World War period airfield, with many of the buildings enjoying listed status. The airfield opened in August 1917 and was primarily used to train aircrew. It did not close after the armistice and flying continued throughout the interwar period. By 1941 the airfield had acquired a satellite field at Oatlands Hill but the airfield itself was still being mainly used for training purposes. An amazing 25,000 vehicles were massed in and around the airfield prior to the Normandy landings. Three squadrons actually operated from Old Sarum and these were Squadron Nos 658, 659 and 662. In the post-war period support for the airfield continued and it was used for training, and it acquired helicopters but in 1971 the RAF ceased using it, although it remained in military use with the British Army until 1979. It was then acquired by a private aircraft manufacturer and civilian aircraft began using it from 1986.

## Ossington, west of Sutton on Trent

Ossington Hall was part of the accommodation for the airfield that opened in January 1942. The site was used for advanced pilot training and in January 1945 it was transferred over to RAF Transport Command. It is understood that the airfield closed in August 1946. Not only have nearly all of the airfield buildings been pulled down, but also the hall itself was demolished in the 1960s.

### Oulton, west of Aylsham

This airfield was a satellite station for RAF Horsham St Faith and then for RAF Swanton Morley. It was then decided that it should become a heavy bomber base and construction work finished in April 1944. The last flights took place in July 1945 but it was used to store aircraft until its closure in November 1947. The airfield also saw the 803rd Bombardment Squadron working alongside RAF Bomber Command in the summer of 1944. The control tower has since been demolished.

### Ouston, northwest of Newburn

Ouston opened in March 1941 and the Polish-manned RAF Squadron No 122, with their Hurricanes, were the first arrivals. Subsequently they were equipped with Spitfires. The airfield would see several other fighter squadrons during the course of the war and French pilots were also based there. Flying continued from the airfield in the post-war period but it is now known as Albemarle Barracks and is home to The Royal Artillery.

### Panshanger, southeast of Welwyn Garden City

This is also known as Holwell Hyde and is home to the North London Flying School. The airfield was already being used as a landing ground before the Second World War. In the first years of the war it was used as a decoy field and then from June 1941 to 1953 as an elementary flying school. It was not renamed RAF Panshanger until September 1943.

### Papplewick Moor, north of Hucknall

This site maintained almost 30 years of association with aviation, first with the Royal Flying Corps in 1916. Amazingly it never had any permanent buildings and was only ever a grass runway. In fact in 1940 it was an emergency landing ground, so when the RAF stopped using it in November 1945 it was quickly returned to farmland.

## Penkridge, northwest of Cannock

The Staffordshire Aero Club is based at the former relief landing ground of RAF Penkridge. The airfield was also known as Pillaton and it closed in July 1945. Today the site is also an industrial estate and a caravan park.

## Penshurst, northwest of Tonbridge

Penshurst had a 30-year association with aviation. It was first opened in December 1916 and was used by Royal Flying Corps aircraft and for training courses. The main accommodation was at Knotley Hall. By March 1919 the school had been closed down and Knotley Hall was put up for sale. In the interwar years it was still being used as an emergency landing ground and in 1930 Home Counties Aircraft Services was based there. The airfield was also used by Imperial Airways, particularly if there were poor weather conditions over Croydon. It saw considerable civilian traffic but when the lease expired the airfield was closed in July 1936.

The RAF took over in 1940, using it as an elementary flying school and a satellite for RAF Redhill. Knotley Hall was again used for accommodation. Several squadrons used the airfield over the course of the Second World War, notably RAF Squadron No 653, which was involved in air observation and liaised with British artillery. The airfield also had its fair share of emergency landings, including one on the night of 6th July, 1944, when a B-17 landed on its belly on the airfield. The airfield closed in May 1946 and since then the infrastructure has gradually disappeared.

### Charles Lindbergh
Charles Lindbergh left from Penshurst on 22nd July, 1936 in answer to an invitation to Berlin from Hermann Goering.

## Peplow, south of Market Drayton

This airfield, despite the fact it was only open between 1941 and 1949, was known by no fewer than four different names. The RAF called it Peplow or Child's Ercall and the Royal Navy called it RNAS Peplow or HMS *Godwit II*. It would seem that the RAF originally used it

The coast path above Hanover Cove skirts the perimeter of Perranporth Airfield. [*Image courtesy of Philip Halling*]

between 1940 and 1945 with aircraft including Wellingtons operating from the base. By 1945 it was being used by Fleet Air Arm squadrons and it would also seem that it was a satellite field for Hinstock, which was known as *Godwit I.*

### Perranporth, northeast of St Agnes

At various times between 1941 and 1946 the RAF Transport Command used this site as a fighter base. From 1941 to 1944 it was primarily used by aircraft patrolling the coast, or by fighters making sweeps over France. Coastal Command took it over in April 1944 and established three Fleet Air Arm squadrons there. They were involved in actions against German E-boats. Towards the end of 1944 Transport Command took it over to ship men to mainland Europe, principally France. It was used by the Air Training Corps from May 1945 through to April of the following year. Since 1950 it has been used for private aircraft and for gliding.

### Pershore, southeast of Worcester

Pershore was extensively used in 2001 for the burial of animals during the foot and mouth disease outbreak. The airfield itself closed in 1978 but it had opened in 1934 and was the Worcestershire Flying School. It retained this role until 1939 when it was requisitioned by the RAF.

From 1941 to 1944 it had a significant association with Canadians who would train there on Wellington bombers. From the spring of 1944 until 1948 it was used as a base from which aircraft could be ferried to other locations. In the early 1950s it was an advanced flying school and its final use was as the Royal Radar Establishment Flying Unit headquarters.

### Perton, west of Wolverhampton

Opening in 1941, Perton operated as an advanced flying school and was involved in flight training until its closure in 1945. In the post-war period the site became a refugee camp until 1950 when it was then converted into housing, which remained occupied until the early 1960s. Some of the area is now a newer housing development, although there are some original buildings still in existence.

### Peterborough, northwest of Peterborough

This area is now better known as Westwood and the original airfield is now a housing estate. It would seem that the site was primarily used by the RAF for flight training and was open between February 1935 and August 1948. It seems to have been a private airfield before the Second World War. It is reported that the airfield itself had opened in 1932 and was to be used mainly as a centre where aircraft would be received, stored and then delivered. There were many changes in the types of training carried out at the airfield over the course of the war. It was also temporarily a home for displaced persons between 1948 and 1952. Most of the land was sold off in the 1960s and the original Officers' Mess has become a training and development centre.

### Plainville, north of York

This airfield had a short life, opening in 1939 and closing in 1941. It was a relief landing ground for RAF Linton.

### Pocklington, east of York

Canadians using Wellingtons and then Halifax bombers used this base from 1941. This was RAF Squadron No 405 and afterwards No 102 began using the airfield. The airfield was closed in 1946 and most of the site was returned to agricultural use, with parts of it becoming an industrial estate. A gliding club operates from the original field.

> **Dangers of flying**
> Australian Pilot Officer George Lambert had a close shave when his Whitley bomber overshot the runway at Plainville on 31st May, 1941. Later in the war, in April 1943, his Lancaster was shot down over France. Four of the crew were killed, two were captured but he evaded capture. Unfortunately, he was killed when his aircraft crash-landed on 5th July, 1944.

### Poole, the Blue Lagoon, west of Poole

This is also known as RAF Hamworthy and was a seaplane base in Poole Harbour, which operated from 1939 until 1948. Catalina and Sunderland flying boats operated from here and it was also a BOAC base both before and after the war. It would seem that the last flying boat used the area in 1958.

### Portland, north of Portland

The site was an anti-submarine training school between 1924 and 1941 and known as RNAS Portland. The area became a Royal Naval base once again in the post-war period and was closed in 1995. Many of the buildings still exist, although in an increasingly dilapidated state.

The old administration building, RNAS Portland. [*Image courtesy of Simon Palmer*]

## Portreath, northeast of Redruth

This base opened in the spring of 1941 and although designated as a fighter station it was in fact used by many aircraft coming over the North Atlantic and heading for either the Middle East or North Africa. Consequently it saw many American and Canadian piloted aircraft. After this it was used by RAF Coastal Command. By the end of the Second World War it had gone into mothballs and was closed down in May 1950. It was used by the Chemical Defence Establishment and renamed Nancekuke to produce chemical weapons. These buildings were pulled down in the late 1970s and the RAF reopened it as a radar station. Originally it was manned, but now it is all automated.

## Portsmouth, northeast of Portsmouth

Portsmouth laid plans for their own airport back in the 1920s. There was some discussion as to whether it should be a land-based one or a seaplane base. Work got underway on Portsea Island to become a conventional airport. The first aircraft landed there in mid-December 1930. It was subsequently used by private companies running charter flights.

During the Second World War the base was used primarily for glider training and in the post-war period civilian flight recommenced. By the late-1970s the site had been closed and it is now housing and industry.

### Air race

In September 1936 Portsmouth was the starting point for the England to Johannesburg air race. Nine aircraft competed and the winner made it in just less than 53 hours.

## Poulton, south of Chester

This was in operation between March 1943 and the end of 1945. An operational training unit was based here and the airfield primarily saw Hurricanes. It would seem that the airfield was also known as Pulford.

## Predannack, south of Helston

When this opened it was to be a night fighter base. Aircraft operating from here would seek to defend Penzance and Falmouth. It opened in 1941 and was subsequently used by Coastal Command. Their Beaufighters and Mosquitos were primarily engaged in anti-submarine warfare. The airfield was mothballed in 1946 and after the war Vickers used the base until it was taken over by the Royal Navy in 1958. Today it is used by the Royal Naval School of Fire Fighting and by an RAF volunteer gliding squadron.

## Pulborough, southeast of Pulborough

This is also known as Parham Park. It operated as an emergency landing ground between 1940 and 1945. It is still an active airfield and used by a gliding club today.

## Radlett, south of St Albans

This site was used by civil aircraft in the early 1930s and bombs were also manufactured here from 1939. It continued to be used by Handley Page into the 1960s. The company went bankrupt in 1969 and the site closed the following year. The majority of the buildings were demolished soon afterwards.

## Ramsgate, west of Broadstairs

Ramsgate opened as a civilian airfield in 1935. It had actually been chosen as a suitable site during the First World War, but had never been built. During the Second World War it operated primarily as a satellite field for RAF Manston. This was during the battle of Britain period and afterwards, in order to prevent German landings on the site obstructions were placed on the runway. In the post-war period most of the site was returned to agricultural use, but the civilian flights did return in the early 1950s. It was also used by a flying club. The airfield remained open until 1968.

## Ratcliffe, north of East Goscote

The airfield opened in September 1940 and remained open for nearly 10 years. During the war the airfield saw air observation units and flight training. It was also used as a point from which aircraft were delivered across Britain to their squadrons. In the post-war period

Leicester Aero Club used the airfield. The site is perhaps best known for the fact that some 3,000 Auster aircraft were built at the nearby Rearsby factory between 1939 and 1968 and that the airfield was used to ferry these aircraft from the factory.

### Rearsby, east of East Goscote
This was the home of an aircraft factory that began manufacturing in 1939. They built the Auster that was used for air observation. Ultimately this airfield was sold to a car manufacturer and from the 1960s to the 1980s it saw the manufacture of components for the car industry. This was a role it continued from the 1980s until the business failed in 2003. The site is now an industrial park.

### Redhill, southeast of Reigate
Redhill Flying Club began using this airfield in 1934 and the area was also used as an alternative base to Croydon for commercial flights. Flight training was carried out from here from 1937 and for a short time in 1940 the base was virtually abandoned due to its exposed position. Aircraft returned in June 1940 but the base was fairly inactive during the battle of Britain. By May 1941 it had become a satellite station for RAF Kenley and notably it was home to No 1 Squadron and their night fighter Hurricanes.

For most of the war the airfield was used by RAF squadrons to raid occupied France. There were more than 200 fighters here in the build

Redhill Aerodrome. [*Image courtesy of Ian Capper*]

up to the Normandy landings in June 1944 and it was then used to help defeat the V-1 flying bomb threat. Towards the end of the war, Redhill was being used as a satellite field for Biggin Hill and then as a bomb store. In 1948 it was a reserve flying school but this unit was disbanded in 1954. Today it is used by helicopters and private light aircraft.

### Rednal, east of Oswestry
The RAF opened this airfield in the spring of 1942 and it was used by an operational training unit until June 1945. From July 1944 the USAAF made extensive use of the airfield in order to bring back casualties from northern France to military hospitals in the area. The airfield itself closed in 1945. Several of the buildings still remain in a derelict condition.

### Riccall, north of Selby
This was opened as a satellite field for RAF Marston Moor and it was only in 2010 that a memorial was established to commemorate those that served at Riccall during the Second World War. Riccall opened in September 1942 and remained operational until the beginning of 1957. The bulk of the site is farmland or woodland now and there is also a mine on the site. It was mostly used as a training airfield for bomber crews and one of the runways is now part of Skipwith Common, a National Nature Reserve.

### Ringway, Manchester Airport
Back in the 1920s Manchester council recognised the need to develop a municipal airport. It took until 1935 for building work to begin at Ringway and scheduled flights began in 1938. There was considerable development during the Second World War and by the late 1940s

---

**Did you know?**
One of the individuals assigned to the No 1 Parachute Training School at Ringway was the comedian Frank Muir. He took slow-motion film of parachute drops and was also responsible for taking photographs of SOE agents for their faked identity cards.

---

additional development had taken place and then periodic upgrades, culminating in a second runway being built in 2001. The RAF remained active at the airfield until around 1957 when the final squadron using it was disbanded. During the Second World War all Allied paratroopers that would be operating in Europe were trained here and it was also used by the agents belonging to Special Operations Executive for their parachute training. Nearby was also an aircraft factory and nearly 4,500 aircraft were made here and flown out of Ringway between 1940 and 1945.

### Rochester, southwest of Chatham

This was a relatively small airfield that was chosen by Rochester council in the early 1930s as a municipal airport site. The first flight took place from there in 1934. Close by was the aircraft factory belonging to the Short brothers and they took over the airfield and shared it with a flight training school belonging to the RAF. The Short brothers were primarily building flying boats. In the post-war period the RAF continued to use the site for training and it was also used by the aviation industry. In 1999 the site was saved from destruction and it is now an operating small airfield for light aircraft.

### Rollestone, northwest of Amesbury

This was a landing ground and also the RAF Anti-Gas School. We know that the airfield was mothballed in 1945 and that the camp probably closed in 1946. Since 1978 it has been used by the army.

**Did you know?**
In July 2011 the old camp was used to replicate an Afghan village, with some 200 individuals pretending to be Afghan villagers. Two of the individuals actually turned out to be illegal immigrants.

### Rufforth, west of York

Work began on this site in 1941 with the runways being ready the following year. Its official opening was in November 1942 and the first squadron was No 158, which were bombers. They spent four months at the airfield, losing eight of their aircraft and 61 air crewmen. Rufforth became the home to Halifax bombers in March 1943 and they remained there until 1945. In the post-war period there was a gliding school and a maintenance unit on the site. The RAF relinquished the site in 1974 and it was sold off seven years later. Some of the site is still used by light aircraft and gliders.

### Samlesbury, northwest of Blackburn

Originally, the site was due to be a municipal airport for Blackburn and Preston and plans were afoot from 1922. Despite this, construction did not begin until the spring of 1939. In the period February 1940 to 1942 nearly 800 Handley Page Hampden aircraft were distributed to squadrons from the airfield. Meanwhile a second factory was constructing Halifax bombers. This meant that by the end of the war some 3,000 aircraft had been built on the airfield and then flown to their squadrons. The site retained its aircraft production links in the post-war period and in fact today the site is owned and run by a company that builds modern fighter aircraft. However, the airfield itself is now closed.

### Sandbanks, southeast of Poole

This was a Royal Naval Air Station that used the Royal Motor Yacht Club during the Second World War. The station was open between May 1940 and October 1943.

### Sandtoft, west of Scunthorpe

This airfield opened in February 1944 to operate as a satellite base for RAF Lindholme. The base was under the control of Bomber Command and used to convert crews to heavier bombers. The station closed in November 1945 but in 1953 it was offered to the USAF. They did not take up the offer and consequently it was marked for disposal in 1955. Today there is a museum on the site and the Imperial Flying Club also operates from there.

### Sawbridgeworth, southwest of Bishop's Stortford

It is reported that this was used as a night-time landing ground in the First World War and that in the 1920s the site was taken over by a gliding club. The RAF showed an interest in it during 1937, at which time it was known as Mathams Wood. The intention was to use it for Army Cooperation aircraft. Great Hyde Hall became the headquarters. In addition to housing the Tomahawk, Mustang and Lysander aircraft, along with Spitfires, the airfield also held a secret role. Agents were taken from Sawbridgeworth into German-occupied Europe. By the summer of 1944 the airfield was being used less and less and it closed in March 1947. Several of the buildings still exist, including some being used by light industry.

### Scampton, north of Lincoln

Scampton is the current home of the Red Arrows but the airfield actually dates back to 1916 when it was called Brattleby Cliff. It was actually renamed Scampton in 1917 and used primarily for training. The land was returned to agriculture in the 1920s, but it reopened in 1936 and in 1939 was handed over to Bomber Command. The first two squadrons to be based there were Nos 49 and 83, who were engaged in attacking enemy shipping and dropping mines at sea. At

Hangar at RAF Scampton, showing the grave of Guy Gibson's dog. Gibson was the Squadron Leader of 617 Squadron, of Dambusters fame. The black Labrador was killed the day before the raid on the Mohne, Eder and Sorpe Dams and was buried outside Gibson's office as the raid was taking place. [*Image courtesy of Linda Mellor*]

first they used Hampdens and then Manchesters and finally Lancasters.

It was at Scampton that No 617 Squadron was set up to carry out the famous Dambuster Raid on 16th May, 1943. By 1944 the airfield underwent an upgrade and welcomed back bombers towards the end of the year. Throughout the course of the war, 266 aircraft were lost from Scampton. For a brief time between 1948 and 1949 it was used by the USAF's B-29 Superfortresses. It then returned to RAF use and was the home of bombers until 1982. It became the home of the Red Arrows in 1983. It faced closure in the early 1990s but in 2000 the Red Arrows returned and since then it has continued to be a key base for the RAF. There is a station museum on site.

### Scorton, north of Catterick

Scorton opened towards the end of 1939 as a satellite field for RAF Catterick. It was first used by Fighter Command and then by Blenheims of RAF Squadron No 219. After a significant upgrade to the airfield in 1941, Spitfires of No 122 Squadron and the Beaufighters of the Royal Canadian Air Force's No 406 Squadron used the site. From the spring of 1943 to April 1944 RAF Squadron Nos 26, 56, 130 and 604 were all based here. In May 1944 for two months USAAF night fighters, in the shape of the P-61 Black Widow, operated from Scorton. It was used for storage until the end of 1945 and sold off in 1958. Some of the original buildings still exist amidst the farmland.

### Sculthorpe, northwest of Fakenham

The Americans began their long-term association with Sculthorpe in 1949. During the post-war period it was an important US airbase and the entire base had a significant infrastructure: in 1957 10,000 personnel were housed there. The Americans finally abandoned the base in 1992 and since then there has been a series of demolitions, notably the hangars in 2009. Many of the other buildings have been sold off and the US quarters are now known as Wicken Green. However the airfield began life in the spring of 1942 and was to be used as an RAF heavy bomber airfield.

The site was home to the Free French Air Force's No 342 (Lorraine) Squadron, who remained there until the summer of 1943. Squadrons belonging to the Royal Australian and the Royal New Zealand Air

Forces then used the airfield. American involvement first began in 1944, when RAF Squadron No 214 arrived with their Flying Fortress aircraft and worked alongside Americans from RAF Snetterton Heath. Towards the end of the war it was redeveloped into a very heavy bomber base, which would be ideal for future American use. Parts of the airfield are still used for training by the Ministry of Defence.

### Seighford, northwest of Stafford
In 1950 this became a camp for Polish displaced persons. It is now home to the Staffordshire Gliding Club and is also used as a race circuit. Many of the original buildings still exist. It was originally opened in 1943, primarily as a satellite station for RAF Hixon. It was used by Wellington bombers and then for gliders. The airfield itself closed in 1947 and the RAF relinquished control in 1966.

### Selsey, south of Chichester
This was a short-term airfield, which opened in May 1943 and closed just a year later. It was built primarily for fighter squadrons using Spitfires in the run up to the Normandy landings. Effectively it was an advanced landing field.

**Did you know?**
Selsey has significant military connections. There was a First World War listening post here to warn of the approach of Zeppelins and the Mulberry Harbours, which were prefabricated sections for the Normandy beaches were stored here. Also, a Spitfire operating out of Selsey shot down the first German aircraft on D-Day.

### Shawbury, northwest of Shrewsbury
Flight training and aircraft repair was carried out here from 1917. By 1920 the site was once again farmland. The airfield was reactivated in 1938 and it became a flight training school once more. It saw many pilots of different nationalities, including a significant number from America. At the beginning of 1944 it became the Central Navigation School and in the post-war years it was taken over by School of Air

Traffic Control (ATC). In the 1960s it was involved in ATC training also. Helicopters moved in during the 1970s and today the site is still used for training pilots and air traffic controllers.

### Shobdon, west of Leominster

Shobdon was originally an army camp and many wounded British troops returning from the continent after France surrendered in 1940 were routed through here. The Americans became involved in the site in 1943, setting up their own hospitals and assisting in the building of a runway. It was also used as a glider training school. This school remained open until 1953. The airfield is now used by flying clubs.

### Shellingford, southwest of Faringdon

At first this site was a practice landing field in the early 1930s. The RAF began using it for night flying in 1941 and based here was an elementary flying school. Later glider pilots were also trained on the site. In the post-war period the airfield saw Dutch pilots being trained and then, in 1948, the airfield was closed but used for a short time in the 1950s by the Americans. They left in 1957 and since then the airfield has been used for quarrying. Some of the buildings still exist and a proportion of these are used as part of an industrial estate.

### Shepherds Grove, northeast of Bury St Edmunds

The intention was to use this as a USAAF base but instead the RAF began working there in April 1944. In January 1945 RAF Squadron No 196 used the airfield to launch their operations for the airborne part of the crossing of the Rhine. In the post-war period, Americans were based there; fighter interceptors came to the airfield in 1951. The Americans remained on the base until the end of 1958 and after this the Ministry of Defence used it to store nuclear weapons. The base was finally closed in 1966. Some of the airfield is now an industrial estate, but most of the site was demolished by 2008.

### Sherburn in Elmet, west of Selby

The Royal Flying Corps used the airfield to monitor recently received aircraft during the First World War. In the mid-1920s it was used by the Yorkshire Aeroplane Club. Fighter Command squadrons based at RAF Church Fenton used the airfield as a satellite landing ground until 1941. The site was then developed by Blackburn Aircraft to make Fairey Swordfish aircraft. They continued producing aircraft here until 1944, by which time 1,700 had been built. Large parts of the airfield have been redeveloped but nonetheless the Sherburn Aero Club still uses the runways.

### Shoreham, west of Brighton

Shoreham is now home to an annual air show, maintaining its links to the RAF. The airfield is rather grandly called Shoreham (Brighton City) Airport and has a claim to being the oldest licensed airfield in Britain, with an Art Deco terminal building. The airfield can trace its aviation history back to 1910. During the First World War it was requisitioned and primarily the Royal Flying Corps used it as a training base.

It was also used to evaluate captured enemy aircraft. It largely returned to civilian use in the interwar years, but the RAF was based there towards the end of the 1930s to train volunteer pilots. RAF Squadron No 225 used it to patrol the English Channel and the airfield also saw use as an emergency landing ground. It was returned to civilian flying in January 1946 and since then has continued its role as a general aviation airport.

### Sibson, west of Peterborough

RAF Sibson was open for six years, between 1940 and 1946. The Royal Navy used it to train their pilots between July 1940 and the beginning of 1941. It was then used by the RAF for flight training. The airfield was effectively closed by 1945 although the official closure did not happen until October 1946. It would appear that very little now remains of this airfield. Nearby is another airfield known as Sibson, which is home to the Sibson Peterborough Flying School. This was a post-war development.

### Silloth, north of Silloth

Silloth opened in 1939 and quickly became a Coastal Command base. It underwent significant improvement in 1941 and was subsequently used to train bomber crews. A maintenance unit was retained on the site and transport aircraft flew from here during the Berlin Airlift. It was then used to dismantle surplus aircraft. The last flight took place in 1960 and by 1962 the site was being used by light industry and much had been returned to farmland. A number of the buildings, including some of the hangars, still exist.

### Silverstone, Silverstone Circuit
Before Silverstone became the world-renowned Grand Prix racing circuit it was an RAF bomber base, with three runways. It opened in 1943 and was primarily home to the Wellington bombers of an operational training unit. The airfield was actually sold off in 1947 and the first Grand Prix took place in 1948. Some of the old buildings have retained their value; the control tower is used as a changing room and one of the original hangars is still in place.

Silverstone from the air, viewed from a Prague-bound flight from East Midlands. The home of the British Grand Prix is on the site of the former RAF Silverstone airfield. [*Image courtesy of Thomas Nugent*]

### Skellingthorpe, southwest of Lincoln

Today part of the Lincoln bypass and the Birchwood estate stands on most of the former airfield. It opened in 1941 and was at first home to RAF Squadron No 50, a bomber unit flying Hampden aircraft. Also based there was Royal Australian Air Force's No 455 Squadron. By 1942 it was clear that in order to cope with Lancaster bombers the runways would need to be extended and by 1943 both 50 Squadron and 61 Squadron were operating from Skellingthorpe. Towards the end of the war the airfield was mothballed and used by a maintenance unit who dealt with crashed aircraft. Over the course of the war the squadrons operating from the base lost 208 aircraft.

### Skipton-on-Swale, west of Thirsk

Livestock farms and fields now occupy the site that was once this base. It opened in August 1942 and became operational in May 1943. It was designed to be a satellite station for RAF Leeming. The first arrivals were Canadians who had a brief stay between August and October 1942. This was the RCAF's No 420 Squadron flying primarily Wellington bombers. Between May and September 1943 the RCAF's No 432 Squadron, also with Wellingtons, operated from the base. The RCAF No 433 Squadron stayed the longest, operating there from September 1943 until August 1945.

The final squadron was again a Canadian one, 424, who had flown in from duties in North Africa. They arrived in November 1943 and stayed until August 1945. 424 Squadron lost a total of 52 aircraft whilst at the base. Both 424 and 433 were disbanded in October 1945 and just over a year later a Polish bomber squadron moved in, in order to be disbanded. Shortly afterwards the airfield was closed. There is a memorial to a Canadian crew who died when their bomber crash-landed on the way home to the base.

### Sleap, southeast of Ellesmere

This was a satellite field to RAF Tilstock and opened in January 1943. Throughout the war it was used for operational training by bomber crews and was also used to train air crews that would work with Special Forces. The airfield was effectively mothballed shortly after Christmas 1945 but it reopened as a satellite station for RAF Shawbury in 1956. For a time it was a training school. The airfield finally closed in 1964. Today there is an aero club on the site, along with a museum.

## Smith's Lawn, Windsor Great Park

This is actually located within Windsor Great Park and was operational from the 1920s until the end of the Second World War. It is believed that it also contained the private airstrip of the Prince of Wales, who would later abdicate and become the Duke of Windsor. This was apparently located in the southeast corner of the park. From 1940, Wellington bombers were constructed in a hangar on the site. It was used also as a relief landing ground and it may also have been the case that some USAAF aircraft used it occasionally. It would appear that this site would have been the emergency airstrip, had the Germans invaded and the Royal family had to be evacuated.

## Snaith, east of Knottingley

This was primarily a bomber base and it saw Wellington and Halifax bombers. It opened in 1941 and would appear to have been operational until at least May 1946. Squadrons that served there, although some for only a matter of days, included:

- 51 (the longest stay – 1942 to 1945)
- 150
- 266
- 578

Some of the buildings still exist, although part of the site is now beneath the M62.

## Snitterfield, north of Stratford-upon-Avon

For the most part this airfield was used to train crews and it operated as a relief landing ground. It was also home to Belgian pilots and aircrew from 1944. The airfield was ready for use in June 1942 but did not open until the following year. It is believed that the airfield closed in 1946. Most of the site is now a golf course, although there is the Stratford Armouries Museum on the southern part, which opened in 2007.

## Somerton, south of Cowes, Isle of Wight

When an aircraft factory was opened in Cowes there was a need for a nearby airbase. This was also used by the RAF just after the First

World War. By 1919 the aircraft factory had closed and the airfield was being used by gliders and other light aircraft. In the late 1920s, flight tests were carried out from the airfield and in 1931 another company took over the old aircraft factory. There were some commercial flights in the 1930s, which offered travel to Gatwick and Ryde. It was not used to a great extent during the Second World War, however, due to its exposed position. There were plans to develop the site in the post-war period as a civilian airport but eventually the airfield was sold off and closed for flying.

### South Cerney, southeast of Cirencester
The base is now used as a major hub to send British troops overseas and is known as the Air Mounting Centre. The history of the site goes back to the summer of 1937 when it began its role as a flight training school. This was the purpose that it sustained until the spring of 1946. After the war it continued in this role until 1971 when the base was transferred over to the control of the British Army.

### South Marston, northeast of Swindon
Aircraft production was important around the Swindon area and South Marston was chosen as the so-called shadow factory. In the event of the main factories coming under air attack by the Luftwaffe, production could continue in these other locations. The factory was opened in the summer of 1940 and by 1941 they were producing around 80 aircraft each month. The Miles Master aircraft they were making were used as training aircraft for fighter pilots.

Later in the war they began producing Stirling bombers at a rate of around 16 per month. This also meant that an airfield was necessary and this was camouflaged in order to disguise the purpose of the site. By 1943 the decision had been taken that the factory would begin producing Lancaster bombers, but instead they began producing Spitfires and they produced their last aircraft in 1949. In the post-war period they refurbished aircraft and produced a number of different aircraft, both for the Royal Navy and for foreign air forces. The final aircraft they produced was the Supermarine Scimitar in 1961. The factory continued production, now for Vickers, and in the 1980s a car manufacturer bought the site and the airfield began to be used to test vehicles.

## Southam, southeast of Royal Leamington Spa

Little remains of this airfield, which was only open between 1940 and the end of 1944. It was home to flight training and the airfield operated as a satellite for RAF Ansty.

## Southrop, east of Cirencester

Southrop was a relief landing field that opened in August 1940 and the last use was towards the end of 1947. It was primarily used by training aircraft. Some of the original buildings do still exist, but in a dilapidated state. It would seem that the airfield was certainly originally used as a relief ground for Brize Norton and then later for South Cerney.

## Speke, Liverpool John Lennon Airport

This site is now much better known as Liverpool John Lennon Airport, which handles 5.2 million passengers a year. It got its original name as it was located in the grounds of Speke Hall, which is a Tudor mansion that now belongs to the National Trust. There were civilian commercial flights from the site in the 1930s and it became known as RAF Speke during the war.

Also on the site was an aircraft factory that produced a number of British aircraft, including Blenheims, as well as being home to Lockheed who had American aircraft that had been shipped from the US in parts and assembled on site. The airfield returned to civilian use shortly after the end of the war in Europe and was gradually developed, assuming its new name in 2002.

## Spilsby, east of Spilsby

This opened as a satellite field for RAF East Kirkby, but in October 1943 it became home to RAF Squadron No 207. Later they were joined by No 44 Squadron. Towards the end of the war 44 Squadron left to be replaced by RAF Squadron No 75 (New Zealand) Squadron. By the end of 1946 the airfield had been mothballed, but it was reopened in 1955 and at this point it was also used by American bombers. The airfield was finally abandoned in the late 1970s, with the runways being used to provide aggregates for the Humber Bridge. There are still some of the original buildings in existence and a memorial to 207 Squadron on the old airfield site.

RAF Spilsby memorial. [*Image courtesy of Richard Croft*]

**Did you know?**
A Hawker Hurricane piloted by Flight Lieutenant Denys Gillam took off from Speke on 8th October, 1940. His aircraft had literally just been assembled and was ready for testing. Suddenly, a German bomber appeared and Gillam promptly shot it down. This is believed to be the quickest kill during the battle of Britain, as Gillam's undercarriage was still retracting when he made the attack.

*Squires Gate, Blackpool Airport*
Before the First World War there was an aerodrome based here to serve Blackpool. It became Clifton Park horse racing course and during the First World War the site was used as a convalescent hospital. By the 1920s the airfield had reopened but was now in competition with Stanley Park. In the Second World War there was not only a Wellington factory on the site, but also it was home to a Wellington squadron and No 63 Squadron flying Fairey Battles. Today, the site is used for Blackpool Airport, as well as a shopping centre and home to industrial units.

### St Just, Land's End
In 1937 there was a passenger service operating from here to the Isles of Scilly. During the Second World War it was primarily used for coastal patrolling. The flights between St Just at Land's End to St Marys in the Scilly Isles continued throughout the war and the base seems to have been used until around June 1945. The base was very small and consisted of a simple grass field.

### St Mawgan, northeast of Newquay
Originally this was called RAF Trebelzue and was a satellite station for St Eval. It had already been operating as a civilian airfield from the 1930s and it received the name St Mawgan in February 1943. By the summer the USAAF had taken over the airfield and, incredibly, after improvements it became one of the busiest airfields in Britain, also being used as a transit point to send aircraft to North Africa. By 1944 over 150 aircraft were arriving there each day. After the victory in Europe the RAF took back control and the airfield was mothballed in July 1947, reopening as a training school in 1951. Helicopters began using it in 1956 and the Newquay Cornwall Airport now operates from part of the original airfield. Military flying ceased in 2008.

### St Merryn, southeast of Padstow
When this airfield opened in August 1940 it was a naval air station and called HMS *Vulture*. From this point until the end of 1943 it was primarily home to the Fleet Air Arm Squadron Nos 774 and 792. In the autumn of 1942 Fleet Air Arm Squadron No 748 was also created here. In 1943 it became the School of Air Combat and by 1944 this was renamed as the School of Naval Air Warfare. Many of the pilots and crew were training up to be shipped to the Far East. When the war ended the resources that had been thrown at the base continued to be used all the way through to June 1955. It closed in January 1956.

### Stanley Park, east of Blackpool
Stanley Park is now part of Blackpool Zoo and one of the old aircraft buildings is now the elephant house. The site was originally designed to be Blackpool's airport when it opened in 1931. During the Second World War it became a technical training school. The site closed in 1945. Several of the buildings, including the hangars, are thought to

be still in existence, although the rest of the site is now a golf course and hotel.

### Stanton Harcourt, southeast of Witney

The Abingdon Air and Country Fair and flying clubs now use this airfield. Flying began in September 1940 and the site was used as a satellite station for RAF Abingdon. It was primarily a bomber base and used to train pilots for night flying. It was also used for gunnery training. The airfield was closed in January 1946 and since then the area has seen extensive gravel excavation. Several of the buildings still exist.

**Did you know?**
On 13th January, 1943, Winston Churchill flew out of Stanton Harcourt in a Liberator to attend the Casablanca Conference.

### Staverton, west of Cheltenham

This is now Gloucester Airport and it is still used by the RAF and by civilian aircraft, as well as being an aviation museum. The airfield was opened in 1936 as an RAF training school. This role continued throughout the course of the Second World War and it was also later used for the first flight of the Gloster jet aircraft.

### Stoke Orchard, southeast of Tewkesbury

When this opened in 1941 it was an elementary flight training school but it later went on to become the centre where glider pilots would be trained. Significantly it was also an aircraft production factory, run by Gloster. Today the airfield is mainly farmland with industrial units and part of the site is also used as a refuse dump.

### Stradishall, northeast of Haverhill

HMP High Point now stands on the site, along with a Ministry of Defence training area. The original airfield opened in 1938 and remained operational until 1970. It was primarily home to bombers and over the course of the war the airfield saw many different units and was also extended in 1941. At any one time around 3,000 personnel would be on the base. Over the course of the war 104 aircraft operating out of Stradishall were lost.

In August 1945 RAF Transport Command took over the airfield and towards the end of the 1940s it was mothballed and then used once again by the RAF, this time for flight training. The training moved out in August 1970 and shortly afterwards the site was selected for the construction of a prison.

### Stratford, southeast of Stratford-upon-Avon
This was a satellite station for RAF Wellesbourne Mountford and Wellingtons operated from here between July 1941 and November 1942. More Wellingtons also operated from the airfield, again as an operational training unit, until the war in Europe ended. It was also then used by the RAF Signals Flying Unit. The airfield closed in 1945 and it was returned to farmland, although some of the buildings still remain, including a derelict control tower.

### Stretton, west of Altrincham
Although the RAF originally intended to use this site, the airfield was in fact used by the Royal Navy and called HMS *Blackcap* when it opened in June 1942. It was to see dozens of Fleet Air Arm squadrons based here. It was used as a transit point for aircraft flying to or flying from aircraft carriers in dock at Liverpool. It was also used to repair aircraft. It would seem that the Royal Navy retained an interest in it until at least 1959 but since then the airfield has been largely retained. Most of the outlying area is now farmland, part of the M56 crosses the site and the rest is an industrial estate.

### Strubby, southwest of Mablethorpe
The Lincolnshire Gliding Club uses the former RAF base today. The airfield was originally designed to be used by Bomber Command but in the end it was first used by Coastal Command, mainly for air-sea rescue. Bomber Command did, however, then take it over and certainly operated there from September 1944. In all operations RAF Squadron No 619 lost some 65 aircraft. Strubby was used to bring back British prisoners of war from Europe and by September 1945 the airfield was being used mainly for storage. It was used as a satellite landing ground for RAF Manby by 1949. The airfield closed again in

Winch launch from snow-covered airfield at Lincs Gliding Club, formerly RAF Strubby. [*Image courtesy of Ian Butler*]

1972 and was sold as farmland in 1980. It then became a helicopter base for rigs in the North Sea.

### Sturgate, east of Gainsborough

Sturgate is still being used as a private airfield today. It was actually developed very late and only opened in 1944. It was used as a training school throughout the remainder of the war and it would appear that the RAF ceased operations there at the beginning of 1946. It was used between 1953 and 1964 by American fighter units. Some of the original buildings, including the control tower, still stand today.

### Sutton Bridge, west of King's Lynn

The site was originally a training camp, and in the 1920s aircraft would use it to practice ground attacks. It was not called RAF Sutton Bridge until 1932 and in fact there was no airfield there until 1936. At the beginning of 1940 RAF Squadron No 266 operated from the airfield.

Throughout the course of the war the airfield was primarily a gunnery school, which was a role it continued in through to the spring of 1944 when the school moved to RAF Catfoss. The airfield was still in use as a training camp until 1958, but it would seem that flying ceased in 1946. Today the site is the Sutton Bridge Power Station and an agricultural research station.

### Swannington, northwest of Horsham St Faith

This was a late opening airfield, which only became operational in the spring of 1944. The first arrivals were RAF Squadron No 85, who operated Mosquitos in a night fighter role. They destroyed in excess of 40 enemy aircraft before leaving the base in June 1945. They were also joined by No 157 Squadron, another Mosquito unit, which scored nearly 30 kills before being disbanded in August 1945. Both units were also involved in trying to deal with the V-1 flying bombs and between them they managed to destroy at least seventy of them. Mosquito aircraft were scrapped on the site in the post-war period and the airfield closed in 1947, being sold off 10 years later. There are many buildings still on the site, albeit in a derelict state.

### Swanton Morley, north of Dereham

Swanton Morley was a major Bomber Command operational base, which opened in the late summer of 1940. At various time it was home to RAF Squadron Nos:

- 88
- 98
- 105
- 226
- 305

It also saw Hurricanes and Mosquitos in 1943 and Beaufighters, Lancasters and Spitfires in the last six months of the war. The RAF retained an interest in the site until it closed in 1995. It then became Robertson Barracks in 1996 when it was taken over by the British Army and today it is home to The Light Dragoons.

### Swinderby, southwest of Lincoln

This was a Bomber Command airfield that opened in 1940. It would see a huge variety of different aircraft, including:

- Fairey Battles
- Hampdens
- Wellingtons
- Manchesters
- Lancasters

During the course of the war approximately 84 aircraft were lost whilst operating out of the airfield. The RAF continued to use the airfield in the post-war period primarily for pilot and recruit training. Flying activities ceased in the early 1990s and the airfield was sold in 1995, with the plan to level the whole site in preparation for the building of a business park and housing.

### Swingfield, south of Barham
Swingfield was originally a Royal Flying Corps airfield that opened in 1917. It was to remain in use until April 1945. During the course of the Second World War it saw RAF Squadron Nos 50, 119 and 819 based there. The airfield is also alternatively listed as an advanced landing ground, which was prepared in advance of the Normandy landings in 1944, but it was apparently not used for this purpose. Also there are references to Fleet Air Arm aircraft being used from Swingfield. These may be ones that were temporarily loaned to RAF Coastal Command in 1944. Little remains of Swingfield and most of the site is now farmland.

### Syerston, southeast of Newark-on-Trent
The airfield is now an RAF cadet gliding school and most of the original buildings, apart from the control tower, have been pulled down. It opened in December 1940 and was used by Polish-manned Wellington bombers. It was later also used by the Royal Canadian Air Force. By 1942 several Lancaster bomber squadrons were using the airfield and it was also being used for flight training. By October 1945 RAF Transport Command were using the facility and it was still being used for flight training. This training school was disbanded in 1970 and for a while the airfield's future seemed in doubt. A gliding school moved there in 1975 and the Nottingham University Gliding Club have also used the site in the past.

### Sywell, southwest of Kettering
An aero club opened here in 1928 and the RAF began using it for their own pilot training in the mid-1930s. During the Second World War it retained this role, training around 2,500 pilots and also they carried out flight training and repairs to bombers, including Wellingtons and Lancasters, on site. The RAF continued to use the airfield in the post-

war period but by the 1960s it was once again a civilian airfield. The current control tower is not the original one and is believed to have been constructed on the site during the 1950s.

### Tarrant Rushton, east of Wimbourne
The airfield opened in November 1943 and was used by RAF Squadron No 298 and their Halifax aircraft. The airfield also saw a number of other squadrons, including:

- 190
- 196
- 295
- 298
- 620
- 644

These squadrons were all stationed here at various times over the period from the spring of 1944 to the autumn of 1946. The airfield was used for flight refuelling and servicing between 1948 and 1980. It was also intended that the airfield should house V-bombers but this never came to fruition. The airfield was closed in September 1980 and since then it has been used as farmland.

### Tatenhill, east of Burton-upon-Trent
Tatenhill was both an operational training unit base and also used for flight training. Bombers left here on night bomber training flights after it opened in 1941. In the post-war period the RAF School of Explosives was based here and they left in 1947 with the airfield being sold a short time later.

**Did you know?**
Just three miles away from Tatenhill, was a huge, underground bomb store. There was an accidental explosion there on 27th November, 1944. It is said that the crater created by the explosion was the largest ever to have occurred in Britain.

## Tatton Park, south of Altrincham

Tatton Park is an estate that is now owned by the National Trust, but during the Second World War it was used to train paratroopers that were based at RAF Ringway. It saw an incredible amount of activity and in the period 1940 to 1946 some 60,000 paratroopers used the facilities. These included Europeans and those that would be dropped covertly into Europe as members of the Special Operations Executive.

## Tempsford, south of St Neots

It is still possible to see the outline of the runways at this former airfield. However, its role was a closely guarded secret, as it was responsible for taking SOE agents and their equipment into German-occupied Europe. It also picked them up for debriefing. Over the course of the Second World War it was used by a variety of units who were largely fulfilling this ferrying role, including:

- 53 Squadron with their Liberators
- 109 Squadron in Wellingtons
- 138 Squadron using the Halifax
- 149 Squadron with Stirling bombers
- 161 Squadron with Lysanders
- Royal Canadian Air Force's No 426 Squadron in Liberators
- 617 Squadron in Lancasters

**Did you know?**
The agent Violette Szabo, who was an SOE operative, flew back from her first mission into Tempsford on 30th April, 1944. She left again in the June but this time she was captured after a gun battle and was subsequently tortured and murdered in Ravensbrück concentration camp.

## Theale, southwest of Reading

This was also known as RAF Sheffield Farm. The site is now a series of gravel pits used by industry and for leisure. It was originally designed to be used as a relief landing ground and also as an elementary flying school. By 1944 a gliding school had been established here and we know that the flights ceased towards the end of June 1945. The airfield was disposed of in 1948.

### Tholthorpe, east of Easingwold

For many months of the Second World War this airfield saw more Canadians than British. It opened as a satellite for RAF Linton-on-Ouse in the latter part of 1940. It underwent an extensive building programme until the summer of 1943 to bring it up to scratch as a bomber station. From June 1943 through to June 1945 it was home to a succession of Royal Canadian Air Force units, these were:

- 420 (Snowy Owl)
- 425 (Alouette)
- 431 (Iroquois)
- 434 (Bluenose)

Collectively, they launched an enormous number of operations, most of them flew Halifax aircraft throughout the war years and 119 aircraft failed to come home. It is understood that the airfield closed in June 1945 and that one of the control towers was subsequently converted into a house.

Old huts at Tholthorpe Airfield. [*Image courtesy of Gordon Hatton*]

## Thornaby, southwest of Middlesbrough

Thornaby's aviation connections lasted at least 30 years from 1928. It is likely that it was also used as a landing ground during the First World War. The airfield itself, however, opened in 1928 and two years later was home to first a light bomber squadron and then a fighter squadron. It was also in considerable use all the way up to the outbreak of the war. Coastal Command operated from here between September 1939 and the spring of 1941. It saw enormous numbers of squadron movements, with a huge variety of aircraft, including:

- Blenheim
- Beaufighter
- Hudson
- Spitfire
- Warwick
- Anson

In the post-war period night fighters were based here, first Mosquitos then Spitfires and finally Vampires. They ceased to be held there in the spring of 1957. Helicopters operated in an air-sea rescue role from 1954 to 1957 but the final unit based here was RAF Squadron No 92, who was stationed here for 13 months from September 1957. At this point the airfield was closed and the site is now given over to industry and housing.

## Tilstock, southeast of Whitchurch

Whitley and Wellington bombers operated from this site between the autumn of 1942 and the late summer of 1944. It was also used by aircrews training to use gliders and drop agents for the SOE. In the latter part of the war the airfield also saw Stirling, Halifax, Wellington and Albemarles bombers. It would seem that the airfield closed in March 1946 and remained mothballed until it was sold off in the 1950s. The airfield is still used for parachuting and is also a butterfly reserve; the remainder has been given over to agriculture.

## Tollerton, southeast of Nottingham

In 1930 Tollerton, or Nottingham Airport, opened for civilian flights. During the Second World War it was used as a relief landing ground for RAF Newton, where there was a training school for the Polish Air

Force. It was also used to repair damaged aircraft. It became a commercial airport shortly after the war but largely failed and since then it has been restricted to private aircraft and flight training. It is now known as Nottingham City Airport.

### Topcliffe, southwest of Thirsk
Originally this was a satellite station for RAF Linton-on-Ouse. It was used by Whitley bombers belonging to RAF Squadron Nos 77 and 102. After improvements to the runways the Royal Canadian Air Force's Squadron Nos 419 and 424 began flying their Wellington bombers from the base. By the beginning of 1943 the Canadians were using it primarily as a training base.

The RAF retained an interest in the site until the early 1970s, mainly for training. The British Army took it over in 1972, renaming it Alanbrooke Barracks. The Royal Navy used it as a flying school in the 1980s and the RAF and the Royal Navy based navigation training here until a decade ago. It is still used to this day by the RAF. There are two parachute clubs on site and it is also used by an air ambulance.

### Townsend, east of Chippenham
RAF Townsend was opened in the spring of 1938 and remained operational until the summer of 1944. It was a satellite station for RAF Yatesbury. The site was used to train pilots before the outbreak of the Second World War. Townsend would often have a variety of different aircraft parked on it during the war. It would seem that Townsend was not used to a great extent beyond the autumn of 1942 and it was retained until the middle of 1944. The area is now farmland.

### Treligga, east of Slaughter Bridge
This airfield was known as HMS *Vulture II*. The site was already being used for gliders before the Second World War. Essentially it was a satellite station for RAF St Merryn, or HMS *Vulture*. Its primary purpose was as an aerial bombing and gunnery range and it retained this role after the war, with the range closing in 1955. What remains of the airfield and buildings can still be seen near Treligga village.

### Tuddenham, northwest of Bury St Edmunds
RAF Tuddenham had a 20-year association with the RAF and the USAF, who used it in the post-war period. It was opened in the

> **Did you know?**
> The Women's Royal Naval Service exclusively ran HMS *Vulture II*. Their accommodation was at Port Gaverne.

autumn of 1943, with the long-term tenants RAF 90 Squadron at first with Stirling bombers and later with Lancasters being based here until November 1946. The base had a brief association with RAF Squadron No 186, who were reformed at Tuddenham in the winter of 1944.

From Christmas 1944 RAF Squadron No 138 operated from the airfield, through to the end of 1946. The last RAF squadrons to use Tuddenham were 147 and 207, who were at the base from the spring of 1946. The USAF chose Tuddenham as a satellite station and used it for five years from 1954. It was then used from 1959 to 1963 as a missile base by the RAF. After this the airfield closed. There are some buildings still in existence, although most of the area is now farmland.

### Turweston, north of Bicester
This airfield was used for barely three years. It saw Anson and Wellington bombers for a short time towards the end of 1942 to the spring of 1943. It was then briefly used by Mitchell and Boston bombers and finally, from July 1943 to the summer of 1945, Wellington bombers. The site is now thought to be a private airfield, although several of the derelict buildings were still in existence until quite recently.

### Twinwood Farm, north of Bedford
Twinwood opened in the summer of 1941, receiving concrete runways a year later. It was primarily used by light bombers belonging to RAF Squadron Nos:

- 26
- 169
- 239
- 268
- 613

**Did you know?**
This airfield will have immortality if for nothing else that it was the place from which Glenn Miller took off heading for Paris on 15th December, 1944. His aircraft of course disappeared over the English Channel and was never found. There was an attempt some years ago by relatives of Glenn Miller to have Twinwood's control tower dismantled brick by brick and shipped to the United States. This did not come to fruition, but instead there is a Glenn Miller Museum in the restored tower.

By 1944 the airfield was being used by the 8th USAAF and it closed in June 1945.

### Upavon, north of Amesbury
The RAF has a gliding squadron here, although in 1993 the British Army took over the base and it is now part of HQ Land Forces. The airfield dates back to 1912 and was used by the Royal Flying Corps.

Upavon airfield, Taken from a glider on a cold winter's afternoon. [*Image courtesy of Chris Talbot*]

In 1918 it became the RAF Central Flying School but the school moved out in 1926 and the base was used by fighter squadrons. The flying school returned to the base in 1935, remaining there until 1942. It was used extensively by the RAF in the post-war years until it was handed over to the British Army in August 1993.

### Upper Heyford, northwest of Bicester

The first aircraft to fly out of Upper Heyford did so just weeks before the end of the First World War. Flying seems to have ceased in around May 1919, at which point the station was closed and many of the buildings demolished. Nonetheless flying recommenced in 1927 and by the 1930s it was intended that Upper Heyford should have three bomber squadrons on site. It was used for a combination of training and by bomber squadrons during the Second World War. It was then home to parachute training in the immediate post-war period.

In 1950 the USAF began to develop the base as a major site for their heavy bombers. It was officially handed over to them in May 1951. The base was especially important in the mid-1960s when the French told the Americans that all of their military forces had to leave France. Many of the units found a new home at Upper Heyford. In 1982, because Upper Heyford's aircraft were armed with nuclear weapons, a peace camp was set up here. The base was important during Operation Desert Storm in 1991, but in 1993 it was closed and to this day many of the buildings are still unoccupied, although it now belongs to the Ministry of Defence.

### Upwood, southwest of Ramsey

Farmland was requisitioned by the Royal Flying Corps in 1917 and it was then known as Bury or Ramsey, due to its location and the proximity of the two towns. It was renamed Upwood in 1918 and was primarily used for night training. It would seem that the squadrons there were disbanded in 1919, the buildings pulled down and the site returned to farmland. Upwood was selected as an ideal site in the 1930s for the RAF. It was designed to be able to handle up to three bomber squadrons. Work was underway to make considerable improvements when the Second World War began and during the war it saw Blenheim, Anson, Wellington and, later, Mosquito aircraft.

Towards the end of the war the airfield also saw Lancaster bombers belonging to RAF Squadron No 156. This squadron was involved in dropping food supplies into Holland and to fly Allied prisoners of war home in Operation Exodus, which culminated in bringing home thousands of prisoners of war. Upwood continued to be used extensively by the RAF. Not only was it involved in the Suez Crisis, it also deployed squadrons to Singapore during the Malay Uprising, to Kenya during the Mau Mau Uprising and then to Cyprus. The USAF was given control of Upwood in 1981 and they remained there until 1994, but the last of the USAF did not move out until 2005. There is still an American presence at Upwood and it is considered part of the larger Alconbury and Molesworth group of bases.

### Waddington, south of Lincoln

Waddington can trace its roots back to 1916 when it was used as a training school, not just for British pilots but also for Americans too. It remained open until around 1920 when it was mothballed. Considerable improvements were made in the mid-1930s and it was designated as a bomber base in 1937. It would at first be home to Blenheim and Hampden aircraft. By 1941 Lancasters were in service at the airfield and in 1943 Australian Lancasters took over the base. They launched their last raid towards the end of April 1945.

The airfield was involved in helping to bring back the thousands of Allied prisoners after the collapse of Germany in May 1945. Post-war the airfield was a V-bomber base and it reopened in 1955 in this guise. Today RAF Waddington is the primary operating base for the RAF's airborne intelligence systems and there are six squadrons present there.

---

**Did you know?**
RAF Squadron Nos 44 and 50, based at Waddington, launched an attack on the German naval base at Kiel on the very first day of the Second World War.

---

## Walney, east of Barrow-in-Furness

Plans were afoot in the late 1930s to develop a site on Walney Island as a civilian airfield. The work did not get underway until 1940 and consequently the first users of the airfield were in fact the RAF. It was primarily used as an air gunnery school and for flight training. Around 5,000 RAF personnel were trained here during the war. The airfield closed in 1946 and it was retained until it was sold in the late-1950s. It is now owned by BAE Systems and there is also a gliding club on the airfield.

## Warboys, northeast of Huntingdon

This airfield was ready for use by the summer of 1941 and it was originally intended that it would be a satellite for RAF Upwood. Stirling bombers were the first to use the airfield, belonging to RAF Squadron No 15. It was then used by an operational training unit, with the first main squadron, RAF Squadron No 156, arriving in the summer of 1942. They first used Wellington aircraft, and later, Lancasters. Various aircraft belonging to Bomber Command used the site, and it would also see Lancasters and Mosquitos in the last months of the war.

RAF Squadron No 571, using Mosquitos that had arrived in July 1945, was disbanded here in the September. By December 1945 the airfield had been mothballed and many of the buildings and other infrastructure were demolished to make way for farmland. In the period 1960 to 1963 missiles were based there, but then the RAF gave up the site. There are a handful of buildings still in existence.

## Warton, east of Lytham St Annes

BAE Systems still use this site and it was an important centre for the development of post-war aircraft, including the Eurofighter, a Nimrod, as well as the production of the Tornado. The site began, however, as a satellite field to be used by Coastal Command based at RAF Squires Gate. It was also used by the USAAF as a stop-off point for aircraft to be distributed to operational squadrons in Europe and in North Africa. The RAF appears to have taken over the station towards the end of the Second World War and then passed it into private hands in 1947.

> **Did you know?**
> Two B-24s left Warton on a test flight on 23rd August, 1944. There
> was a violent storm and the aircraft were called back. One of
> them crashed into the village of Freckleton in Lancashire and hit
> the Holy Trinity Church of England School, three houses and a
> business premises. Amongst the 61 killed, 38 were children.

## Warwick, southeast of Warwick

Warwick opened towards the end of 1941 and was primarily used to
train pilots. Essentially it was a relief landing ground and it is reported
to have been open until February 1946. At various times it was used
in conjunction with RAF Church Lawford and Hockley Heath.

## Watchfield, northeast of Swindon

Watchfield was an important training command base and it has been
suggested that around 90 per cent of all RAF bomber pilots were once
at Watchfield to learn how to land in poor weather conditions. The
base seems to have been operational between 1939 and 1946. It was
certainly an air observation and navigation school between 1940 and
1941, but during the course of the war it saw a blind approach school,
an airfield controllers school and, after the war, it was a school of air
traffic control. The airfield closed in 1950 and wind turbines are now
on part of the old airfield, although the rest of the site seems to be
farmland.

## Waterbeach, north of Cambridge

This airfield opened in 1941 and many RAF squadrons passed
through this base, as it was used to convert squadrons from one type
of aircraft to another. The first squadron arrived in March 1941, in the
shape of Wellington bombers of RAF Squadron No 99 and they
remained there for a year. The airfield saw Lancasters, Liberators,
Wellingtons and Stirling bombers.

The bombers left the airfield in August 1945 and it was taken over
by Transport Command, who remained there for some years and
certainly until 1950 when Waterbeach became a Fighter Command
base. There were considerable changes to the structure of the base to

accommodate the new jet fighters. During the 1980s the site was turned over to the British Army and it is now primarily used by Royal Engineers. The main runway is still in use.

### Wath Head, southwest of Carlisle

This was a satellite landing ground that opened in the spring of 1941 and was linked to RAF Kirkbride. It soon became clear that the site was not ideal as it often became waterlogged. After some work, it was reopened in the spring of 1942 and saw Mitchell, Halifax and Wellington aircraft. It became an offshoot of RAF Dumfries at the beginning of 1944 and Wellington bombers were stored here before being broken up for scrap. The airfield finally closed in September 1945. Very little is left of the site, although there are original buildings amongst woodland.

### Wellesbourne Mountford, east of Stratford-upon-Avon

Opening in 1941, the airfield was primarily used to service aircraft, to train ferry pilots and, later, for glider training. In the post-war period it was used by the School of Photography and also had a maintenance unit. The airfield would appear to have closed in 1963. Some 9,000 aircrew were trained here by the end of the Second World War. Today there is a museum in the underground emergency command and control bunker. The airfield is still operational and provides a range of services for private aircraft users.

### Wellingore, south of Lincoln

From the late 1930s this was used as a relief landing ground for RAF Cranwell. It was then attached to RAF Digby and saw Hurricanes, Beaufighters and Blenheims. From the autumn of 1942 to Christmas 1943 four squadrons were based here:

- 154
- 288
- 416
- 613

The airfield was then used by Hurricanes and Spitfires until the spring of 1944. It then appears to have been used as a relief landing ground for RAF Cranfield until its closure in 1945. Some of the original features still exist but most of the area is now farmland.

### West Hartlepool, south of Hartlepool

This site is variously known as RAF Greatham and West Hartlepool Civic Airport. Industrial buildings now cover this site, which was once owned by British Steel. In the period June 1942 to January 1943 it was home to RAF Squadron No 403 and their Spitfires, but it would seem that only a handful of aircraft were ever based here, as the squadron actually operated from RAF Catterick. Little now remains of the old airfield, although there are some pillboxes still in place.

### West Raynham, southwest of Fakenham

The Ministry of Defence sold off this site in 2006, with the RAF having left in 1994. The intention now seems to be to develop the site for housing, although there is considerable pressure to list many of the buildings in order to prevent them from being demolished. The airfield opened to accept the Blenheims of RAF Squadron No 101 in May 1939. West Raynham even acquired a satellite field of its own at Great Massingham.

In July 1940, RAF Squadron No 101 launched its first mission; they would be involved in more than 600 in the coming year. New squadrons were also formed at this airfield in 1942 and in 1943 French-manned Boston aircraft of No 342 Squadron was formed. There was

West Raynham airfield, Norfolk. [*Image courtesy of Rodney Burton*]

considerable investment in the site in 1943 and by the time the work was finished it was capable of housing more than 3,000 personnel.

By the end of 1943 Mosquito bombers were operating from West Raynham. The airfield saw continued RAF support into the post-war years and a huge variety of aircraft. It was also the home of the Royal Observer Corps' annual summer training camp. The last squadron to leave the airfield was RAF Squadron No 85, which was disbanded in 1991.

### Westcott, northwest of Aylesbury

Not only was Westcott used extensively by Wellington and Lancaster bombers of various squadrons between September 1942 and August 1945, but it was also extremely important as part of Operation Exodus. The defeat of Germany in May 1945 saw thousands of Allied prisoners of war needing to be returned home. Westcott was the major British staging post for their repatriation. Around 53,000 Allied prisoners of war saw their first taste of freedom when they touched down at Westcott. The airfield closed at the beginning of April 1946 and for a time in the 1960s and 1970s it was the home of the Rocket Propulsion Establishment. The site is now called Venture Park and is a light industrial estate.

### Westenhanger, west of Folkestone

This is Folkestone Racecourse today, which has a long history of its own, having been set up in 1898. Aircraft first landed on the racecourse in September 1910. During the early stages of the Second World War the only contribution that the site made was as a decoy airfield and there were dummy aircraft scattered around the fake airfield. In late April 1944 an Army Cooperation Squadron No 660 began using the site. They flew air observation aircraft and it would seem that they used Westenhanger primarily for training purposes. The squadron left in July 1944 and at that stage it became a racecourse once again.

### Weston-on-the-Green, west of Bicester

The site was used for training in the summer of 1918 but it was closed by January 1920. It was again selected as an airfield that could be used by bombers and it was linked to West Raynham. It then became a satellite station for RAF Bicester and then for RAF Kidlington. By the end of 1941 it was a glider training school and it was a satellite landing ground for Kidlington, with its own satellite at Kingston Bagpuize. The airfield was closed for flying by the end of May 1945 but by March 1946 it had been transferred to Transport Command. It then became a drop zone for the parachute training school, which is the current purpose of the site.

### Weston-super-Mare, southeast of Weston-super-Mare

This airfield achieved over 50 years of association with aviation before it closed in 1987. However, it is now The Helicopter Museum, which was founded in 1958 but moved to this site 20 years later. Weston-super-Mare opened in 1936 and was primarily a flight training school and an air observer and navigation school. It was also briefly home to RAF Squadron No 286 towards the end of 1942. It too served as the Polish Air Force Staff College for two years from the spring of 1944. In the post-war years the site was owned by Westland and they were involved there from 1966 until 1978.

### Weybourne, west of Sheringham

This is home to The Muckleburgh Military Collection, which is an eclectic selection of military artefacts. The site has a long association with the military. It was an army barracks during the First World War, an anti-aircraft base in the late 1930s and an airfield during the Second World War. It was only ever bombed on one occasion during the Second World War and it was home to anti-aircraft cooperation units. When the current owners took over the site in the 1980s they had to remove over 200 derelict buildings that were beyond repair. The museum is currently occupying the workshops and storage area of the base.

### Wheaton Aston, east of Telford

Wheaton Aston was used for pilot training and opened in 1941 with operations beginning in the spring of 1942. It was used until at least the end of 1946 and closed at some point in 1947. The site is now farmland, although some of the original buildings can still be seen.

### Whitchurch, southeast of Bristol

This site is now South Bristol Community Hospital. The airfield was originally opened by Prince George, The Duke of Kent, in May 1930.

Hengrove Park. A view of the old Whitchurch Airfield from the air. [*Image courtesy of Steve Bailey*]

It was a municipal airport for Bristol and was also the home to a flying club. Commercial flights were developed during the 1930s and towards the end of the decade it became a training school for RAF Volunteer Reserve pilots. The Air Ministry requisitioned the site in

**Did you know?**
During the war commercial flights were continued to Lisbon in Portugal and via Shannon airport there was also a connection to the United States. Bob Hope and Bing Crosby were two such passengers. The actor, Leslie Howard, was killed when his aircraft was shot down *en route* from Whitchurch to Lisbon on 1st June, 1943.

August 1939. For the most part the airfield was used to ferry aircraft to combat squadrons.

After the Second World War the airfield was used by flying clubs and it also reopened for scheduled flights. Due to encroaching housing it was not chosen as the site for the future Bristol Airport and flying stopped in 1957. It opened two years later as a motor racing circuit. The area is now known as Hengrove Park and as late as 1993 an aircraft made an emergency landing there.

### White Waltham, southwest of Maidenhead

This is still an active airfield and owned by the West London Aero Club. Back in the late 1920s the airfield was established as the de Havilland Flying School. Between 1940 and 1945 it was home to the civilian Air Transport Auxiliary who was responsible for ferrying military aircraft on behalf of the RAF and the army. The RAF used it as a headquarters for their Home Command Communications Squadron between 1950 and 1959 but they relinquished control of the field in 1982.

**Did you know?**
White Waltham was where Prince Philip, the Duke of Edinburgh, learned to fly in 1952. The airfield also doubled as a 1950s version of Heathrow Airport for the 2011 film *My Week with Marilyn*.

### Wickenby, northeast of Lincoln

This site is now a private airfield and it has a memorial to the RAF personnel that served there between 1942 and 1945. It opened as a bomber base in the autumn of 1942 and RAF Squadron No 12's Wellingtons and then later Lancasters remained there until September 1945. It was also home to RAF Squadron No 626 and they too flew Wellingtons and Lancasters and launched 300 operations between November 1943 and October 1945.

Over the course of the war more than 1,000 RAF crewmen lost their lives from this base. After the war it was briefly used for flying but mainly to store bombs until the mid-1950s, at which point it was sold to become a private airfield.

## Wigsley, west of Lincoln

Wigsley opened in February 1942, primarily as a satellite airfield for RAF Swinderby. Initially aircraft flying from there were involved in laying mines. More bombers moved in during mid-1942 and many operational missions were launched from the airfield. The airfield finally closed in the summer of 1958. Some buildings still exist, although most of the site is now farmland.

## Windermere, northeast of Windermere

There are in fact two sites associated with Windermere; the first was used from 1911 through to 1920 and was a Royal Naval Air Station variously known as Hill of Oaks or Cockshott Point. It is still possible to see the slipway used by the seaplanes. The Second World War site is now known as White Cross Bay Leisure Park and Marina. It was used between September 1942 and September 1945. There was a factory producing Sunderland flying boats nearby, where 35 were built and then the factory concentrated on maintenance and repair. The slipway still remains.

## Windrush, west of Burford

This airfield was only open during the war years and was linked to RAF Chipping Norton and RAF Little Rissington. It opened in 1940 and closed in the summer of 1945. The airfield was still used in the post-war period by a flying club and then for parachuting, but it closed in 1997.

---

**Did you know?**
On 18th August, 1940 Sergeant Pilot Bruce Hancock of the RAF Volunteer Reserve was killed when he rammed a German bomber with his unarmed Avro Anson. A memorial to him can be found in the Church of St Peter in Windrush village.

---

## Wing, southwest of Leighton Buzzard

Wing airfield had a satellite station at Little Horwood. It opened in the late autumn of 1941 and was a bomber airfield. In the post-war years it was considered as the location of an additional London airport, but in the end Heathrow was expanded and the plans were shelved. Wellington bombers routinely left the airfield bound for raids on Germany during the war. In the immediate post-war period it was used as a reception centre for Allied prisoners of war being returned home. Large numbers of Dakotas and Lancasters were used in this airlift. The airfield was mothballed in the summer of 1946 and the RAF finally disposed of the site in 1960.

### Winkleigh, north of Okehampton
Originally this airfield was to be used by Coastal Command, but it was actually used by Fighter Command at the beginning of 1943. By the end of that year, squadrons belonging to the 9th USAAF began using the site. It was subsequently used by other RAF squadrons and relegated to flight training by the end of 1944. It seems that flying ceased in the summer of 1945 but the RAF retained the site until 1958. The control tower still exists but is in a derelict state.

### Winthorpe, northeast of Newark-on-Trent
Opening in the late summer of 1940, Polish crews flying Fairey Battles and Wellington bombers used this airfield. It was then closed in order for concrete runways to be installed. Heavy bombers flew from the site from October 1942 until August 1945. At this point it became an RAF Transport Command base until the summer of 1947. It was then effectively mothballed for 12 years before disposal. It is believed that the bulk of the buildings were demolished in the 1990s. It is, however, the home of the Newark Air Museum.

### Wisley, southeast of Wisley
This airfield has an interesting history, even though it was only opened in 1944. It was used for flight testing and apparently several German jet aircraft were tested on this site towards the end of the war. It is understood that the airfield closed in the early 1970s and that the bulk of the buildings were pulled down a decade later. The runways, however, still survive. It is now proposed that a huge composting plant is to occupy the site, which is close to RHS Wisley.

### Witchford, southwest of Ely
Both Wellington and Lancaster bombers operated from this airfield during the Second World War, notably RAF Squadron Nos 196 and

Office Building at Witchford which
has a display of memorabilia about
the former wartime airfield RAF
Witchford. [*Image courtesy of Paul
Shreeve*]

then 115. The airfield opened in 1942 and closed in 1946. Today there
is a museum dedicated to the airfield and the personnel in the village
of Witchford.

## Wolverhampton, north of Wolverhampton

This was to be a municipal airport for Wolverhampton and was
known as Pendeford Airfield. Close by was an aircraft factory, owned
by Boulton Paul. The airfield was primarily used for flight training
during the Second World War and it retained this role in the post-war
period until around 1953. It was then used by private aircraft and
some scheduled services. The problem was that the airfield was too
small and it was too close to housing. It finally closed at the end of
1970.

## Wombleton, northwest of Helmsley

This was mainly a training base and a satellite to RAF Topcliffe. It saw
Halifax and Lancaster bombers during the Second World War but the
site closed in 1949 and for some years during the 1950s it was used to
house the homeless. The site is still used today for private aircraft.

## Woodbridge, northeast of Ipswich

Woodbridge is still being used by aircraft and can trace its history back to the late summer of 1943 when it was primarily used as an emergency landing field. It retained this role until the spring of 1948. In fact during the course of the Second World War some 4,000 emergency landings were made at the site. The Americans moved in during the early 1950s and they used it extensively for around 40 years. It is still used today for army and RAF training and is an engineer barracks.

## Woodford, south of Bramhall

The aircraft manufacturer Avro began using the airfield in the mid-1920s. It was an incredibly important site, as over 4,000 Lancaster bombers were built at the factory and the factory retained its importance, building the Lincoln, Shackleton and Vulcan in the post-war period. By the 1960s they were building civilian airliners and then Nimrod reconnaissance aircraft. The site closed in 2012.

## Woodhall Spa, southeast of Woodhall Spa

This was a satellite airfield for RAF Coningsby. At various times over the course of the Second World War it was used by RAF Squadron Nos:

- 97
- 617
- 619
- 627

After the end of the war in Europe the airfield was used to store bombs and then in the 1960s was used as a missile base. Most of the site was sold off in the mid-1960s, but part remained open until 2003.

## Woodley, east of Reading

This is the home of the Museum of Berkshire Aviation. Woodley was the home of an aircraft factory and also home to a flying club. The aircraft factories were based here until around 1947.

**Did you know?**
In 1931 Amy Johnson visited Woodley and, in the same year, whilst flying with an RAF aerobatics team, Douglas Bader had a serious crash at Woodley in which he lost his legs.

## Woodvale, northwest of Liverpool

This is still used by the RAF for gliding and it is an Air Training Corps base and also used by a university air squadron. It was originally built in 1941 to act as a base for night fighters to protect Liverpool. It was also used to give squadrons based further south a relative break from daily combat in the early stages of the Second World War. By the spring of 1945 the Royal Navy's Fleet Air Arm was also using the site, and as it was a satellite field for Burscough airfield, it was known as HMS *Ringtail II*.

## Woolfox Lodge, northwest of Stamford

When the airfield opened in 1940 it was used as a satellite field for RAF Cottesmore but later concrete runways were added and it became a satellite for North Luffenham. It was the home of RAF Squadron No 61 and they launched 180 missions, losing some 16 aircraft. Further extensions were made to the airfield and the site reopened in the summer of 1943 and saw Stirling bombers.

By August 1944 the USAAF were using the airfield, primarily for their transport aircraft that would be involved in Operation Market Garden. After this it became a satellite field for North Luffenham again, with a unit based there converting from Stirling to Lancaster bombers. In the immediate post-war period it was mothballed and the runways began to deteriorate. In 1960 it became a missile base and the RAF relinquished control of the site in 1965, selling it the following year.

## Woolsington, northwest of Newcastle

Originally this was a civilian airport that had opened in 1935. It is now much better known as Newcastle International Airport, which handles approaching 4.5 million passengers a year. It was primarily used as a satellite field for RAF Acklington and RAF Ouston.

Immediately after the war it returned to civilian flying and has since gone on to become an important regional airport.

## Woolston, east of Southampton

In 1913 an aircraft factory opened here and throughout the First World War seaplanes were constructed at the site. In the interwar years the factory was involved in converting flying boats to civilian use and there was also passenger services laid on.

By the late 1920s, Supermarine, as the company had been called, was now owned by Vickers and they continued to build flying boats. The Woolston site is perhaps most well known for its involvement in the development and construction of the Supermarine Spitfire. Even though the factory is now gone, there is a memorial to R.J. Mitchell, who designed the Spitfire.

## Worksop, west of Retford

This site was opened towards the end of 1943 and was a satellite field for RAF Finningley. Primarily it was an instructors' school linked to Bomber Command. The airfield was used for flight training until 1948 but it was then mothballed for four years and reopened as a flying school. It seems that the airfield finally closed around 1958 and was sold off towards the end of 1960. The area has now been returned to farmland.

## Worth Matravers, west of Swanage

This site is perhaps best known for its involvement in the development of radar. Considerable progress took place between 1940 and 1942 and in fact the radar towers continued to be used after the Second World War and were not demolished until the 1970s. At Swanage there is an exhibition of the early radar work carried out at this site. The landing strip at Worth Matravers was originally used to help calibrate and test the radar. A memorial to those that carried out the work was unveiled in 2001.

## Worthy Down, north of Winchester

This is now an army barracks but it was opened on the site of Winchester racecourse by the Royal Naval Air Service in the autumn of 1917. It was again used during the Second World War by the Royal

Navy and called HMS *Kestrel*. It was only used between 1939 and 1942, primarily because of the awkward siting of the runway. It was mothballed for 10 years and then reopened as HMS *Ariel* and remained with the Royal Navy until 1960 when it was handed over to the army. The airfield part of the site is now farmland. Several of the original buildings still exist.

### Wratting Common, southeast of Cambridge

It was intended that this site be used by the USAAF but instead the first arrivals were RAF Stirling bombers. This was RAF Squadron No 90. Originally the airfield was to be called West Wycombe but there was already an airfield in Kent called this. RAF Squadron No 90 was there between the end of May and mid-October 1943. It was then home primarily to RAF Squadron No 195 who flew nearly 1,400 sorties from the airfield. It was finally home to RAF Squadron No 51, who arrived in October 1945 and remained there until mid-January 1946. After this, the airfield was used to cope with the many hundreds of prisoners of war and displaced persons. The airfield was abandoned shortly after the end of the war in Europe, although most of the site is now agriculture some of the original buildings are still believed to exist.

Three old Nissen huts left over from the nearby Second World War airfield RAF Wratting Common. [*Image courtesy of Keith Evans*]

## Wroughton, south of Swindon

The site has been owned by the Science Museum since the late 1970s. The airfield was a major site where as many as 7,000 aircraft were repaired, modified or serviced during the course of the Second World War. It was also used as a major base for wooden gliders that were being carefully built by furniture makers in the build-up to the D-Day landings. As many as 600 gliders were assembled here. After the war it was used to dismantle Lancaster bombers and in the 1950s as a support base by the RAF. In the 1960s it was used as a helicopter base and the RAF handed it over to the Royal Navy, who also serviced their helicopters there until the site closed in 1978.

## Wymeswold, east of Loughborough

The airfield opened as a training base in the summer of 1942. It was then used by RAF Transport Command as a training base. For a brief time in the late 1940s it was used by Fighter Command but it closed in 1957, although it continued to be used by private aircraft until 1968. Today the runway is used for motorsport and there are businesses in many of the original buildings. It may be that the site will be subsumed by a new town that is planned to be built around the area.

## Wyton, northwest of Cambridge

RAF Wyton is now part of the larger RAF Brampton Wyton Henlow complex and is home to university air squadrons, flight training, air equipment support and technical services. It was originally opened in 1916 and used for training by the Royal Flying Corps.

It was primarily a bomber base during the Second World War with Lancaster, Mosquito and Blenheim bombers. In 1942 it became the base of a Pathfinder unit. In the post-war years, Wyton was the home of the Strategic Reconnaissance Force. It has retained an importance to the RAF and there is also a microlight club and flight school on the site.

## Yate, Chipping Sodbury

There was an aircraft repair depot and a Royal Flying Corp base here in the First World War. In 1925, the aircraft manufacturer Parnalls moved into the empty depot. From here they produced a range of aircraft into the 1930s. During the Second World War, the factory made airframes and gun turrets and the airfield was still in use. Today the factory is still running, making household appliances.

**Did you know?**
German aircraft bombed the factory in February and March 1941. In the March raid, 53 factory workers were killed.

### *Yatesbury, west of Swindon*

The Royal Flying Corps used the site to train pilots from 1916 and the airfield remained open for a short period after the First World War but was closed in 1920. At that point it was returned to farmland, but reopened in 1936. A flying school opened and ultimately the RAF used the site to train aircraft mechanics and to teach radar operators.

During the course of the Second War World over 50,000 personnel were trained at Yatesbury and in the post war period another 70,000. The airfield was finally sold off in 1965. Four years later many of the buildings were demolished. A decade ago work began to revitalise the airfield and establish a flying school on the site.

### *Yeadon, northeast of Leeds*

This airfield is far better known as Leeds Bradford International Airport. It originally opened in October 1931 as a flying club base and later in 1935 North Eastern Airways set up services there. The airfield was requisitioned by the RAF and was used by a maintenance unit, as a training school and also as a relief landing ground. A factory was also set up here which produced bombers from 1942. The RAF remained at Yeadon until 1957 and the airfield officially closed in 1959. Since then it has been gradually developed as the international travel hub it is today.

### *Yeovil*

Back in 1915, the site became an aircraft production facility known as the Westland Aircraft Works. Aircraft production continued throughout the interwar years and it was also used to service and repair aircraft. It retained this role during the Second World War and

Spitfires, amongst others, were built at the site. It is still used today for helicopters and flight evaluation.

### Yeovilton, north of Yeovil
This is still a Royal Navy base and the home of the Fleet Air Arm Museum. To the Navy it is better known as HMS *Heron*. The base opened in June 1940 and saw a huge range of aircraft being used by the Royal Navy and several of their Fleet Air Arm squadrons. The base has retained its importance in the post-war period and is still being used by their squadrons. Until 1985, there was also a Westland Aircraft repair facility on site, but the Royal Navy now runs this. The current control tower is not the original, having been built in 2006.

### York, northern York
York City along with Yorkshire Aviation Services established this as a civilian airport in 1936. It was a primitive affair, but nonetheless the RAF took it over in 1939 and by 1942 it had three runways. To begin with it was intended for use by Bomber Command, but the first tenants were Lysanders involved in Army Cooperation duties. As the airfield grew it was variously known as York, Clifton and Rawcliffe owing to the land it was now covering. Seafires belonging to 809 Squadron of the Fleet Air Arm used the airfield for a month in the spring of 1943 and then the site was transferred over to Fighter Command. After the war a maintenance unit scrapped aircraft here until closure in 1948. It was returned to civilian use soon afterwards. The site is now covered with housing and a golf driving range.

### Zeals, east of Wincanton
The Royal Navy called this base HMS *Hummingbird*, although this was after the end of the war in Europe in May 1945. Fighter Command used this as a landing ground from 1942 to October 1943. From August 1943, the USAAF began using it for maintenance and repair of their C-47s, but later it was used to deal with P-47 Thunderbolts.

In the spring of 1944, the RAF ran Mosquito night fighters out of Zeals and continued to do so until the spring of the following year. In May 1945, the Royal Navy began using it for their Fleet Air Arm squadrons until the airfield closed for flying in January 1946 and the land returned to agriculture some six months later.

## The former Blackburn Aircraft Factory

Construction of these factory buildings began in 1937, as a result of a business partnership between Sir Maurice Denny, Managing Director of the Dumbarton firm Denny Shipbuilders, and Robert Blackburn, of Yorkshire's Blackburn Aeroplane and Motor Company. The site on which the factory stood was called Barge Park; completed machines would be taken across the River Clyde by barge to Abbotsinch airfield.

Aircraft built here included the Blackburn Shark B6 Mark III (a torpedo/spotter/reconnaissance biplane, assembled from components manufactured in Yorkshire), the Short Sunderland (a flying boat patrol bomber, built entirely at this site), and many others.

By early 1961, the factory had closed. As the photograph shows, the factory buildings survived rather longer, becoming part of a bottling plant. They have since been demolished. [*Image courtesy of Lairich Rig*]

# Chapter Three

# Scotland, Ireland, Wales and the Isle of Man

ALL PARTS of the British Isles played a vital role in either the defence of Britain or the offensives against German-occupied Europe. Some of these outlying airfields had specific purposes, which included:

- Covering key transport routes
- Operating as hubs or assembly points for incoming aircraft from the United States
- Major training bases
- Protecting key installations or factories
- Rest areas for squadrons who had been in the thick of the fighting
- Secret bases to test new equipment, aircraft or captured aircraft

## SCOTLAND

### Abbotsinch, west of Glasgow

This site is now much better known as Glasgow International Airport, which handles nearly seven million passengers a year. Glasgow Airport opened in 1966, but the site actually dates back to 1932. The first squadron there was RAF No 602 Squadron (City of Glasgow), who moved there in January 1933.

It became an official RAF station in 1936. In 1940 there was torpedo training there, which saw a long-term association with the Royal Navy, who called it HMS *Sanderling*. The Royal Navy left in 1963 and it was then chosen as the site for Glasgow's new airport.

### Alness, west of Invergordon
This base was used for seaplanes and was known as RAF Invergordon before the Second World War. In fact it was called RAF Alness from February 1943. An Air-Sea Rescue Marine Craft Unit, No 1100, was based there from July 1946 until its closure in 1985. There was a flying boat unit based at Alness between February 1943 and December 1944 and there was also a flying instructors school there briefly in 1945.

### Annan, northeast of Annan
A nuclear power station sits on this former airfield, known as Chapelcross Power Station. The plant was designed to produce weapons-grade plutonium. It was decommissioned in 2005. We know that the airfield opened in December 1940 and remained operational until July 1955. During the war it was used for training and exercises. Both of the airfields apparently still remain; one underneath the remains of the power station and the other is overgrown. Several of the buildings remain, although the tower was demolished.

### Arbroath, northwest of Arbroath
Strictly speaking, this is a Royal Navy establishment. It was set up in 1938 and originally used as a training school for observers. The Royal Navy called it HMS *Condor*. It was attacked by German aircraft in October 1940. The airfield remains operational to some extent in the present day. There were upgrades only a decade or so ago and it is home to 45 Commando of the Royal Marines.

### Ayr, northeast of Prestwick

**Did you know?**
One of the earliest duties that the RAF Ayr had to carry out in 1941 was to send men to pick up the deputy German leader, Rudolf Hess, who had parachuted into Scotland.

The airfield was opened in 1941 and, confusingly, it is known by several different names: RAF Heathfield and, by its Royal Navy name, HMS *Wagtail*. To confuse matters further, it is next door to Glasgow Prestwick Airport. The airfield was actually used during the First

World War, but initially it began life as an RAF airfield in the Second World War, before passing into the hands of the Royal Navy. The USAF used it for storage in the early 1950s. The site closed in 1957 and is now primarily a retail park.

### Balado Bridge, west of Kinross

The airfield opened in March 1942, primarily for training but also as a satellite airfield for RAF Grangemouth. Spitfire pilots were trained here between March 1942 and June 1944. The airfield was taken over by the War Department in November 1944 and the site was used as a scrap area for former Royal Naval aircraft. These activities ceased in around 1952. It was also used for private light aircraft and gliding until the airfield itself closed in 1957. Today there are poultry farms, an activity centre and the site is also used for music festivals.

### Banff, northwest of Aberdeen

The airfield is also known as Boyndie and work got underway in 1942, with construction completed in April 1943. It had three intersecting runways and became a base for a pilots' advanced flying school, which had moved from Nottinghamshire. The unit was disbanded in August 1944, but Banff had trained over 2,000 pilots by that time. The base was then used for aircraft of RAF Nos 143, 144, 235 and 248, along with the 333rd Royal Norwegian Air Force squadron and the 404th Royal Canadian Air Force squadron. They were engaged in seeking out and destroying German vessels around Scandinavia, particularly Norway. They operated in incredibly dangerous conditions and the Germans carefully guarded their convoys with vital resources from Scandinavia. The last mission flown from Banff was on 4th May, 1945. The units were stood down towards the end of the month. The airfield closed in the middle of 1946 and Banff Flying Club began using it in 1976, but the club closed in the early 1980s. The site is now a wind farm. There is a memorial near the airfield and there are still vestiges of the buildings and the runway to be seen.

### Benbecula, on the Isle of Benbecula in the Outer Hebrides

Originally the airfield was used by Scottish Airways and was known as Balivanich. This ran between 1936 and 1939. Between June 1942 and October 1943 RAF No 206 Squadron operated from the airfield on anti-submarine patrols. The airfield was also briefly home to several other squadrons between March 1943 and June 1945, including Nos 36, 179, 220 and 304 Squadrons. The airfield is still operational, having been transferred back into civilian hands in 1946.

### Black Isle, north of Inverness
This airfield was also known as Blackstand. It was a satellite landing airfield and many of the buildings still exist. We know that the airfield opened in August 1941 and remained operational until around October 1945. As many as 117 aircraft were kept here as of July 1944. It was a secret location and much of the area is now covered with post-war trees.

### Bowmore, Isle of Islay
Bowmore was an RAF seaplane base that opened in September 1940 and remained operational until around March 1946. In March 1941 it was home to a flight of RAF No 119 Squadron, as part of RAF Coastal Command.

### Brackla, in the County of Nairn
The airfield opened up as a relief landing ground for RAF Dalcross in 1941. It was abandoned during the late 1940s or early 1950s. Some of the hangars were used by the Royal Brackla Distillery. It is believed that the airfield was used primarily to dispose of aircraft. It had grass runways and only vestiges of the original airfield remain.

### Buttergask, northeast of Perth
Buttergask opened towards the end of 1942 and remained in operation until the end of November 1948 as a relief landing ground. It is not believed that anything now remains of this site.

---

**Did you know?**
On 24th January, 1943 a Sunderland flying boat was coming back from the North Atlantic towards Bowmore with 12 men on board. Eye witnesses say the Sunderland circled up to 10 times. It then crash-landed on the beach. 11 of the men got out but the rear gunner was trapped. Eight of the crew went back in to help get him out but a depth charge exploded and killed all nine of the men.

War graves at Bowmore. [*Image courtesy of Andrew Wood*]

### Campbeltown, south of Tarbert

This site is also known as RAF Machrihanish and confusingly it is also known as HMS *Landrail*. It was opened in 1916 and used through to 1918 by marine patrol aircraft. The airfield was again opened in June 1941, but under another name, Strabane Naval Air Station. The airfield was also used during the Korean War and there were significant improvements made there in the early 1960s. American Navy Seals were also based there, and there were further upgrades in the 1990s. The airfield is now a civilian airfield and has scheduled flights to Glasgow. The base was finally abandoned by the military in May 2009.

### Castle Kennedy, east of Stranraer

Opened in July 1941, this airfield was also known as Cults Farm and flying continued there until around November 1957; although by this stage it was civilian flying. However the first aircraft to have landed there did so in 1913. Initially during the Second World War it was an air gunnery school but it was then used to store Wellingtons and Mosquitos. In the post-war period it was still used by private aircraft and also a kart club.

### Charterhall, west of Berwick-upon-Tweed

This was the base of RAF No 54 Operational Training Unit. It ran as a training base from 1942 until 1946. The Battle of Britain pilot, Richard Hope Hillary, an Australian, died after taking off from Charterhall on 8th January, 1943. He and his observer died and in 2001 a memorial was unveiled to them.

### Connel, south of Oban

During the Second World War the Oban Bay area was used by RAF flying boats. Later it was used as a stopover point for air crews and it was known as RAF Connel Ferry. The Royal Observer Corps was based here until the late-1990s and it was then used for private aircraft. It is now Oban Airport. It is believed that the original airfield was opened in the 1930s.

### Crail, southeast of St Andrews

Towards the end of the First World War, the Royal Flying Corps used Crail airfield. There were also Americans based there in 1918. The airfield closed in 1919 but in 1940 through to 1947 the Royal Navy took it over as an air station, naming it HMS *Jackdaw*. In 1947 it became a foreign language school, under the name of HMS Bruce. It is believed that Crail closed in 1958 and it is now a motorsports racing course.

### Crimond, southeast of Fraserburgh

Crimond airfield has had various names, including Rattray Aerodrome, and when it was a Royal Naval Air Station it was called HMS *Merganser*. The airfield was opened in late-1944 and closed in 1946. It was then used as a wireless station until 2004.

### Dalcross, northeast of Inverness

This is now Inverness Airport. It opened as an airfield in 1940 and is believed to have been the first runway that ever had tarmac in Britain.

---

**Did you know?**
Dalcross airfield was used during the filming of *633 Squadron*, which was released in 1964 and starred Cliff Robertson.

It opened as a civilian airfield in 1947. RAF 614 Squadron operated from the airfield and it was later used for training pilots and aircrew.

### Dallachy, southeast of Lossiemouth

Originally this was a training station when it opened in March 1943, but it was then used by Beaufighters belonging to RAF Squadron Nos 144, 404, 405 and 489. It was then used between October 1944 and June 1945 by the Royal New Zealand Air Force's No 489 Squadron on anti-shipping missions. Towards the end of 1944 the Royal Navy's No 838 Squadron began using the airfield and in the post-war period, until around 1958, it was used as a training centre for the Territorial Army. Some derelict buildings still remain on the site.

### Donibristle, east of Rosyth

This airfield site has a bewildering selection of names. It is now probably better known as Donibristle Industrial Park, but since it has been home to the Royal Flying Corps, the Royal Naval Air Service, Fleet Air Arm and the RAF it is unsurprising that the names have changed over the years. The Royal Navy, for example, called it HMS *Merlin*. It was opened in February 1917 and did not close until October 1959.

The site is now covered with housing and an industrial estate, although some of the buildings have the hallmarks of being former airfield structures. The airfield began life as a landing ground for the Royal Naval Air Service and it was used as a shore

The Donibee Sculpture. In recognition of all civil and military personnel (The Donibees or sometimes misspelled Donnybees) who served at nearby Donibristle airfield and aircraft repair yard 1917–1959. Millennium Award. Sited at Dalgety Bay railway station. [*Image courtesy of Simon Johnston*]

base for naval aircraft from 1925. None of the original hangars have survived, but some of the other buildings, including the barrack blocks, are still being used. The area is now known as Dalgety Bay, a suburb effectively of Edinburgh.

### Dornoch, close to Dornoch, north of Inverness
Dornoch was a golf course when aircraft began landing on the grass airstrip in the 1930s. The RAF took it over in 1941 and it officially opened in the August. It was used to store aircraft and also operated as an emergency landing field. It continued to be used to store aircraft, including Lancaster bombers, until operations ended in September 1945. The airstrip was returned to private use and in 1967 there was a service running to Wick and Inverness, which operated until 1972. There is still a grass airstrip on the site, but much of the surrounding area is a golf course once again and on the perimeter there is a caravan park.

### Dumfries
This is now the Dumfries and Galloway Aviation Museum. It served as a bombing and gunnery school, an air observers' school and an advanced flying school during the war. The airfield was open between 1940 and 1957. In the post-war years it had been used to train recruits to the Royal Air Force Regiment but the site was sold off in 1960.

### Dundonald, southeast of Irvine
This is now known as the Olympic Business Park. It was home to RAF 516 Combined Operations Squadron. This unit had an important role as they provided close support for amphibious landings. In October 2010 a memorial to the airfield and to the men that served there was opened. Dundonald was a fairly secret airfield and a wide variety of different aircraft operated from there. In December 1944, 516 Squadron was disbanded and the airfield itself closed in August 1945. The hangar that can be seen in the area is not the original one.

### Dunino, southeast of St Andrews
Initially Army Cooperation aircraft of 309 and 614 Squadrons operated from here between April 1941 and November 1942. It then became HMS *Jackdaw II* in the December, when the Royal Navy took

it over. Swordfish, Barracudas and Walruses all operated from the base certainly until the beginning of 1944. It was then used for storage until 1946 and was finally sold off in 1957. It is reported that the control tower is still there, but in a derelict state.

### East Fortune, south of North Berwick
Back in 1916 the Royal Naval Air Service used the site as a base for aircraft and for airships. It was then used in the post-First World War period for torpedo bomber training. The airfield apparently closed in around 1920, to be opened 20 years later as a satellite station for RAF Drem. It was used to train aircraft crews from June 1941 to May 1946. The airfield closed in 1947 and was finally sold off in 1960. It had a very short life as a civil airport but this did not work out. The National Museum of Flight, Scotland is on the site and this opened in 1976.

### Edzell, northwest of Montrose
This base did not close until 1997. Some of the housing now on the site has been renamed Edzell Woods. An airfield was set up towards the end of the First World War but it closed in 1919. It was a civilian airfield in the 1930s and became RAF Edzell in 1940. It was primarily used to maintain and store aircraft. Post-war it was used as a motor racing circuit and the last race took place in 1959. The US Navy took it over in 1960 and at its high point 3,000 personnel were based there. This facility closed in October 1997. During the Second World War the airfield was primarily used by RAF No 612 Squadron. They ran their aircraft out of the airfield, which included Avro Ansons and Whitleys.

### Elgin, south of Lossiemouth
This was a satellite airfield for RAF Lossiemouth and opened in June 1940. It was also known as Bogs O'Mayne. It was primarily used for flight training and then to house aircraft between 1945 and its closure in 1947. Much of the site is now farmland, although some huts and other buildings appear to have survived.

### Errol, southwest of Dundee
Strangely Errol has a Russian connection, as it was used as a training base for Russian aircrew receiving British aircraft. This arrangement continued from 1943 through to 1944. The RAF gave up on the base

in 1948, as during the post-war period it had only been used to store equipment. The site is still used by light aircraft and there are numerous open-air events and car boot sales on the site.

### Evanton, north of Inverness

This airfield has been known by two other names: HMS Fieldfare and RNAS Evanton. The airfield opened in 1922 and was used by the Royal Navy to support the Home Fleet. The airfield was extended in 1937 and as a consequence of the fact that the Home Fleet had moved to Scapa Flow it was in fact shared with the RAF. It was mainly used to train air gunners. By 1943 up to 250 aircraft were there for maintenance by Coastal Command. The base was also being used by seaplanes. Although the base closed in 1947 it is believed that the Americans were still using it in the 1950s. Some of the site is now an industrial estate.

### Fearn, northeast of Invergordon

Originally built as a satellite station for RAF Tain, it was actually opened as HMS *Owl* when it was transferred into the hands of the Royal Navy in July 1942. It was mainly used as a torpedo training school and Royal Naval units remained there until the summer of 1946. The airfield was also known as Balintore. The control tower is a listed building and several of the other buildings still remain intact on the site.

### Findo Gask, west of Perth

This opened for flight training in June 1941 but it was never a successful airfield because the area was always prone to flooding. Ultimately it was used by the Polish Army for training and towards the end of the war as a German prisoner of war camp. The RAF relinquished control of it in 1948 and there is very little left of the original airfield.

### Fordoun, northeast of Montrose

A road now cuts across the two runways of this airfield and some of the original site is now used by a sawmill, a pipe company and a caravan site. The airfield was active between 1942 and 1944, mainly training pilots and crews. Several of the buildings on the outer perimeter of the site still exist.

## Fraserburgh, southwest of Inverallochy

This is also known as Inverallochy airfield, which opened in December 1941. It was used for pilot training and also by Coastal Command and Air-Sea Rescue. The airfield closed in 1945 and was used by a gliding club in the 1950s. Much of the site can still be seen, including the runways.

## Ganavan Sands, in the bay of Oban

This was a seaplane base near Oban. Officially it closed in 1946 but it was home to not only RAF flying boats but also those manned by Americans, Australians and Canadians. Oban has a War and Peace Museum with many artefacts from the area's history of aviation.

## Greenock, southeast of Greenock

Between September 1942 and June 1945 this was used by flying boats. A maintenance unit kept it open until the October. The site was variously known as Caird's Yard and Gourock. The site is now the home of industrial units.

## Grimsetter, southeast of Kirkwall

This is now better known as Kirkwall Airport. It was originally built in 1940 to help defend the naval base at Scapa Flow. In 1943 the Royal Navy took it over, renaming it HMS *Robin*. It remained in military hands until 1948 and was finally sold to the Highlands and Islands Airports Ltd in 1986. It is the Orkney Islands' main airport.

## Hatston, northwest of Kirkwall

This was a Royal Naval Air Station and called HMS *Sparrowhawk*. It was designed to provide air cover for Scapa Flow, which was the base of the Royal Navy's Home Fleet. The airfield became Orkney's main airport in the immediate post-war period, but in 1948 the aircraft moved to Kirkwall. The airfield remained associated with aviation until 1957, with a flying club based there, but it is now closed and an industrial estate occupies the site.

## Helensburgh, northwest of Helensburgh

During the Second World War RAF Helensburgh was a Marine Aircraft Experimental Establishment. There were certainly flying boats based here and it is understood that the facility remained open in the immediate aftermath of the war. This was a top secret establishment and according to rumours there were jet seaplane research tests there in the final two years of the war.

### Inverness, in Inverness
RAF Inverness was operational between February 1941 and August 1945. It was home to several different squadrons, some for relatively short periods of time. These included:

- 241
- 289
- 309
- 526
- 527
- 598
- 614

It was also the headquarters of the No 70 Signal Wing. The airfield was also known as RAF Longman. Today, the site is an industrial estate.

### Islay, on the Island of Islay
There is a potential confusion here, as Islay Airport is also known as Glenegedale and is a small, rural airport. Its history dates back to 1940 when construction began and the concrete runway was put in during

Islay Airfield from the end of a runway. [*Image courtesy of Andrew Wood*]

1942. Further south, however, there is RAF Port Ellen, which was home to an operational training unit, a unit responsible for ferrying aircraft and an RAF Air-Sea Rescue Marine Craft Unit. Port Ellen itself closed in 1947, but Islay remains open and runs scheduled flights to the Scottish mainland, principally Glasgow.

### Kidsdale, southeast of Port William
Often this airfield is referred to as Burrow Head and opened in 1939. Primarily the aircraft based here towed targets for anti-aircraft gunners. It would appear that flying ceased in around 1943. It had a grass runway, three hangars and a number of other buildings, including pillboxes. Some of the hut bases still remain, as do the two pillboxes.

### Kinloss, north of Kinloss
Regular RAF flying from this base ceased at the end of July 2011. The intention is to turn the base into an army barracks. The history of the airfield dates back to its opening in April 1939 where it was used to train bomber crews.

Shortly after the Second World War Kinloss began a long association with maritime flying and it would become an important base for search and rescue and anti-submarine warfare. It would provide crews and aircraft for a number of post-war conflicts, including the liberation of the Falkland Islands and Kuwait.

### Kinnell, southwest of Montrose
This airfield operated as a satellite field for RAF Tealing, to the north of Dundee. From the spring of 1942 to the summer of 1944 Lysander aircraft operated from the airfield, towing targets for Hurricane and Spitfire pilots. In the latter half of the war it was a satellite station for RAF Montrose. The airfield was finally closed in 1945 and it would appear that the RAF finally relinquished it in 1948. Although the runways are still clear on aerial maps, it is unknown how many of the original buildings still exist.

### Kirknewton, south of Edinburgh
From humble beginnings as a radar base, RAF Kirknewton has a bright future, having been selected as the site for the British Army's

new multirole brigade. This should ensure the base's survival for a number of decades. The base did see RAF Squadron No 289 created here in November 1941. In the post-war period it became a prisoner of war camp and during the 1950s until 1966 the USAF used the base. Since then it has been used by the Air Cadets and the British Army.

**Did you know?**
Peter Guy Ottewill was a squadron leader in June 1943. He ran to the aid of two airmen whose Bristol Beaufighter had crashed into the ammunition store on Kirknewton airfield. Despite the fact that the ammunition was already exploding, Ottewill and two others dragged the two men clear. This was despite the fact that Ottewill had already been severely burned when an aircraft he had been flying had been shot down. He was awarded the George Medal for his gallantry.

### Largs, north of West Kilbride
Largs opened in September 1942 as a seaplane base and was involved in dealing with aircraft that would be used against German submarines. The original slipway is now used by the Royal National Lifeboat Institute. The facility closed in September 1945 and there is a memorial to the units that were based there, including 231 Squadron.

**Did you know?**
The TV presenter Hughie Green was a ferry pilot based at Largs. His logbook is one of the artefacts held at St Columba's Parish Church.

### Lennoxlove, south of Haddington
Lennoxlove was a satellite field for RAF Dumfries and was primarily used as a secret landing ground to store replacement aircraft. Many of them were hidden under trees and at one point in late 1944 there were almost 120 aircraft there. It would appear that the airfield closed in the late summer of 1945.

## Lerwick, The Shetland Isles

This would appear to have been a flying boat base. We know that the Royal Norwegian Navy used Lerwick between 1942 and 1945. It would seem that the bay was also used by flying boats.

## Leuchars, northwest of St Andrews

Back in 1911 British Army Royal Engineers set up a balloon squadron here. In the First World War the Royal Flying Corps chose it as a base, but work was still underway when the armistice was signed in November 1918. It became a Naval Fleet training school, but in 1920 it became RAF Leuchars. The navy still maintained a presence here and in 1935 it became a training school for the RAF before Coastal Command moved in, in the shape of Squadron Nos 224 and 233. They were involved in anti-submarine warfare and patrolling the shipping channels.

Leuchars became a jet aircraft base in 1950 and in 1954 search and rescue helicopters were based there. In subsequent years Lightnings, Phantoms and Tornados all used the base. In 2010 the first Typhoon squadron in Scotland was based at Leuchars. Leuchars remains in the hands of the RAF and is still an important base.

**Did you know?**
A Hudson from 224 Squadron out of leuchars found the German prison ship Altmark in February 1940. This allowed it to be intercepted by HMS Cossack, which led to the freedom of 200 British prisoners of war.

## Lossiemouth, southwest of Lossiemouth

The most important raid to have been launched from Lossiemouth took place on 12th November, 1944, when RAF No 617 Squadron attacked the Tirpitz. During the course of the war several raids were launched from here, but it was also used as a training centre. Coastal Command took it over towards the end of the war and in 1946 Fleet Air Arm took up residence and it was renamed HMS *Fulmar*.

The RAF got the station back in 1972 and it was used for, amongst other things, a helicopter search and rescue flight. The station is now one of the busiest fast jet airbases used by the RAF and currently there are Tornado aircraft and Sea King helicopters based there.

### Low Eldrig, north of Kirkmaiden
A maintenance unit was based here and the airfield was open between June 1941 and November 1944. The site proved problematic due to the peat and it was only possible to use it during the summer months. Some aircraft were kept here, but the last aircraft were apparently flown out in September 1942 and it was not used for aircraft again.

### Machrihanish, northwest of Campbeltown
RAF Machrihanish is now called MOD Machrihanish and is actually part of the bigger Campbeltown Airport complex. For many years it was used by the United States and there was a special warfare detachment based there. It was officially handed back to the Ministry of Defence in 1995. The history of the site, however, goes back to 1916. It was used for maritime patrol airships and aircraft until the end of the First World War. In June 1941 the airfield reopened as Strabane Naval Air Station.

The Royal Navy called it HMS *Landrail* and later it was renamed RNAS Machrihanish. During the Second World War it was used by both the Royal Navy and the RAF. By 1946 it had been mothballed, but it was reactivated during the Korean War. There was considerable redevelopment in the early 1960s and in the late 60s the US Navy established a presence there. The British Army now use the base, although the base has reportedly recently been put up for sale.

### Macmerry, west of Haddington
In 1929 the Edinburgh Flying Club started using this airfield and there were scheduled flights in the late 1930s. The RAF took it over in 1941 and it was subsequently used by Hurricanes, Blenheims, Lysanders and other aircraft. Towards the end of the war the airfield was passed over to the Royal Navy, but it was never used. It became a satellite field for RAF Drem and was called HMS *Nighthawk II*. The RAF regained control of it in March 1946 and the Edinburgh Flying Club began using it again in August that year, but the airfield closed in 1953. Several of the original buildings still exist.

## Methven, northwest of Perth

Methven opened in April 1941. Repairs to aircraft were carried out here and we also know that it was used as a prisoner of war camp for both Italians and Germans in 1945. The airfield was also home for a time to RAF Squadron No 652, which was an air observation unit. They worked in close cooperation with the artillery of the British Army.

**Did you know?**
It is popularly believed that 652 Squadron was involved in firing the very last artillery shots by the British Army during the Second World War. They directed artillery fire onto Dunkirk, which was still being held by German forces, on 7th May, 1945.

## Milltown, southeast of Lossiemouth

This site has associations with the RAF and with the Royal Navy. From 1941 through to 1943 it was effectively a satellite field for RAF Lossiemouth. In 1946, when Lossiemouth became a Royal Naval base, so too did Milltown and it was christened HMS *Fulmar II*. The airfield saw no flying after 1977 and instead has become a communications centre.

## Montrose, northeast of Montrose

This is an airfield that stakes the claim as being Britain's very first operational military airfield. It was originally used by the Royal Flying Corps from 1913. Towards the end of the First World War it was also used by American pilots. In fact the airfield would see many nationalities and this would continue when the airfield was used during the Second World War, with many pilots being trained at the airbase, or serving from the airbase.

The site today is now the Montrose Air Station Heritage Centre. Many of the buildings and artefacts have been preserved as a result of the work of the volunteers and Heritage Lottery grants. The airfield celebrated its 100th anniversary in 2013.

## Perth, northeast of Perth

This was also known as RAF Scone and is now the municipal airport of Perth. The airfield itself opened at the beginning of 1936. In the early part of the war it was home to an experimental flight, as well as an air observation and navigation school. RAF Squadron Nos 309 and 666 also used it. A Polish fighter reconnaissance squadron, 309, flew Hurricanes and later Mustangs. An air observation unit, 666, worked with the Canadians during the war, but by the time it was at Perth, between 1949 and 1957, it was part of the auxiliary of the RAF.

### Peterhead, west of Peterhead

This airfield was originally known as RNAS Longside, as it was an airship base set up in 1915. It became RAF Peterhead in 1941 and it was closed in 1945, being sold off 14 years later. Today it is used by aircraft supporting the oil industry. The primary job of the squadrons based here was to protect Allied shipping. Notable squadrons included 309 and 416. Today, apart from the hangars, a large number of the original buildings still exist but the control tower was pulled down in the late-1960s.

### Port Ellen, the Isle of Islay

This airfield was opened in August 1935. The first flight into Islay actually took place in 1928, but the present site, which is now the home of Islay Airport, is also known as Glenegedale, which was established in 1940. Concrete runways were added in 1942 and it was primarily used for training RAF pilots but between April 1943 and April 1946 No 67 Air-Sea Rescue Marine Craft Unit was based here. The RAF relinquished control of the airfield in 1947 and it was returned to civilian use, which is its current role.

### Prestwick, northwest of Prestwick

This is now the home of Glasgow Prestwick Airport, handling around 1.3 million passengers a year. It began life as a training airfield in the mid-1930s and was primarily used as a ferry point for aircraft arriving from North America. It also saw front line squadrons, such as No 610, who operated there between April and May 1940. It was also home to No 615 Squadron in the early autumn of 1940.

By July 1942 the first B-17 Flying Fortress touched down at Prestwick. It was to be the first of some 12,000 to fly in from America. It was also used to fly back wounded US personnel after the Normandy landings. In the post-war period it returned to civilian use in April 1946 but it was still used for a time during the 1950s by the Americans. In 1970 it became known as HMS *Gannet*, with Royal Naval helicopters being based there and they renamed it RNAS Prestwick in 1994.

### Renfrew, south of Renfrew
Renfrew was first established in 1916 and in the period running up to the Second World War it was used for military and civilian aircraft. The airfield dealt with scheduled flights from 1933. The problem was that the airfield was never an ideal location for a large civilian airport and consequently the last flights left the airfield in 1966. The runway became part of the M8 and the rest of the airfield was pulled down in the late-1970s. There is now a supermarket where the terminal building used to be located.

### Scatsta, Shetland Islands
This airfield was built in 1940 in order to provide fighter cover for the flying boat base on the eastern shore of Sullom Voe. Scatsta had a

Final approach, Scatsta Airfield. [*Image courtesy of Mike Pennington*]

second runway built, which was completed by April 1942. Perhaps its most famous role was as a support base for No 617 Squadron when they launched their successful attack on the German battleship the Tirpitz in November 1944. The airfield was mothballed until the late-1960s. It became a civilian airport in 1978 and is now used primarily to provide helicopter flights for the oil industry.

### Skeabrae, north of Sandwick, Orkney

The Royal Navy's Fleet Air Arm was first to use this airfield from around August 1941 and it was known as HMS *Tern II*. It was then at some point transferred to the control of the RAF who used it in order to provide fighter cover for the Orkney Islands. The airfield closed in 1957. Today there are several of the buildings still in existence, including the old cinema and gymnasium.

### Skitten, northwest of Wick

This was a satellite station for RAF Castletown but the decision was made to turn it not into a fighter base but into an airfield that could be used by Coastal Command. This also meant Bomber Command could use it for emergency landings. Towards the end of 1944 Coastal Command used it almost exclusively. It closed down fairly soon after the war in Europe ended and was then sold. Skitten's most famous contribution during the Second World War was as a base used to train crews to use the bombs known as Highball. These would be used against the Tirpitz.

**Did you know?**
The inspiration for the film *The Heroes of Telemark* can also date back to Skitten. Two gliders towed by Halifax bombers left Skitten on 19th November, 1942. The idea was to coordinate with the Norwegian resistance to destroy part of Germany's atomic weapons research programme in Norway. One of the bombers, along with a glider, crash-landed into a mountain, killing everyone. The second crash-landed and the survivors were picked up. After interrogation they were murdered by the Gestapo.

### Stornoway, east of Stornoway
Coastal Command used this airfield, which was a former golf course, to hunt for German U-boats. RAF Squadron No 612 and their Avro Ansons were the first arrivals, even before the airfield was finished. They were replaced in November 1940 by RAF Squadron No 48. The Fleet Air Arm also operated from here, in the shape of 827 Squadron. In the post-war period it was used by a signals unit of the RAF, and the station closed in 1998. The runway is now part of Stornoway Airport. Many of the other buildings were demolished.

### Stracathro, northeast of Brechin
The airfield was in use between July 1941 and 1948. Aerial photographs still show the outer perimeter track and the footprint of several buildings. Stracathro was effectively a satellite station of RAF Montrose and flights began in July 1941. It was primarily used for flight instruction.

### Stravithie, southeast of St Andrews
Apparently flying took place here from the 1930s and we do know that the airfield closed at the beginning of May 1945. Since then it has become farmland and housing. It was a satellite landing field and over the course of the war it saw aircraft as diverse as Wellingtons, Halifaxes and Hurricanes.

### Sullom Voe, northeast of Brae, Shetland Islands
This was a flying boat station during the Second World War and was used not only by the RAF but also by the Norwegian Air Force. The base opened in August 1939 and seems to have remained operational until 1957. The area is currently used as an oil terminal.

### Tain, east of Tain
Tain was used by Fighter, Bomber and Coastal Command, as well as the Royal Navy. It opened in the autumn of 1941 and was first home to the Hurricanes of RAF Squadron No 17 who remained there for just a month, to be replaced by RAF Squadron No 123. In the spring of 1942 Sea Hurricanes of Fleet Air Arm Squadron No 801 were based there and over the same period the Tirpitz was attacked by the Halifaxes of RAF Squadron No 76, who were also using the airfield.

Coastal Command used the airfield for almost a year from the summer of 1942. By the beginning of 1943 it was used to train both Royal Navy and RAF crews to use torpedoes. This role was retained until the winter of 1946. The base was also used by Coastal Command to carry out anti-shipping attacks and then from July 1944 until August 1945 the Liberators of RAF Squadron No 86 were there and from August 1944 until June 1945 so too were 311 Squadron and their Liberators. The airfield closed towards the end of 1946 and the area is now farmland.

### Tealing, north of Dundee
There was an operational training unit based here between the spring of 1942 and the summer of 1944. It was also used for training purposes. It would seem that training continued here until at least June 1945, at which point the airfield was closed. Although the site is now given over to agriculture, a number of the buildings are still thought to exist.

### Tiree, on the Isle of Tiree
This is still an airport and it originally opened as a civilian airfield in 1934. It operated in this way until 1940 when the RAF began using it primarily for Coastal Command. It was closed for a period towards the end of 1942 but flights recommenced in September 1943 and the airfield saw Halifax, Anson and Warwick aircraft. The RAF relinquished control in June 1946 and in the following year the civilian airfield opened once again. Many of the original buildings still remain and are in daily use.

### Turnberry, southeast of Maybole
Turnberry was briefly open between 1917 and 1918 and was reopened in the 1930s. It seems to have been used for anti-aircraft training. It was considerably improved during the early years of the Second World War and was used for air-sea rescue and to train torpedo bomber pilots. It would seem that the airfield closed for flying towards the end of 1945, but it was used as a prisoner of war camp until at least 1946. At that point the bulk of the buildings were demolished. The runways can still be seen. The site is now much better known as Turnberry golf course. The control tower is now a home, and a road runs through part of the site.

Pillbox, former RNAS Twatt, Orkney. The pillbox lies on the southern edge of the airfield and is adjacent to the minor road to Bryameadow. The ridges on the walls show that corrugated iron was used as shuttering when it was built. The airfield control tower can be seen on the left. [*Image courtesy of Claire Pegrum*]

## *Twatt, southeast of Kirwall, Orkney Islands*
Royal Marine engineers built this base, which opened in April 1941 as HMS *Tern*. It is probably the most complete of all airfields in Scotland with many of the original features and buildings still existing. Essentially it was a reserve station and it remained in this role until January 1949. The Royal Navy disposed of the site in 1957. It was primarily used for Fleet Air Arm squadrons who were moving to or from Royal Navy vessels.

## *West Freugh, southeast of Stranraer*
West Freugh was not this airfield's original name, as it was opened as a naval airship base called RNAS Luce Bay during the First World War. By the late 1930s it had become a training camp. It was an ideal place for the training of bomb aimers, observers and navigators and this was its role during the Second World War. At various times it was designated as an air observers' school, a servicing base and for anti-aircraft cooperation. Although the RAF closed the airfield in 2001, it is still used for aviation-related testing and is owned by a private company that produces bombs and air-to-ground missiles.

## Whitefield, east of Bankfoot

This airfield opened as a satellite field for RAF Perth. It had a grass runway, some buildings and additional Nissen huts. It is believed that the airfield closed in July 1945 and it then reverted to farmland. At one stage the airfield had six hangars and it would appear that the airfield was used as an elementary flight training school.

## Wigtown, south of Wigtown

Originally this airfield when it opened in the late summer of 1941 had a grass runway with two concrete runways built at some time during 1942. It was exclusively used by Air Observation aircraft, which remained there until late 1945. It was then a sub-field of RAF Dumfries and closed in the summer of 1948.

## Winterseugh, southeast of Dumfries

This site was used for a brief period from 1940 until the spring of 1944. The main problem it posed was its size, as it was too small for most aircraft. The area is now known as Millside Plantation.

## Woodhaven, south of Dundee

This was a seaplane base, which opened in the spring of 1942. It was first home to the Catalinas of the Royal Norwegian Air Force. By May 1943 the Norwegians had become part of RAF Squadron No 333. Their Catalinas still operated out of Woodhaven and they were still engaged in hunting German U-boats and generally attacking any German shipping around Norway. It is understood that Woodhaven closed in 1945. The 333 Squadron still exists as a part of the Royal Norwegian Air Force.

## NORTHERN IRELAND

### Aldergrove, northwest of Belfast

The site of this airfield neighbours Belfast International Airport. Aldergrove has a long and illustrious history; it opened in 1918 but was not formally adopted by the RAF until 1925. RAF No 502 Squadron was the main tenant of the airfield between 1925 and 1941. RAF No 10 Squadron was briefly there in 1936 and in the period 1936 to 1940 it was a training camp and in 1939 an air observer school. Between November

1939 and July 1940 the Royal Navy posted 774 Squadron at the airfield. RAF No 245 Squadron and their Hurricanes used Aldergrove between July 1940 and July 1941.

Throughout the war the site was also extensively used by Coastal Command squadrons, who were mainly on anti-submarine duties. From February 1944 through to August 1945 Flying Fortresses, Halifaxes and Liberators were all at the airfield. Other squadrons were based there for considerable periods of time in the post-war years. RAF No 518 Squadron was present between September 1945 and July 1964, 202 Squadron between March 1948 and August 1951, 502 Squadron between July 1946 and March 1957. There was also 118 Squadron between May 1960 and August 1962.

In later years, RAF No 72 Squadron flew Wessex helicopters from Aldergrove between 1969 and 2002. The airfield was also used by American aircraft when US presidents visited Northern Ireland. The last unit to leave Aldergrove was RAF No 230 Squadron. They had been operating Puma helicopters from 1992 and left in 2009 when the station formally closed. In effect the airfield has now been subsumed by Belfast International Airport.

### Ballyhalbert, southeast of Newtownards

RAF Fighter Command used the airfield from its opening in May 1941, with the first operational aircraft arriving in the shape of the Hurricanes belonging to RAF No 245 Squadron. Over the wartime years the airfield was responsible for protecting Belfast and the rest of Northern Ireland. Not only were the RAF based there, but also the British Army, the Royal Navy and the USAAF. The airfield received a famous guest on 19th May, 1944 in the shape of General Eisenhower, who stopped off at the airfield on the way to RAF Bovingdon. In the post-war years it became known as HMS *Corncrake* and was used by the Fleet Air Arm. The airfield was closed in November 1945 and transferred to RAF Coastal Command, but in March 1960 the site was sold off. There are a number of buildings and structures still on the site, although the majority of the airfield is now a large caravan park.

### Ballykelly, northeast of Londonderry (City of Derry)

The airfield opened in June of 1941 and was primarily a base used by RAF Coastal Command. From here they launched flights aiming to locate and destroy German U-boats. The squadrons operating from the airfield are credited with at least 12 U-boat kills. The airfield was significantly extended in 1943. It was closed at the end of the Second World War, but reopened in 1947 to be used as an anti-submarine school.

By 1955 three squadrons were operating from the airfield. In the early 1960s the Royal Navy began using the airfield and called it HMS Sealion. The aircraft left in March 1971 and in the June of the following year the British Army took it over, calling it Shackleton Barracks. The army left Shackleton Barracks in 2008 and the site has since been sold off to be converted into housing.

### Belfast (Sydenham), east of Belfast
Back in 1937 this airport was established alongside an aircraft factory. It became Belfast's main civil airport and was requisitioned during the Second World War and used as a flight training school. For just over a year, from June 1940, RAF Nos 88 and 226 Squadrons were based there. From the end of November 1941 it became known as RAF Belfast. From July 1943 to April 1944 the USAAF had fighter aircraft assembled and flight tested from the site. In June 1943 the airfield was officially transferred to the Royal Navy and became HMS *Gadwell*.

In 1973 it was transferred back to the RAF and closed in 1978. The site is now, of course, the George Best Belfast City Airport, which opened in 1983 and assumed its new name in 2006.

### Bishopscourt, northeast of Ardglass, County Down
This airfield boasted many years of history when it closed in 1990. It had opened in April 1943 and ran until 1947 as an air observers' school. Advanced flying took place in 1945 and between August 1943 and May 1945 it also served as an air gunnery school. Liberators belonging to Coastal Command operated from the airfield from June 1943 to September 1944. By 1948 it appeared that the airfield had run its course, but it was reopened in March 1952 and remained open until April 1954. It had another new lease of life in 1988 until its final closure in July 1990 when part of the RAF Regiment was stationed there.

### Boa Island, Fermanagh
This was opened as a flying boat base at the end of May 1944 and only remained open for a year. The buildings are still in relatively good

condition. It is based on an isolated stretch of coastland some 15 miles from Enniskillen.

### Cluntoe, southeast of Cookstown

This was a training airfield and also used for emergency landings. For a year, from November 1943, the USAAF used it as a training centre for their B-17s. The RAF took back control of the airfield towards the end of 1944 and temporarily it closed. It reopened in 1953 as a training school and it was finally closed in 1955. There are several derelict buildings still on the site.

### Eglinton, Derry, Londonderry

Coastal Command's 504 Squadron with their Hurricanes began using this airfield in 1941. For a short time, towards the end of 1941 until January 1942, RAF No 133 (Eagle) Squadron and their Spitfires also used the base. Throughout 1941, Spitfires of RAF Squadron Nos 134 and 152 also operated from Eglinton. It was also used in 1942 by the USAAF's 52nd Fighter Group and 82nd Fighter Group. In May 1943 the airfield had a new lease of life as HMS Gannet. It was used by the Royal Navy until April 1959 for fighter training. In 1960 through to 1966 it was known as HMS *Sea Eagle* and was used by Royal Navy

Former USAAF technical site at Dunnaval. These are the best-preserved buildings of the former RAF/USAAF Greencastle airfield. [*Image courtesy of Eric Jones*]

helicopters. In 1994 the airfield became the City of Derry Airport, although civilian flights had actually begun there in 1978.

### Greencastle, southwest of Kilkeel, County Down
Originally, the RAF intended to use this to train bomber crews but instead the USAAF began using it in August 1943. The RAF regained control of the airfield in May 1945, at which point it is believed that it closed. The control tower still stands but most of the rest of the base has now been pulled down.

### Killadeas, north of Enniskillen
This was a flying boat base. Construction began at the beginning of 1941, and Catalinas and later Sunderlands began arriving in the spring. The site is now the home of the Lough Erne Yacht Club. The base is linked to another site at St Angelo, which is now Enniskillen Airport, which also has connections with Coastal Command aircraft. It is understood that the base closed down towards the end of February 1947.

### Kirkistown, south of Ballyhalbert
This was a satellite airfield for RAF Ballyhalbert. It opened in July 1941 and in January 1942 it became the base of RAF No 504 Squadron. When Ballyhalbert became a Royal Naval Air Station in 1945 and was renamed HMS *Corncrake*, Kirkistown followed suit in the July and became HMS *Corncrake II*. The airfield now is a venue used by motor vehicles for racing.

### Langford Lodge, west of Crumlin
The RAF was to utilise this airfield, which opened in 1942, but in fact it was used by the USAAF to carry out repairs and modifications instead. Many aircraft were assembled and flight-tested from this airfield and in fact over the period November 1942 to August 1944 no fewer than 14,000 aircraft were either modified or serviced at this base. The RAF took back control of the airfield in the spring of 1946. The control tower is now the Ulster Aviation Society Museum.

### Limavady, north of Limavady
This Coastal Command station opened in 1940 and was used by RAF Squadron No 502. They were involved in anti-submarine patrols. Also

serving at the airfield over the course of the war were Squadron Nos 172, 221, 224, 407 and 612. It would appear that the RAF left in August 1945 and it became a satellite station for the Royal Naval Air Services base at Eglinton.

### Long Kesh, southwest of Belfast

Long Kesh is most associated with hunger strikes and the political situation in Northern Ireland. Its infamous H-blocks were actually built on top of the former RAF base. The site became known as Maze Prison, but this was closed in 2000 and demolition began in 2006. There are current negotiations regarding the historic value of the site. It was all to be levelled and a multi-purpose stadium built, but for the time-being this has been postponed.

The airfield opened in November 1941 and the USAAF considered it as a potential base in August 1942. As it was, it became primarily a training base and in 1944 the Fleet Air Arm also started using the airfield. It closed in 1946 and was used by the British Army in the post-war period. It was extensively used during the Northern Ireland conflict and in 1971 it became an internment camp.

### Maghaberry, southwest of Belfast

This is the site of the high security prison Maghaberry, which opened in the 1970s. This replaced the Maze prison. Initially Maghaberry airfield was part of a bigger complex used to manufacture bombers. In November 1943 the site was turned over to the USAAF and from here aircraft flew in from America and then onto their squadrons in the rest of Britain. For a time the airfield was also used by Coastal Command and also apparently paratroopers did initial training there. After the war many aircraft were broken up at this site.

### Maydown, northeast of Londonderry

This was a satellite station for RAF Eglington and was known as HMS *Shrike*, as the Royal Navy used the site. It was open between 1942 and 1949. The airfield was also apparently used by the USAAF and we also know that RAF Coastal Command used the base and that the Americans there were involved in anti-submarine training. There were many Fleet Air Arm squadrons based at Maydown, flying aircraft including Swordfish, Barracuda, Avenger, Wildcat, Seafire and

Corsair. We also know that in 1942 USAAF units flew Spitfires and P-38s from here.

### Mullaghmore, southwest of Ballymoney

Although this airfield had a short existence between August 1942 and May 1945, three different services used the site during this time. It was first used as an operational training centre for Wellington crews and, simultaneously, as a replacement and training centre by the USAAF. In fact, the Americans stored aircraft on the site until the summer of 1944.

RAF flight training continued at Mullaghmore until March 1945 and this also coincided with the end of the use of the airfield by the Royal Navy, who had posted several Fleet Air Arm squadrons there since November 1944. It would seem that the airfield closed in May 1945 and was sold off shortly afterwards. The site still has some of the original buildings, including the control tower which is now a house. Microlights are launched from the site and other parts are used for car racing.

### Nutts Corner, northwest of Crumlin

To begin with this was a civilian airfield and there were actually regular flights to London from 1934. During the Second World War it was used by Coastal Command, notably RAF Squadron No 120. It was also used as a stopping-off point for US aircraft. The airfield was temporarily used as Belfast's main civilian airport in the post-war period, but in the end it lost out to what had been RAF Aldergrove. Today the airfield is used for karting but it did enjoy a period of being a superbike and rallycross centre.

### Sandy Bay, west of Belfast

Sandy Bay was on the eastern side of Lough Neagh. There were 12 mooring positions on the east side and a further four to the east of Ram's Island. Whilst the site was primarily used for training, it was also used by Sunderland aircraft flying between Britain and the United States. The most frequent visitor was the PB2Y Coronado, which was used by both the RAF and the US Navy. This function began in around May 1944 and continued until October. The route was usually via Bermuda or North Africa.

St Angelo Airport, Enniskillen. The small plane is proceeding to the runway for take-off. [*Image courtesy of Kenneth Allen*]

## St Angelo, north of Enniskillen

This site is probably better known as St Angelo's Barracks, as it was used by the British Army from the 1970s. It was actually originally designed to be a satellite airfield for RAF Aldergrove. By 1943 it had become a Coastal Command base and aircraft from the airfield protected the Irish Sea and the Atlantic.

The station was also used by the Fleet Air Arm, who called the base HMS *Pintail*. Aircraft were stored and dismantled here in the immediate post-war period and it was then used for helicopter operations, eventually becoming a British Army base. Today the future of the site is uncertain and it may be significantly redeveloped in years to come.

## Toome, northwest of Toomebridge

Toome was opened at the beginning of 1943 and the original intention was that it would be a satellite field for RAF Cluntoe, to the southeast of Cookstown. Wellingtons operated from here in the late summer of 1943 and in the July the 8th USAAF began using it as a combat crew replacement centre. The 9th USAAF also trained bomber crews here. This arrangement ended towards the end of 1944 and the RAF took it over but not for flying, as one would expect. In fact it was just used to store equipment until the spring of 1947.

There seems to have been intentions to continue to use the airfield, as additional work was carried out in the early 1950s but the RAF closed the site in 1954. The Royal Navy then carried out aircraft repairs on the airfield until around 1959. The airfield was disposed of two years later. Most of the site is now turned over to agricultural use, although the control tower has been converted into a house.

## WALES

### *Aberporth, north of Cardigan*

As this airfield is situated close to the village of Blaenannerch, it was originally named this and did not become Aberporth until November 1941. Work began in 1939 and two hangars and some concrete areas were constructed, but the airfield was originally grass.

The airfield stayed open until 1946. Then the Royal Aircraft Establishment took over the airfield and reopened it in 1951. In the mid-1950s they replaced the grass runways with concrete ones. Over the next few years the airfield was improved and extended. The Ministry of Defence still uses the airfield, but it is currently under development as West Wales Airport.

### *Angle, west of Pembroke*

Angle was opened in 1941 and was used by the Hurricanes of RAF No 32 Squadron. Shortly afterwards RAF No 615 Squadron was also based there, along with Hurricanes and then the Spitfires of RAF No 312 Squadron. The base was also used by the Royal Navy but they moved out in September 1943. Other RAF squadrons that served at Angle were Nos 152, 263, 412 and 421. Angle played a significant role in the testing of Barnes Wallis' bouncing bombs when tests were carried out at the beginning of October 1943. There are a number of pilots buried at Angle in St Mary's churchyard.

---

**Did you know?**

Jan Doucha was born in Czechoslovakia and fled to Britain to join the RAF. He was a Battle of Britain veteran and flew both Hurricanes and Spitfires. He was killed on 7th November, 1942 at the age of 28. Jan is one of the pilots buried at St Mary's churchyard in Angle.

---

## Beaumaris, Isle of Anglesey

During the Second World War the aircraft manufacturer Saunders-Roe had a flying boat-works at Beaumaris, where they modified and serviced Catalina seaplanes. The base was also known as Friars Works. Much later, in 1968, the factory on the site was incorporated into a larger business that focused on engineering related to shipping. From the same site buses were made in the post-war period.

Many Catalinas were built at Beaumaris and we know, for example, that RAF No 259 Squadron received its Catalinas at Beaumaris in January 1943. The squadron then flew out to South Africa to undertake patrols in the Indian Ocean. A great deal of the station still exists today.

## Bodorgan, Isle of Anglesey

RAF Bodorgan was originally called RAF Aberffraw, but the name was considered too hard to pronounce. In turn, the locals called it

A pillbox built for the defence of RAF Bodorgan. This is a gem of a pillbox. It is designed for a multi-weapon defence of the airfield, using mortars as well as machine guns. Its elaborateness reflects the fact that RAF Bodorgan had a Battle Group lodger unit charged with providing infantry training for RAF personnel with the aim of defending airfields from terrestrial as well as aerial attack. [*Image courtesy of Eric Jones*]

Penrhyn Halen. It was used as a landing ground and as a base for aircraft towing targets for air gunners. We know that the airfield closed down in 1945. There are several of the buildings still in existence but the land was given back to the Bodorgan Estate after the airfield closed in September 1945.

### Brawdy, northwest of Haverfordwest

The army took over this base in 1996, renaming it Cawdor Barracks. There was considerable demolition in the mid-1990s and some of the airfield is now Brawdy Business Park. The airfield was originally opened in February 1944, to be used as a satellite field for RAF St David's. By the beginning of 1946 Fleet Air Arm were using the airfield and in September 1952 it became known as HMS *Goldcrest*. For just over 20 years, from 1974, the US Navy had a base next to the airfield. There are still numerous original buildings on the base, particularly the concrete runways.

### Cardiff, west of Cardiff

This airfield began life as Cardiff Municipal Airport, which was a role that it readopted after the Second World War until it was closed in 1954. The only real vestige of the airfield is the names of some of the roads on the former site, which are now houses, a school and industrial units. It was also known as RAF Pengam Moors. The site's aviation history dates back to 1905 when airships were built there. There were commercial flights to locations such as Birmingham in the 1930s and later to France.

In 1936 it was decided that an Auxiliary Air Force station would be built there and work was completed in 1938. It was also briefly occupied by a naval air squadron and in 1940 a maintenance unit was established there. It was their job to dismantle aircraft and pack them

---

**Did you know?**
Wing Commander Guy Gibson, who commanded the famous Dambuster Raid, flew in from Lincolnshire to Pengam Moors, Cardiff in a Blenheim for his wedding to the actress Eve Moore in 1940. He then flew her back to Lincolnshire three days later.

up to be shipped overseas. A pair of hangars was built in 1941 and a concrete runway replaced the grass airstrip in 1942. The RAF ceased using the airfield in January 1946.

### Carew Cheriton, north of Tenby
This airfield was built in the late-1930s and work continued to make it a major airfield. It was built on the site of RNAS Pembroke, which had been used during the First World War and was then decommissioned. The airfield was effectively a support base for Pembroke dock and it was also used to train aircrew, but it closed in 1945 and much of the airfield still remains intact. A restoration project has allowed the control tower to become a museum and the site is now used for various activities, including a Sunday market.

### Chepstow, northwest of Chepstow
This is now the site of Chepstow Racecourse. We know that the airfield opened in 1941 and remained operational, or at least under RAF control until the end of the conflict. It is well known that the site was used as a horse racing venue before the war and it quickly returned to this purpose in the mid to late-1940s.

### Dale, south of St Ishmaels
Construction began on this site in 1941 and the opening took place in June 1942. It was a satellite field for RAF Talbenny and was to be originally called RAF Marloes. In 1943 it was passed over to the Royal Naval and it remained open until December 1947. Much of the airfield was pulled down in the early 1980s and the site is now farmland.

### Fairwood Common, Swansea
This site is now Swansea Airport. Its construction took place in 1941 and it was used as a fighter base. The squadrons operating out of the airfield were tasked with the role of protecting South Wales. Over 40 squadrons worked from the airfield, including Nos 125, 263, 312, 456 and 595. RAF involvement ended in 1946 but it took 10 years for the RAF to hand the airfield over to the Swansea Corporation. As a commercial airport for passengers it has not been hugely successful and it is mainly used for light aircraft and helicopters.

Control Tower,
Haverfordwest (Withybush)
Airport. The airfield was
first established in 1941 by
the Ministry of Defence for
use by the RAF. [*Image
courtesy of Pauline Eccles*]

## Haverfordwest, north of Haverfordwest
Coastal Command used this airfield from 1943 through to 1945. It is now known as Haverfordwest Aerodrome and is also known as Withybush Aerodrome.

## Hawarden, west of Chester
BAE Systems own this airfield and there is a large Airbus factory on the site. During the Second World War it was a factory that produced Wellingtons and Lancasters. The RAF was on site during the course of the war until 1957, mainly engaged in storing, repairing and then scrapping aircraft. It was also used by the RAF to ferry aircraft from the factory to their squadrons.

## Hell's Mouth, southwest of Llanengan
RAF Hell's Mouth was both a satellite for RAF Penrhos and used as a bombing range and for air gunnery practice. The airfield was a grass one and consequently, although the runways have long since disappeared under farmland, it is still possible to see some fragments of the original site, such as small shelters, slabs of concrete and a pillbox.

## Lawrenny Ferry, southeast of Haverfordwest
This was better known as HMS *Daedalus II*, as the Royal Navy used it from October 1941. Although the site was probably in use until the beginning of 1946, it is likely that not much activity took place beyond the autumn of 1943.

## Llanbedr, south of Harlech
Originally this opened as a navigation school, but for the winter months of late 1941 to early 1942 Spitfires operated from here, protecting convoys. This was repeated during the summer of 1942. For a short time, in the spring of 1943, the USAAF used Llanbedr to help train their P-47 Thunderbolt pilots, so aircraft towed targets for them from there.

After the war it continued to be used by the RAF and by the Royal Aircraft Establishment until 1992. The site itself finally closed in 2004 and since then there has been a wrangle about the site, with environmentalists campaigning against the development of a civilian airport there. Eventually it was agreed that the airport can be used for limited flights.

## Llandow, southwest of Cowbridge
A maintenance unit established itself here in April 1940 and training units soon moved in, along with transport aircraft. In the post-war years it was used by jet aircraft until the late 1950s. The airfield closed in 1957 and it is now a trading estate, but many of the original buildings are intact.

---

**Did you know?**
On 12th March, 1950 an airliner carrying home Welsh rugby fans from Dublin crashed on the final approach at RAF Llandow. All but three of the 85 passengers and crew were killed.

---

## Llandwrog, southwest of Caernarfon
Today this is Caernarfon Airport and open to private aircraft. It was founded in January 1941 as an air gunnery school. Later it was a base for air observers and the RAF Mountain Rescue Service was established here in June 1943. The RAF ceased operations in 1945.

This was the largest airfield in Wales during the Second World War. In the post-war period over 70,000 German bombs that were said to contain a nerve agent were housed in the open on the site. In 1954 they were loaded onboard ships and sunk off the northwest of Ireland.

### Manorbier, southwest of Tenby

An anti-aircraft training school was set up here in the 1930s but it was to become an airfield that would host a Pilotless Aircraft Unit. Catapults were set up to launch radio controlled aircraft, known as Queen Bee Drones. The RAF continued to use the airfield for this purpose until after the Second World War, but it is reported that they ceased operations in September 1946. The airfield is now used by the British Army.

### Mona, southwest of Anglesey

The Royal Naval Air Service opened this as an airship base in 1915. In 1942 it was reopened as an air gunnery school. From late 1943 to the end of the war it was being used for advanced flight training. It would seem that the airfield closed towards the end of the war, but reopened in 1951 as a satellite field for RAF Valley. It is still home to RAF training and is also used by a flying club. A new control tower was built here in 2004.

### Pembroke Dock, northwest of Pembroke

Pembroke Dock had closed as a Royal dockyard in 1926 but it was given a new lease of life in 1930 when it was chosen as an ideal base for flying boats. It would play an incredibly important role during the Battle of the Atlantic. Nearly 100 flying boats were operating from the base by 1943 and they roamed the Atlantic hunting for submarines. The flying boats, notably the Sunderlands, stayed at Pembroke Dock in the post-war period until they were finally phased out in 1957. Throughout the whole period, the RAF Air-Sea Rescue and Marine Craft Section were notable residents of the station. Two of the hangars still exist but much of the rest of the station was demolished.

### Penrhos, north of Llanbedrog

The base was opened in 1937 and it was primarily used as a bombing and gunnery school. The airfield came under attack on two occasions in October 1940. Following this, detachments of Spitfires and Hurricanes were stationed here for protection. These were the Spitfires of RAF Squadron No 611 and Hurricanes of No 312. Squadron No 312 was manned by Czechs.

Later the airfield was used by the Polish Resettlement Corps and it is understood that it closed in October 1946; however, several of the buildings are still in existence. Most of the site is now housing or agricultural land, part of the area is a golf course and there is also a caravan park. Significantly there is also a Polish housing society building on the site, dedicated to the care of elderly people with a Polish background.

### Rhoose, Cardiff Airport
This was a satellite field for RAF Llandow and it opened in April 1942. It was used by Spitfire pilots, primarily for training. The site is now, of course, much better known as Cardiff Airport. This is an international transport hub with around 1.2 million passengers a year.

### Rudbaxton, north of Haverfordwest
RAF Rudbaxton was a satellite landing ground that was only open between April 1941 and July 1943. It was home to an RAF maintenance unit. The Ministry of Aircraft Production used the site from September 1942, with aircraft being stored there. When it was returned to the original owner in July 1943 the hangar and the Nissen huts were taken down and put up at Withybush. It has now been returned to farmland.

### Sealand, north of Queensferry (Flintshire)
RAF Sealand managed to reach its 90th anniversary, but only just. It was marked for closure in 2004 but the actual end of the base would not take place until 2006. The Royal Flying Corps used it from 1916, although before that it was a civilian airfield. It was used for flight training during the interwar period and it retained this role during the Second World War. The Americans used the base between 1951 and 1957 and then it became a support base and was also home to a volunteer gliding squadron. There is still a link with aviation, as an avionics company works on part of the site.

## St Athan, southeast of Cardiff

St Athan is now owned by the Ministry of Defence but it began life as a technical training centre and school of air navigation shortly before the Second World War. At its peak some 14,000 ground crew and aircrew were being trained here at any one time. It continued its training role into the post-war period and has also been home to a number of British Army units. It was supposed to be the home of the Defence Training Academy but this was cancelled.

Military graves in St Deiniol's graveyard. Many local cemeteries and graveyards have war graves, containing the remains of First World War and Second World War casualties, and St Deiniol's has a number scattered among the locals' graves. The proximity of the RAF airfields at Sealand and Hawarden led to a dedicated section being established at its northeast corner, opposite the Council Cemetery, where there are further war graves. Those buried here include men killed between the wars and since the Second World War. Their graves are similar to those of wartime casualties, but they are not listed on the War Graves Commission's website entry for the cemetery. RAF Hawarden, where Second World War bombers were built, is now the Broughton Factory of British Aerospace, building wings for the European Airbus. [*Image courtesy of David Long*]

### St Brides, south of Bridgend

For a short time, between April 1941 and September 1945, this was a satellite landing ground. It would seem that there were two different landing grounds, known as St Brides East and St Brides West. It would also appear that the airfield became fully operational as a satellite landing ground to St Athan by the spring of 1941. It was used to store Hurricanes, Beaufighters and Beauforts. The RAF retained control of part of the airfield between July and September 1945 to dismantle some aircraft but at that point it was then returned to the ownership of the farmer.

### St Davids, east of Solva

Originally the US Navy was going to use this airfield for their Liberators, but when it opened in September 1943 it was in fact used by Coastal Command, notably 206 and 220 Squadrons were based here. RAF Squadron No 58 arrived in November 1943, along with 502 Squadron. They both remained at the airfield until the late summer or early autumn of 1944. By the end of 1945 the airfield was mothballed but was then passed on to the Royal Navy and it was used by them until around 1958. Today it is possible to still see the runways and taxi areas, along with some of the concrete pads for the other buildings.

### Stormy Down, northeast of Porthcawl

The airfield opened in June 1939 and remained operational until February 1947. It was an air gunnery school and around 10,000 air crewmen were trained here. It was not only used by the RAF but also by the USAAF. Apparently the runway was susceptible to dangerous crosswinds and consequently, flying stopped in August 1944. Today the site is used for motorcycle training and by industry.

### Talbenny, southeast of Haverfordwest

In June 1942 Wellington bombers manned by Czech aircrews belonging to RAF Squadron No 311 moved into Talbenny. They patrolled, hunting for submarines, as far as the Bay of Biscay. The squadron was supported by Beaufighters, who were also based at the airfield. Simultaneously, the airfield was used for gunnery practice and for training. Shortly after the war most of the site was demolished and it was returned to farmland. There was a service carried out in St Mary and Virgin Church in 1985 to commemorate the 82 servicemen that died whilst stationed at RAF Talbenny.

---

**Did you know?**
Brigadier Vivian Dykes had attended the Casablanca Conference and was returning to RAF Talbenny on 29th January, 1943. His aircraft crashed as it approached the airfield, killing Dykes and 10 others.

---

### Templeton, southeast of Haverfordwest
This airfield had a very mixed history, being first used by a unit that ferried aircraft then by Coastal Command and then by the USAAF who flew aircraft to tow targets out of there. The airfield also saw Spitfires and Mosquitos towards the latter part of the war. It is understood that the airfield closed around June 1945 and that the site was then returned to farmland.

### Towyn, north of Aberdovey
On the memorial to those that served at this airfield, the station is referred to as RAF Morfa Towyn. Its primary purpose was to provide aircraft to tow aerial targets for the anti-aircraft guns of the Royal Artillery. We know that it was operational from 1940 and that it closed in July 1945. Other sources suggest that it opened as early as 1939.

### Wrexham, east of Wrexham
Sometimes this airfield is known as Borras, which is an area to the northwest of Wrexham. Aviation began here in 1912 and the site was first a racecourse and then plans were discussed to turn it into a municipal airport. Towards the end of the First World War it was being used to train pilots and was also home to an aero club. This tradition continued during the interwar years.

During the Second World War it was originally used for flight training but was then upgraded and identified as being a prime location for a night fighter squadron to help protect both Liverpool and Manchester. This meant it became home to RAF Squadron No 96, who moved in from RAF Cranage. During the war it was also used as a landing ground for US Army aircraft. The airfield was mothballed towards the end of 1945 but remained in RAF hands until 1959. It was then sold and quarrying began in the area. Some of the original features still exist despite the quarrying. Also on the site is a nuclear bunker, which is reportedly used as a recording studio. The bunker was built in the early 1960s.

## THE ISLE OF MAN

### Andreas, Isle of Man

Andreas was chosen as an ideal site because it would allow aircraft based there to cover Belfast, Glasgow and Liverpool. Construction began in June 1940 and by the summer of 1941 the first RAF personnel began to arrive. Spitfires belonging to RAF No 457 Squadron arrived from nearby RAF Jurby in October 1941. Andreas was considered fully operational by March 1942, but by then 457 Squadron was required to move south to RAF Redhill. It was replaced by the Australian Squadron 452 who remained there until the June. In turn, they were replaced by 93 Squadron, who were based there between June and October 1942.

From October 1941 an Air-Sea Rescue unit was based there and in the period May 1943 to September 1946 it became an air gunnery school. The Fleet Air Arm's 772 Squadron formed at Andreas in May 1945 but were disbanded by the September. The station closed shortly after the war and it was temporarily used to house people waiting for their homes to be built on the island. The airfield was used for motorcycle racing and then by a gliding club and privately-owned aircraft.

### Jurby, Isle of Man

Jurby is now the site of a prison, a racing circuit and a karting track. There are also parts of the airfield which are now covered by housing. The base was opened in 1939 and initially used for training purposes, but there were a number of squadrons that operated from the airfield, particularly in the period January 1941 to March 1942. These included RAF Squadron Nos:

- 258
- 302
- 312
- 457

The first three of these were Spitfire squadrons and the last was a Hurricane squadron. The airfield was used in the post-war period for training and it closed in 1964, with some demolition taking place in the early 1970s. It is still used for an annual air show and many of the original buildings, including the control tower, are still in place.

Slieu Curn, Isle of Man. Looking north back down the unmetalled road towards the village of Ballaugh. Jurby airfield can be seen near the coast, as can the Scottish coastline on the horizon. [*Image courtesy of Andy Radcliffe*]

## Ronaldsway, Isle of Man

This was a private airfield dating back to the 1920s, with flights to Blackpool and Liverpool then later to Glasgow and Leeds established in the 1930s. In the period 1939 to 1943 it was used as a gunnery school. The airfield underwent significant development in 1944 when it became HMS *Urley* and was used by Fleet Air Arm squadrons for training purposes. The Isle of Man government bought the site in 1948 and made improvements to it. It now serves as the Isle of Man Airport.

## THE ISLES OF SCILLY

### St Mary's, Scilly Isles

There was a regular service between here and St Just at Land's End in Cornwall. There was a small detachment of Hurricanes based here and it would appear that the accommodation was tents and, later, a handful of Nissen huts were built. It was not until the autumn of 1942 that tarmac was added to the landing strip.

The primary role of the aircraft based here was to help protect Allied bombers that had been damaged by German fighters. As a result there were some emergency landings on the field. The pilots would also intercept German flying boats and other aircraft that strayed within range. The flight based here was disbanded after the Normandy landings in 1944 and as far as the RAF was concerned the airfield was then mothballed. In June 1945 civilian flights to Land's End began again.

St Mary's, Scilly, from the air on a clear day, with a good view of St Mary's. The large bay in the centre is Porth Hellick. The airfield runway is just visible centre-left. The small island off St Mary's centre-right is Toll's Island. The larger islands visible in the background are Bryher and Tresco to the left, and St Martin's to the right. [*Image courtesy of John Rostron*]

## Chapter Four

# The Mighty Eighth

O N THE morning of 7th December, 1941 the Imperial Japanese Navy launched Operation Hawaii. Without declaring war on the United States they undertook a surprise strike against the vast US naval base at Pearl Harbor in Hawaii. A day later, President Roosevelt declared war on Japan. On 11th December, honouring their Tripartite Pact promises, Germany and Italy declared war on the United States.

**Did you know?**
The Allies were to determine a 'Germany first' strategy. They aimed to crush Germany with their full strength before focusing on the Japanese.

### The Yanks are coming

In January 1942, the United States Army Air Force (USAAF) was actually comprised of four separate air forces numbered one to four. On 2nd January the 5th USAAF was created, but this was soon renamed the 8th Air Force. It would be the Eighth that would be shipped to Britain to stand alongside the Royal Air Force in the air war against Germany.

The very first US airmen arrived in the shape of an advanced party in February 1942. They set up home at Daws Hill Lodge in High Wycombe. This was just the vanguard of a massive 60 combat groups, consisting of bombers, fighters, reconnaissance aircraft and transports.

In July 1942 the first B-17s and P-38s arrived in Britain. Over the next two years the largest air fleet ever seen was created. It was to spread over 122 air bases, with over 200,000 men. The fleet peaked at around 2,000 bombers and 1,000 fighters.

In early 1941 Britain and the United States had agreed that in the event of the United States entering the war it would need bases in the British Isles. The US Army Observer Group began looking from May 1941 for suitable airfields. It was a vital task, as by 7th May, 1945, just four years later, the USSAFE (United States Strategic Air Forces in Europe) would have 500,000 men and 17,000 aircraft. This huge total dropped dramatically by the end of 1946 to just 75,000 men and 2,000 aircraft.

At first with the 8th Air Force consisted of two main bomber groups, simply called the first and second Wings. By October 1942 a third and fourth had been added. Expansion continued into 1944 and by June of that year the Heavy Bombardment Group alone consisted of three whole air divisions.

It is relatively simple to identify the aircraft that belonged to these three divisions:

- The 1st Air Division had a triangle on the tail
- The 2nd Air Division had a circle on the tail
- The 3rd Air Division had a square on the tail

**Did you know?**
The 1st Air Division was largely based in Cambridgeshire and Northamptonshire. The 2nd was mainly in Norfolk and the 3rd in Suffolk, with some units in Norfolk.

### The steady build up and the first missions
Although the United States aircraft were predominantly the famous B-17s and B-24s, the first attributed mission took place in RAF aircraft. The 8th borrowed six Douglas Bostons for a mission against German airfields in France. The raid took place on 4th July, 1942. This was a significant date, as this marked US Independence Day. USAAF

markings were painted on the aircraft and they were fully crewed by Americans. However, only half of these aircraft managed to return safely home.

One of the men who had landed back in February 1942, as part of the advanced guard, was Ira C. Eaker. He would command the 8th from 1942 until 1944. American bomber tactics were very different to those of the RAF. They focused on high-level, precision bombing, during daylight hours. The aircraft all operated as a tight-knit group. They flew in defensive boxes to fend off enemy fighters. The Boeing B-17 (Flying Fortress) and the Consolidated B-24 (Liberator) were the key aircraft that would be used.

The plan was to build up the 8th until it had some 3,500 operational aircraft. To cope with this amount of aircraft at least 75 airfields would be needed. In order to be in range to hit a wide spread of German-held targets in mainland Europe the majority of these airfields would have to be in the east of England. However, the first of the 8th began arriving in July 1942, and as we have seen, that was the very month that US aircrews launched their first mission. The following month saw the 8th begin missions for real in their own aircraft.

The first mission with B-17s took place on 17th August, 1942. Twelve B-17s took off from Grafton Underwood in Northamptonshire. For this first mission, commanded by Colonel Frank Armstrong, Eaker himself could not resist going along for the ride. Spitfires of the RAF protected the mission against Rouen, and all 12 of the B-17s returned safely home.

The 8th was also beginning to fly its fighters. Towards the end of August, No 31 Fighter Group was created and given Spitfires. No 1 Fighter Group was issued with P-38 Lightnings. In September 1942 the US pilots and aircraft of the RAF's Eagle squadrons (all three of them) were formally handed over to the 8th. The build up of the 8th continued, but it took until January 1943 for them to be strong enough to launch an attack on Germany itself. The first German target on 27th January, 1943 was the Wilhelmshaven naval base.

**Did you know?**
The 1st Bomb Wing settled in the East Midlands. The 2nd and the 3rd were based in Suffolk and Norfolk.

Within a year the 8th had grown to such an extent that in five days in late-February 1944 they were able to send 3,000 aircraft against targets in Germany. Over the five-day period the 8th lost 177 aircraft. German fighter losses were estimated at nearly 500. With enormous numbers of new aircraft and crew arriving in Britain the 8th was more than able to cope with these casualties. Attention now turned to destroying Germany's ability to produce oil.

In May 1944 German oil industry targets became a priority. By June of that year the 8th was directly involved in supporting the D-Day landings in Normandy. On the invasion day itself, 6th June, they flew 2,500 bomber sorties. In September 1944 the 8th supported Operation Market Garden, they dropped supplies to US troops around Nijmegen and Eindhoven. The 8th launched their biggest raid on Germany on Christmas Eve 1944, with over 2,000 heavy bombers engaged.

**Did you know?**
The 8th's last mission was on 25th April, 1945. It was bombing mission 968. Over the course of just three years the 8th had lost some 40,000 men.

## American airfields
Some of the airfields used by the 8th Air Force were formerly RAF bases. Others were civilian bases and still more were built specifically for the new arrivals. Over the course of the war years, some of the airfields were used by both American and British aircraft and personnel. The following sections feature the majority of the airfields used by the 8th Air Force during the war years.

## Bedfordshire

### Podington, southeast of Wellingborough
This airfield was originally built for RAF Bomber Command and became operational in August 1942. It had three concrete and tarmac runways and two main hangars. The 8th took it over officially in April 1942. The first arrivals were the C-47s belonging to the 28th Troop Carrier Squadron. The airfield was used as a base for crew

Tower House, Podington airfield. The former control tower is now a dwelling. [*Image courtesy of Will Lovell*]

replacements between August 1942 and May 1943. Also present during this time was part of 301st Bomb Group. Podington operated as a satellite airfield for Chelveston in Northamptonshire.

Around the same time the runways were lengthened and for a short period the airfield was home to the 15th Bomb Squadron and the 100th Bombardment Group. Between September 1943 and July 1945 the airfield was the base for squadrons of the 92nd Bombardment Group (Heavy). They flew in B-17s and clocked up over 300 missions. After this the Air Ministry took control of the airfield and used it for storage. It was sold off in 1961. There is a memorial to the 92nd and the control tower has been converted into a house.

### Thurleigh, north of Bedford
This airfield was opened in 1941 and was home to the RAF's No 160 Squadron. They flew Liberators. At some point in early 1942 the runways were extended and the airfield became the first combat air base to be officially transferred to the United States. The 367th, 368th, 369th and 423rd Bombardment Squadrons of the 306th Bombardment

Group (Heavy) operated their B-17s out of Thurleigh between September 1942 and December 1945. They were then transferred to Germany, having flown over 340 missions and lost over 170 aircraft. The bulk of this airfield was demolished in 1946.

## Buckinghamshire

### *Cheddington, southwest of Cheddington*
Cheddington was originally opened in 1917 but closed soon afterwards. It was also known as RAF Marsworth. During the Second World War it opened again in March 1942 and was used by Wellington crews that were being trained. It was transferred to the 8th in September 1942 and used by the 66th, the 67th and the 68th B-24 Liberator squadrons of the 44th Bombardment Group. These units subsequently moved to Shipdham in Norfolk in the October.

The RAF used the site as a training base for a short period of time but in August 1943 it was again used by the 8th as a replacement centre for their bomber crews and then as a temporary home for the 50th Fighter Squadron. Some strange units arrived in 1944; they would operate between May 1944 and February 1945. Their particular job was to drop leaflets, carry out special operations and run electronic counter measure missions. Over the period the 850th, the 858th, the 406th and the 36th Bombardment Squadrons all operated out of Cheddington.

In the post-war period the British Army used the air base until it was closed in 1952. It was also allegedly used as a CIA base, although there is no evidence to support this. Very little can be seen of the base now, although private aircraft still use the grass runway there and several of the buildings remain in their dilapidated condition.

---

**Did you know?**
Amongst the leaflets dropped were 'safe conduct passes', which could be used by German military personnel as a means by which to surrender to Allied forces. They were a guarantee that they would be treated well. The squadrons also dropped forged ration cards in order to disrupt the German wartime economy.

---

## Cambridgeshire

### Alconbury, northwest of Huntingdon

This pre-war airfield was opened in 1938 and was initially home to the RAF's No 63 Squadron. It was then used by the RAF's No 15, No 40 and No 156 Bomber Squadrons. The 8th took over the airfield in August 1942. The first arrivals were the 93rd Bomb Group (Heavy) with their B-24 Liberators. They operated out of Alconbury between September and December 1942. In the December, Alconbury was taken over by the 92nd Bombardment Group (Heavy) with their B-17s. Between March and June 1943 the B-17s of the 95th Bombardment Group (Heavy) used the airfield before being transferred to Framlingham in Suffolk.

The longest stayers on the airfield arrived in August 1943, when the 482nd Bombardment Group (Heavy) took over with their B-17s and B-24s. They remained on the base until June 1945. From November 1945 to September 1948 a maintenaince unit used the facilities at Alconbury. It became a main USAF base in 1951 and after modernisation the first units began to arrive in 1953. The base was temporarily closed over the period September 1994 to April 1995. The airfield is still being used today by the RAF and the United States Air Forces in Europe (USAFE).

### Bassingbourn, northwest of Royston

This was opened in 1938 and was used until September 1942 by RAF Wellington squadrons. It was transferred to the USAAF in October 1942. Between the October and June 1945 it was home to the 322nd, 323rd, 324th and 401st Bomb Squadrons of the 91st Bombardment Group (Heavy).

The 91st flew some 340 missions, losing 197 B-17s. After the war the base was used by Transport Command of the RAF and in August 1950

---

**Did you know?**
Bassingbourn was home to the famous B-17 bomber, *The Memphis Belle*. The wartime version of the movie was filmed at Bassingbourn.

---

the US 353rd Bomb Squadron arrived. This was the first of several American squadrons to use the airfield after the war. Bassingbourn was transferred back into RAF hands during the 1950s and used by Bomber Command until the late-1960s. It is now an army training base. Considerable amounts of the original airfield still remain. One of the control towers is a museum dedicated to the 91st Bomb Group.

### Bottisham, east of Cambridge
Opened in 1940 and initially used by Army Cooperation squadrons, it passed over to the 8th in November 1943, to become the home of the 361st Fighter Group. They flew their first missions in January 1944, flying P-47 Thunderbolts and, later, P-51 Mustangs. They moved to Little Walden in Essex in May 1944. During 1945 to 1946 Belgian pilots used Bottisham but the base was largely demolished in 1948, having officially closed in May 1946.

### Duxford, south of Cambridge
The airfield opened in 1918 as an RAF fighter base. The air base was enlarged in the late 1920s and early 1930s. In 1938 the RAF's No 19 Squadron, operating out of Duxford, was the first to be issued with

Spitfire Vb BM597 (G-MKVB) is towed from Hangar 3 at Duxford. Built in 1942 at Castle Bromwich, this aircraft is maintained in flying order by the Historic Aircraft Collection, and is frequently seen at displays. [*Image courtesy of Richard Green*]

the Spitfire. Several RAF squadrons operated out of Duxford during the early stages of the war. In 1942 the USAAF's 350th Fighter Group, with P-39 Airacobras, took over. They were based there between October 1942 and April 1943.

In April 1942 the 78th Fighter Group, who became known as the Duxford Eagles, began operating their P-38 Lightnings out of Duxford. Later the unit would use P-47 Thunderbolts and P-51 Mustangs. They remained at Duxford until November 1945. After this the base returned to the RAF. It is now home to the Cambridge offshoot of the Imperial War Museum.

**Did you know?**
Parts of the movie *Battle of Britain* were filmed at Duxford in 1968. One of the main hangars was blown up in one of the scenes. It was no longer safe enough to be preserved and Duxford airfield agreed that it could be destroyed in the film.

### Fowlmere, southwest of Cambridge
This airfield opened in stages between 1918 and 1922. Most of the original buildings were demolished in 1923. It was reopened in 1940 as an offshoot to Duxford and was home to RAF No 19 Squadron. It was also used by other RAF squadrons, including those manned by Canadians and Czechs. In 1943 the airfield was substantially rebuilt and extended.

The USAAF operated out of Fowlmere between April 1944 and October 1945. The 503rd, 504th and 505th Fighter Squadrons of the 339th Fighter Group used P-51 Mustangs for 264 missions. They were incredibly successful, claiming to have shot down 239 German aircraft and destroying another 440 on the ground for the loss of 97 of their own. The base returned to the RAF and was sold off in 1957. Very little remains of the original base.

### Kimbolton, west of Huntingdon
This airfield was opened in 1941 and had a relatively short life, as it was closed in 1946. It was designed for bombers and the 91st Bombardment Group spent a short time here in September 1942. Over

---

**Did you know?**
The 379th Bombardment Group (Heavy) dropped 26,459 tons of bombs on enemy targets. This was the highest total of all units in the 8th.

---

the next two months it was home to the B-26 Marauders of the 17th Bombardment Group. Longer-term, the 524th, 525th, 526th and 527th Bombardment Squadrons of the 379th Bombardment Group (Heavy) remained at Kimbolton from May 1943 until June 1945. Their B-17s flew some 330 missions.

The site is now agricultural land and the home of the Bicton industrial park.

### Steeple Morden, west of Royston
Opened in 1940 and closed in 1946, only a memorial and a handful of buildings now remain to show the site of this base. It was used from 1940 to September 1942 as a dispersal field for Wellington bombers of the RAF No 11 OTU, based at Bassingbourn.

Elements of the USAAF 3rd Photographic Group operated at Steeple Morden between October 1942 and December 1942. For the first five months of 1943 it was used by Blenheims of the RAF's No 18 OTU. The 355th Fighter Group (USAAF) moved onto the air base in July 1943 and remained there until July 1945. They flew P-47 Thunderbolts and, later, P-51 Mustangs. Before moving to Germany they had gained a great reputation. In July 1945 the 336th Fighter Group was stationed at Steeple Morden until they were shipped back

---

**Did you know?**
The 355th Fighter Group lost 175 aircraft in action. They destroyed 365 enemy aircraft in air battles and claimed another 502 on the ground. This was another groundbreaking figure by the 8th and they were the highest scoring fighter group.

---

to the United States in November 1945. The airfield was closed in September 1946 and sold off in 1961. It is now agricultural land.

## Essex

### *Andrewsfield, west of Braintree*
This airfield was actually purpose-built by the United States between July 1942 and April 1943. It was the first of 14 that would be built by US Army engineers. The first temporary tenants were the 96th Bombardment Group (Heavy) who only stayed there from May until June 1943.

The next arrivals were the 322nd Bombardment Group (Heavy). They remained on the base from June 1943 to September 1944. They would become the first B-26 unit to become operational. They had been previously operating out of Bury St Edmunds. In September 1944 the unit moved to France. During their stay at Andrewsfield they flew 34 missions and lost 12 aircraft.

Overlapping the stay of the Americans was a US Pathfinder squadron who also flew B-26s. In October 1944 the air base returned to the RAF and over the succeeding years would be used by a number of different squadrons. Significantly, No 616 Squadron was the first to ever be equipped with the Gloster Meteor fighter. The airfield still operates for private aircraft, although many of the original buildings have been demolished. The larger footprint of the airfield has now been returned to agricultural use.

**Did you know?**
Two of the unit's B-26 Marauder aircraft could claim significant firsts. The aircraft nicknamed 'Flakbait' was the first USAAF bomber to fly 200 missions and the aircraft, nicknamed 'Mild and Bitter', was the first to fly 100.

### *Boxted, northeast of Colchester*
Boxted was identified as a potential 8th bomber base and originally the 96th Bombardment Group was due to be based there, but instead they were sent to Snetterton Heath in Norfolk. To complete the

confusion, the 386th Bombardment Group (Medium), flying B-26s, moved from Snetterton to Boxted. There was a good reason for this, as the 8th wanted to use Essex as their primary operational area for their B-26 units.

The 386th did not remain at Boxted for very long, but they flew their first mission on 20th July. They were then transferred to Great Dunmow on 24th September. Boxted was still under construction at the time and it then became home to the 354th Fighter Group, who flew in from Greenham Common in mid-November 1943. Their primary role was to escort bombers and for this purpose they flew P-51 Mustangs. The 354th left Boxted in April 1944, to be replaced by the 56th Fighter Group, which had come in from Halesworth in Suffolk.

The 56th Fighter Group also had a major hero in their midst in the shape of the commander of the 61st Fighter Squadron, Lieutenant Colonel Francis Gabreski. He was the top American fighter ace in Europe, with 28 kills. His P-47 Thunderbolt was forced down over Germany on 20th July, 1944 and although he was eventually sent to a prisoner of war camp, he ran rings around the Germans hunting for him for five days.

The final American unit to use Boxted was the 5th Emergency Rescue Squadron. They remained there from May 1944 until January 1945. After this the RAF took over Boxted and the site was eventually sold in 1963. During the 1960s the majority of the infrastructure was demolished, including the control tower, although there are still a small number of Nissen huts on the site.

**Did you know?**
One of the most distinguished pilots of the 354th was Colonel James H. Howard. He was on an operation over Germany on 11th January, 1944 and single-handedly he took on 30 German aircraft. He only broke off when he had run out of ammunition and his fuel was perilously low. During those 30 minutes he had shot down three enemy aircraft. For his bravery he was awarded the Medal of Honor.

## Chipping Ongar, northeast of Chipping Ongar

This was one of the airfields originally identified as being ideal for use by the USAAF back in 1942. It was actually built by US Army engineers and work began in August 1942 and it took around a year to complete. The airfield became operational in the spring of 1943. The airfield was still under construction when the 387th Bombardment Group (Medium) arrived from Kentucky in June 1943. They flew Marauders and there were four operational squadrons, the 556th, the 557th, the 558th and the 559th.

The 387th remained at Chipping Ongar until 21st July, 1944 when they shifted to RAF Stone Cross in Hampshire. Over the course of the eight months that they had been operating there they had flown 204 missions at a cost of 10 aircraft. The next significant use of the airfield was during Operation Market Garden, when it was used as a base for C-47 aircraft flying paratroopers and supplies into Holland. The US 61st Troop Carrier Group then used the airfield and were involved in Operation Varsity, where they dropped British paratroopers across the River Rhine in March 1945. The RAF took over the base again in April 1945 and it became a satellite station for RAF Hornchurch.

Throughout the remainder of the 1940s and into the 1950s the airfield was used as a training base and for reservists. The RAF finally left the base in February 1959. The bulk of the airfield was then demolished and the runways broken up. There is only a tiny fragment of the runway still in existence.

**Did you know?**
There was tragedy when the 387th launched their first mission against coastal defences around Boulogne on 15th August, 1943. They tried to take off from Chipping Ongar in heavy fog. One of the B-26s crashed at the end of the runway. The entire crew was killed, with the exception of the tail gunner.

## Debden, southeast of Saffron Walden

This airfield opened in 1937 and until 1942 it housed many RAF fighter squadrons that were directly involved in the Battle of Britain. The German Luftwaffe also attacked the site on a number of

Former RAF Debden from the air. [*Image courtesy of Thomas Nugent*]

occasions. Over the period May to August 1942 the RAF's Nos 71, 121 and 133 Eagle Squadrons, flown by Americans, were based here and officially transferred over to the 8th. Respectively they would become the 334th, 335th and 336th Fighter Squadrons of the 4th Fighter Group. They retained their Spitfires until January 1943 when they were issued with P-47 Thunderbolts. Just over a year later, in February 1944, they transferred to P-51 Mustangs. They then moved to operate out of Steeple Morden.

The RAF transferred their No 616 Squadron to Debden in October 1944 and between 1946 and 1960 it was a diversion airfield for Duxford. It operated as a training school and an RAF police depot until 1975. The site then became an army barracks and this is its current use.

### Earls Colne, southeast of Halstead
The airfield opened in 1942 and after being used temporarily by RAF No 3 Group of Bomber Command it was transferred to the USAAF in

May 1943. The first US unit to arrive came from Bassingbourn on 12th May, 1943. It consisted of the 331st, the 332nd, the 33rd and the 410th Bombardment Squadrons of the 94th Bombardment Group (Heavy). As it was, they only stayed there for a short period of time, because they were transferred to Bury St Edmunds on 12th June. They were replaced two days later by the 323rd Bombardment Group (Medium), who had flown in from RAF Horham in Suffolk.

The unit flying B-26 Marauders consisted of the 453rd, the 454th, the 455th and the 456th Bombardment Squadrons. Their main job was to attack German military targets across Belgium, Holland and France. Shortly after D-Day in 1944 they moved to Beaulieu in Hampshire. The RAF took over the base again in September 1944 and it was only used until March 1946.

Part of the old airfield is still used by a flying club. The control tower was originally converted into a house, but this was pulled down in 2003. The bulk of the remaining land is now a golf course.

**Did you know?**
The airfield was sold at public auction in 1955. The concrete from the runways was used to make improvements on the A12 in the 1960s. Its greatest claim to fame is that Glenn Miller used one of the hangars on the base for a performance.

*Great Dunmow, west of Great Dunmow*
This was another airfield that was built over the period 1942 to 1943 by US Army engineers. The 552nd, the 553rd, the 554th and the 555th arrived at the airfield towards the end of September 1943 from Boxted in Hertfordshire. These were elements of the 386th Bombardment Group with B-26 Marauders. In October 1943 the 386th became part of the 9th USAAF. They flew 257 bombing missions out of Great Dunmow and then the group moved to France in October the following year. The airfield was then used, until December 1945, by Stirling bombers belonging to RAF Nos 190 and 260 Squadrons. At the end of this period No 260 Squadron was transferred to Palestine and the 190 Squadron was disbanded.

The airfield was then used as a storage facility for army vehicles until 1948, when it was officially closed. Large amounts of the concrete were broken up and used to help build the A12. This means that there is very little left apart from some of the tracks which are now used as agricultural roads. However, there is a small museum in Great Dunmow, which has relics relating to both the 386th and the airfield itself.

### *Little Walden, northeast of Saffron Walden*

Using requisitioned farmland, the base was originally to be called Hadstock. Construction got underway in 1943 but it was assigned to the USAAF in August 1942 and officially opened on 9th March 1944. The first arrivals came from Louisiana in the shape of the 409th Bombardment Group (Light). The four squadrons flew A-20 Havocs and A-26 Invaders. These were light bombers and the men were trained to fly low-level missions. Although their principal targets were coastal defences, they were also involved in hitting V-weapon sites and German airfields. The group moved to France and then on to Germany before flying to North Carolina in the United States for deactivation in 1945.

The 361st Fighter Group came in from Bottisham at the end of September 1944 to replace the 409th. They were involved in protecting US bombers but they also undertook fighter sweeps and ground attacks against numerous German targets. The fighter group was subsequently transferred to Belgium, but it returned to Little Walden to fly its last combat mission on 20th April, 1945.

Initially the hangars were used as warehouses. Across a part of the site there is now a road, and a light industrial estate is situated on another part of the base. The control tower has been restored and is used as a memorial to the US units that were based there.

**Did you know?**
The 493rd Bombardment Group (Heavy) used Little Walden in March 1945 while their home base, Debach, was being repaired. The unit was actually there for VE day. The 56th Fighter Group, known as the Wolf Pack, were also stationed there between September 1945 and November 1945, before they headed back to America to be deactivated at the end of the year.

## Ridgewell, northwest of Halstead

The Essex Gliding Club use part of this airfield and there are two memorials on site: one to the 381st Bombardment Group and another to RAF No 90 Squadron. They are both located where the hospital base used to be situated. There is also a small museum. Ridgewell was originally designed to be used by the RAF's heavy bombers. The base opened in December 1942 and Stirling bombers belonging to RAF 90 Squadron operated out of here until May 1943. At this stage the airfield was being used as a satellite station for RAF Stradishall in Suffolk.

Ridgewell would become the major heavy bomber base used by the 8th in Essex. It was considerably enlarged and updated and the first arrivals were the 381st Bombardment Group (Heavy). They flew in from Colorado at the end of June 1943. The unit, consisting of the 532nd, the 533rd, the 534th and the 535th, would fly nearly 300 missions and would lose 131 of their B-17 aircraft. They remained at Ridgewell until June 1945 and then flew to South Dakota in the July, where the unit was deactivated in the following month.

Post-war, the RAF used Ridgewell to store bombs. It remained a storage base until March 1957. The site was then sold off, although interestingly, some of the old hangars were still being used by the USAF until the 1990s. The vast majority of the site was levelled shortly after it was sold at the end of the 1950s.

## Wormingford, northwest of Colchester

This airfield has an interesting history, as during the First World War it was used as a landing ground for aircraft flying missions against German Zeppelins. The airfield reopened in 1942; it was another site that had been earmarked for use by the 8th. It was intended that Wormingford be used for bombers, but it was subsequently used as a fighter base. Flying in from New York on 30th November, 1943 was the 362nd Fighter Group. Consisting of three squadrons, their job was to protect B-24s that were engaged in bombing missions against German rocket launch sites around Calais. Hence their first mission was in this role on 8th February, 1944.

The unit continued to protect bombers, but they were also involved in attacks of their own in the run up to the Normandy landings. The unit moved to RAF Headcorn in Kent in April 1944 to join the 9th Air Force. Wormingford was then taken over by the 55th Fighter Group.

**Did you know?**
The 55th Fighter Group were awarded two Distinguished Unit Citations. They won the first for their activities over Germany between 3rd and 13th September, 1944. They shot down all the German fighters that were trying to attack the bombers they were protecting and then swept down and destroyed more German aircraft on their airfields. Their second citation was won on 19th February, 1945 where they flew *en masse* across Germany, wiping out tanks, trucks, railway trains, troop carriers and selected buildings.

Originally they flew P-38 Lightnings and, later, P-51 Mustangs. They were involved in escort duty, but primarily ground attacks during the Battle of the Bulge, over the Christmas period 1944 to 1945 and in support of the British paratroopers at Arnhem during Operation Market Garden.

The 55th flew its last combat missions out of Wormingford on 21st April, 1945 and they then moved to Germany. At the end of the war in Europe the air base was returned to use by the RAF, where it was used by training and transport command. The site was sold off in the early 1960s. Much of the site is now occupied by farmland; however the Essex and Suffolk Gliding Club use a small section of the runway for their activities.

**Hertfordshire**

*Nuthampstead, east of Hertford*
This air base was built by US engineers. Construction began in 1942 and it was originally designated as a heavy bomber airfield. However, it was actually used by the 38th, the 338th and the 343rd Squadrons of the 55th Fighter Group, flying P-38 Lightnings until April 1944. They had flown in from Washington on 14th September, 1943. In April the unit moved to Wormingford in Essex and the base was taken over by the 398th Bombardment Group (Heavy), consisting of the 600th, the 601st, the 602nd and the 603rd Bombardment Squadrons. They

Fighter Group Memorial, Nuthampstead. Memorial next to The Woodman pub, dedicated to the pilots of 55th Fighter Group, 442nd Air Service Group, 66th Fighter Wing and VIII Fighter Command, USAAF – who were lost in combat while based at RAF Nuthampstead. [*Image courtesy of Lorraine and Keith Bowdler*]

flew B-17 Flying Fortresses and their primary targets were strategic missions over Germany.

In all, the group flew 195 missions and lost 58 aircraft. The RAF took over Nuthampstead in July 1945 and it was used as a store until the end of October 1954. The air base was officially closed on 1st

**Did you know?**
The 398th Bombardment Group ranged far and wide, attacking Eindhoven in September 1944, targets in the Ardennes over the Christmas period 1944 to 1945, bombing Prague in February 1945 and then flying its last mission, again over Czechoslovakia, on 25th April, 1945.

March, 1959. The site was sold off the following year. The runways and buildings were demolished and it was planned to plant large numbers of trees in their place, until it was discovered that there was a huge amount of bombs still remaining on the site. These had to be cleared before planting could begin. Nuthampstead nearly made it as a potential site for London's third airport, but plans never came to fruition.

## Huntingdonshire

### Glatton, north of Huntingdon
This was specifically built for the 8th and the first arrivals were the 457th Bombardment Group (Heavy). They arrived on 21st January, 1944 and a month later they were involved in their first mission, which became known as 'Big Week'. The idea was to engage the Luftwaffe over Germany and inflict irreparable damage on them in the air, whilst simultaneously pounding the aircraft factories.

Large numbers of German aircraft were destroyed and, more importantly, the Germans lost huge numbers of highly experienced pilots. The 457th's four squadrons continued operations through to 20th April, 1945, by which time they had clocked up 237 missions for the loss of 83 of their B-17s. From June 1945 to April 1946 the RAF used the airfield for Lancaster and Liberator flights to the Middle East.

The site was still being used by an RAF maintenance unit until September 1947 but the following year the site was sold off. Much of the airfield was then returned to agricultural use, but parts of the runway still exist and they are now incorporated into Conington Airport. The original control tower was demolished at some point, but there is now a new control tower and clubhouse on the same site.

### Molesworth, northwest of Huntingdon
The airfield dates back to 1917 when it was used by the Royal Flying Corps' No 75 Squadron. The Second World War base was built between 1940 and 1941 and initially Vickers Wellingtons of the Royal Australian Air Force's No 460 Squadron operated from there between mid-November 1941 and the beginning of January 1942. There was also a brief stay by Bomber Command's No 159 Squadron. In February 1942 it was assigned to the 8th, but it would need a huge amount of work, including the lengthening of the main runway.

The 15th Bombardment Squadron flew in from RAF Grafton Underwood at the beginning of June 1942. They were involved in early training and cooperation with the RAF but they left in October 1942 and Molesworth became home for the 303rd Bombardment Group and their B-17s. They flew their first mission on 17th November and, like many of the other bombardment groups they were focused on destroying German industry. They would go on to complete some 364 missions.

The RAF took back the station in July 1945 to be used to train pilots on the Gloster Meteor. The base was effectively deactivated in the late 1940s, but it reopened in July 1951 with a brand new runway and became home to the US 582nd Air Resupply Group. They flew into Molesworth in February 1954.

By 1959 the base was only being used on an irregular basis, but it was not until 1973 that the airfield was deactivated. Then it was chosen as a site for ground-launched cruise missiles in the early 1980s. Much of the Second World War buildings and infrastructure were removed. In 1986 US missiles were moved onto the base but they only stayed there until October 1988. The site was then chosen as an intelligence analysis centre.

**Did you know?**
The 303rd claimed 378 enemy aircraft shot down. They had 817 of their men killed in action and over 750 became prisoners of war.

## Norfolk

### *Attlebridge, northwest of Norwich*
Officially closed in 1950 as an airfield, since the late 1950s this site has been a turkey farm. Attlebridge was completed in August 1941 and used by RAF aircraft and Coastal Command, primarily for anti-shipping patrols. By September 1942 it had been handed over to the 8th, which meant that the runways and infrastructure had to be enlarged.

The first Americans to arrive came in the September and it operated as a satellite station for Horsham St Faith. The 319th Bombardment Group (Heavy) and their Mitchell bombers only stayed for a short period and then they flew on to Algeria. It was then used as a training airfield but during the period March 1943 to February 1944 the Dutch of RAF No 320 Squadron flew B-25 Mitchells from the airfield.

The airfield returned to US use at the beginning of March 1944, with the arrival of the B-24 Liberators of 466th Bombardment Group (Heavy). They were involved in daylight raids on Berlin, attacking the coastline of Normandy and a wide range of other strategic operations. By the time they flew their last mission towards the end of April 1945 they had flown 232 missions and lost 47 aircraft.

### Bodney, west of Watton

Initially Bodney was used as a satellite airfield for RAF Watton. In this role it was used by RAF Bomber Command, with Nos 21, 82 and 105 Squadrons being based there. The USAAF took over the airfield in the middle of 1943. In order to prepare for their arrival, significant additions were made to the hardstanding for the aircraft, the runways and to the road infrastructure. The 352nd Fighter Group, consisting of the 328th, the 486th, and the 487th Fighter Squadrons arrived over the early summer months. They were responsible for protecting bombers and they flew P-47 Thunderbolts.

By April 1944 they were now flying P-51 Mustangs. Because of the aircraft's paint job they became known as the 'Blue-nosed Bastards of Bodney'. The unit would go on to be involved in operations over Holland, the Ardennes and the Rhine, having been temporarily detached to airfields in Europe before returning to Bodney in April 1945.

---

**Did you know?**
In the early hours of 6th June, 1944 Lieutenant Robert Frascotti of the 352nd was killed when his P-51 Mustang hit the control tower whilst he was taking off at Bodney. The fighter group as a whole flew 420 missions, clocking up over 59,000 combat hours. They could claim 776 enemy aircraft destroyed.

---

FROM THESE FIELDS, AMERICAN AIRMEN JOINED THEIR BRITISH ALLIES IN THE CAUSE OF FREEDOM

352nd FIGHTER GROUP

HQ. & HQS. SQD.                     486th FIGHTER SQD.
328th FIGHTER SQD.              487th FIGHTER SQD.

1st SERVICE GROUP DETACHMENT "A"

HQ. & HQS. SQD. - DET. "A"       1104th QUARTERMASTER CO.
17th SERVICE SQD.                     1141st MILITARY POLICE CO.
22nd STATION COMP. SQD.        1772nd ORDNANCE SUP. & MAINT. CO.
1066th SIGNAL CO.                     2019th ENGINEER PLATOON

1943 ~ 1945

Memorial to the 352nd Fighter Group at the former site of RAF Bodney, Norfolk. The memorial is outside Bodney Camp army barracks this is at the edge of the Army's Stanford training area. [*Image courtesy of Keith Evans*]

The control tower which was hit by Frascotti still remains on the site, along with other now derelict buildings, although most of the airfield is now farmland.

### Deopham Green, north of Attleborough

Although this was originally built during 1942 to 1943, it was not officially opened until the arrival of the 452nd Bombardment Group (Heavy) at the beginning of January 1944. A month later they began operations, mainly against strategic targets in Germany. They were also involved in a number of other key strategic operations and would fly some 250 missions for the loss of 110 aircraft.

Post-war, an RAF maintenance unit remained on the airfield from October 1945 until the beginning of January 1948. The land was sold

---

**Did you know?**
Two members of the 452nd were awarded posthumous Medals of Honor. Flight Lieutenant Donald Gott and Second Lieutenant William E. Metzger Jr remained on their crippled B-17 after it had been hit by anti-aircraft fire on a mission over Germany on 9th November, 1944. There was a fire onboard and at any moment the bombs still in the aircraft could have exploded. Gott and Metzger, ignoring the danger, carried on towards their target and dropped their bombs. They tried to crash-land the crippled aircraft but in vain, as it exploded on landing.

---

in 1961 and all that now remains are some of the old runways and taxiways.

### East Wretham, northeast of Thetford

The airfield was originally opened as a satellite for RAF Honington and used by RAF No 311 Squadron, with Czech pilots. In April 1942 Coastal Command took over but in the November RAF No 115 Squadron moved in, using the base for their Wellingtons and Lancasters. The airfield was then transferred to the 8th and the first occupants were the 359th Fighter Group, who had flown in from Massachusetts. They became operational in December 1943 and followed the same pattern as other fighter units, protecting bombers, to begin with using P-47s and then P-51s. They too were involved in many of the major operations of the liberation of Europe and they remained based at East Wretham until November 1945. By this time they had flown nearly 350 missions.

The site was then temporarily used by Fighter Command and, in 1946, by Bomber Command and then as a training centre. The site's final major use was as a Polish resettlement camp. It is still used by the British Army as a training area and, as such, many of the original buildings still exist, including the control tower.

### Hardwick, west of Bungay

This airfield was originally built with the RAF in mind, but in fact it was assigned to the 20th Combat Bombardment Wing as their headquarters, at first the home of the 310th Bombardment Group (Medium). They were *en route* from South Carolina to Prestwick in Scotland and then they used Hardwick airfield as a stopping off point whilst travelling to Algeria. The 93rd Bombardment Group (Heavy) took up occupation of Hardwick when they came in from Alconbury in Cambridgeshire in December 1942. After detachment to North Africa they came back to Hardwick and, until April 1945, carried out strategic bombing missions across Europe.

The RAF took over the base in June 1945. For a time it was used for maintaining aircraft, but it was closed down in 1962. The bulk of the buildings were demolished but some still remain and are used by a local farm. There is a museum in one of the Nissen huts and part of the airfield was also used for private aircraft.

### Hethel, southwest of Norwich

This base was specifically designed and built for the 8th. Between September 1943 and June 1945 it was the headquarters for part of the 2nd Bombardment Division. Flying in from Florida in September 1942 came the 320th Bombardment Group (Medium) and their B-26s. They were only passing through, heading for Algeria where they arrived in the December. The 310th Bombardment Group (Medium) also used Hethel as a stopping-off point in their journey from South Carolina to French Morocco.

In the meantime, the base was being used for training purposes. Hethel finally thought it would receive its permanent tenants; the 389th Bombardment Group (Heavy) with their B-24 Liberators. They arrived on 11th June, 1943, but within a month they were in Libya, bombing German targets as widespread as Crete and Romania. In the summer of 1945 Hethel became home to the P-51 Mustang squadrons flown by Polish pilots. The site was temporarily used as a transit centre and then for training, but it was officially closed as an airfield in 1948.

In the immediate aftermath of the war the airfield was used to house the homeless and eventually, in 1966, Lotus Cars moved onto the site. The runways were perfect for test driving. As such, the control tower and many of the other buildings have undergone some changes, but they are still in use. Large portions of the runway still exist and the site, which stretches to around 55 acres, is a major factory and engineering works. Some of the outlying parts of the airfield are now farmland.

## Horsham St Faith, north of Norwich

This airfield is now Norwich International Airport. It began life in 1939 and was opened as an RAF station at the beginning of June 1940. It was first used as a dispersal station for RAF No 21 Squadron's Blenheims, which operated out of RAF Watton. The first operational aircraft were Spitfires belonging to RAF Nos 19 and 66 Squadrons. From May 1940 part of RAF No 264 Squadron operated from the airfield and then bombers moved in belonging to RAF Nos 139 and 114 Squadrons.

The Americans arrived in early April 1943, although the airfield itself had been made available to the 8th from September 1942. The new arrivals were the 56th Fighter Group but their stay was relatively brief, as on 8th July they moved to RAF Halesworth so that Horsham St Faith could be enlarged to take heavy bombers. Work took some time to complete and towards the end of January 1944 B-24 Liberators of the 458th Bombardment Group (Heavy) arrived.

Part of their job was to fly fuel into France, a job that they were involved in from around September 1944. In all, the group flew 240 missions and lost 47 aircraft before flying its last mission on 25th April, 1945. Fighter Command took over the station in the July and it was used by Gloster Meteors, which began arriving over the period 1946 to 1948.

The airfield itself was deactivated at the beginning of August 1963 and was then slowly developed as an international airport. Some of the original hangars are still used for maintenance purposes. Other old buildings are now part of the industrial estate situated there.

**Did you know?**
It was from Horsham St Faith that a Blenheim belonging to RAF No 18 Squadron dropped a replacement pair of artificial legs for Wing Commander Douglas Bader. The artificial limbs were dropped onto a German-held airfield in France on 19th August, 1941. The drop was called 'Leg Operation'.

## North Pickenham, east of Swaffham

This was a relatively late airfield, as it only opened in 1944. However, it would remain operational until around 1965. It was always designed to be used by the 8th and the first unit to be assigned to the airfield was the 492nd Bombardment Group (Heavy), who remained there until early August when they were transferred to RAF Harrington near Kettering. Their place was taken by the 491st who flew in from Texas in the August, via Metfield. The 491st flew 187 missions with their last one being flown on 25th April, 1945.

The airfield then became an offshoot of Shipdham and by the late 1940s it was in mothballs. North Pickenham was reopened in December 1958, to be used by RAF No 220 Squadron. The unit left in October 1963 and it was finally sold off in 1967. The site is now a large turkey farm and some of the old buildings still exist.

## Old Buckenham, southeast of Attleborough

This airfield, built for the 8th, is still in use as Old Buckenham Airport. It was built over the period 1942 to 1943 and the first arrivals were the four bombardment squadrons of the 453rd Bombardment Group (Heavy). They flew in from California just before Christmas 1943. The unit flew B-24 Liberators and became operational on 5th February, 1944, when they launched their first mission against an airfield near Tours in France.

The squadrons were primarily concerned with attacking German infrastructure and industry targets. They were also involved in attacking coastal defences in the build up to D-Day and continued

**Did you know?**
The most famous individual who was part of the 453rd Bombardment Group was the actor James Stewart. He served as the group operations officer from March 1944. In all he flew 20 missions and received the Distinguished Flying Cross, the Croix de Guerre and the Air Medal with three oak leaf clusters. In July 1944 he ceased flying combat missions and became chief of staff of the 2nd Combat Bombardment Wing. In just four years of military service he had risen from the rank of private to colonel.

> **Did you know?**
> The other famous member of the 453rd was the actor Walter Matthau. He was a radio man and gunner on a B-24 Liberator. He would reach the rank of staff sergeant before changing his career to that of an actor.

operations through to April 1945 when they were told that they might be transferred to using B-29s in the Pacific.

The airfield was taken back by the British in May 1945 and housed maintenance units until its closure in June 1960. There is a large, granite memorial on the site to the 453rd, which was dedicated in 1990.

### Rackheath, northeast of Norwich

This airfield got underway in 1943, which meant that the base was not opened until March 1944. It would become home to the 467th Bombardment Group (Heavy), who had flown in from Utah. They began their operations on 10th April, 1944, setting the pattern for their attacks on strategic targets, including steel works and chemical plants. They were also involved in September 1944 in flying out emergency fuel supplies to France. They flew some 212 missions and lost 46 aircraft.

The airfield closed in 1945, leading to the demolition of the majority of the infrastructure. However, the control tower is now offices and a light industrial business operates out of one of the hangars.

> **Did you know?**
> The 467th's commanding officer, Colonel Albert J. Shower, was the only commanding officer to remain in command of a unit in the 8th from the time it left the USA until it returned.

Derelict RAF building on the edge of Seething airfield. [*Image courtesy of Adrian S. Pye*]

### Seething, southeast of Norwich
This airfield was specifically built for the 8th and it opened on 1st December, 1943, to become home to the 448th Bombardment Group (Heavy). Their B-24 Liberators were involved in combat missions from 22nd December, 1943 until April 1945. Their last mission was on 25th April and the unit flew to South Dakota in July 1945.

The airfield was formally closed that year and the majority of the airfield became agricultural land. Part of the main runway is the home of the Waveney Flying Group and this portion of the airfield is known as Seething airfield. The control tower has been fully renovated and is a museum to the 448th.

### Shipdham, south of East Dereham
Shipdham still has close associations with flying, as in June 1970 it opened for private flying and is home to the Shipdham Aero Club. There is also a museum on site. Some of the buildings are in a poor state of repair and the control tower is derelict. Part of the site is now an industrial estate.

Shipdham has the honour of being the first base in Norfolk to be used by American heavy bombers. It was also the airfield that was used for the longest period, stretching from October 1942 all the way through to the departure of the last Americans in December 1945. The base itself was built during 1941 to 1942 and it served as headquarters for the 14th Combat Bombardment Wing from September 1943 to June 1945. The base was used as a staging post by the 319th Bombardment Group (Medium) in September 1942, as they moved from Shipdham to Horsham St Faith and then on to Algeria.

The base became home of the 44th Bombardment Group (Heavy) on 10th October, 1942. They flew B-24 Liberators and were engaged from the November until June 1943 against a host of targets across Europe. Parts of the unit were temporarily shifted to Libya in June 1943 and in all, the unit flew 344 missions, losing 192 aircraft. This was the highest number of B-24s lost by any one unit. When the Americans left in 1945 the airfield became a transit centre for German prisoners of war. These were men that had been held captive in the United States. They were screened and processed before being returned to Germany.

### *Snetterton Heath, southwest of Norwich*
This was another airfield that was originally intended to be used by the RAF but with the USAAF needing more airfields it was allocated to them instead in 1943. From September through to June 1945 it was the headquarters of the 45th Combat Bombardment Wing. As an airfield it opened in June 1943 and was to be used by the 386th Bombardment Group (Medium). They were to fly their B-26 Marauders, but in fact were transferred to Boxted just a week later. This left the field free for the 96th Bombardment Group (Heavy) to come in two days later from Andrewsfield. They flew B-17 Flying Fortresses. Amongst their targets were factories and oil refineries.

The airfield itself was closed in 1948 and had been home to an RAF maintenance unit since December 1945. It was sold in 1952. The idea was to turn it into a motor racing circuit. It has now been transformed and is used to test cars and motorcycles, as well as holding racing competitions.

### *Thorpe Abbotts, east of Diss*
The original intention was that this airfield would become a satellite station for RAF Horham, but instead it became a base used by the

100th Bombardment Group (Heavy). They flew B-17 Flying Fortresses and arrived from Nebraska in early June 1943. For the next seven months they pounded German industry and naval targets and also severely damaged a large German aircraft factory at Regensburg in Bavaria. They too were involved in all of the other major bombing offensives, including Normandy, the Ardennes and the crossing of the Rhine. In all they flew some 306 combat missions. They were known as the 'Bloody Hundredth' as they were inaccurately portrayed as having a high combat loss when in fact it was fairly average.

The RAF took the base back towards the end of June 1946 and it was mothballed until its final closure in 1956. The airfield was largely demolished and returned to farmland. There is a small airstrip for light aircraft, but in 1977 the control tower was restored to become a museum to the 100th. Close to the control tower are some restored Nissen huts.

### Tibenham, southwest of Norwich

Tibenham was used by the Royal Flying Corps during the First World War. It was considerably redeveloped as an air base for the 8th during 1941 to 1942. It was used as a transit point for the B-26 Marauders of the US 12th Air Force's 320th Bombardment Group (Medium) on their long flight to Algeria in November 1942. They were only being transported, so the B-26s never actually landed at Tibenham.

As it was, Tibenham was finally assigned as a training base in the summer of 1943, but it would become home to the 445th Bombardment Group (Heavy). They flew in from Iowa at the beginning of November 1943 and were ready for action by mid-December. They launched their first operation against the U-boat pens at Kiel. Like many other bomber units they were involved in a wide range of different missions, including dropping propaganda leaflets, providing supplies to the French Resistance and supporting ground forces.

All in all the 445th flew over 280 missions, losing over 130 aircraft. In July 1945 through to 1952, the RAF used Tibenham mainly for maintenance activities. They sold off part of the airfield in 1952, but in 1955 it was decided to lengthen the main runway so that it could be used by post-war jet aircraft. However, this never came to fruition and Tibenham was mothballed in 1959. It was subsequently sold in the mid-1960s. The site is now used by the Norfolk Gliding Club. The

**Did you know?**
The 445th faced its most perilous combat mission on 27th September, 1944. Due to a navigational error, 35 of the aircraft were separated and came under attack for 150 German fighters. The 361st Fighter Group appeared on the scene, but over the space of a few minutes 29 German and 26 US aircraft had been shot down. Only four of the unit's aircraft made it back to Tibenham.

control tower was still being used in the 1970s but it was apparently demolished in 1978. Several of the other buildings do still remain on the site.

### Wendling, northwest of East Dereham
This was another airfield that had been planned to be used by RAF Bomber Command, but was in fact to become the home of the 392nd Bombardment Group. They were the first tenants, arriving from New Mexico in July 1943. They flew their Liberator aircraft against a wide range of targets and were involved in the Normandy landings, the Battle of the Bulge, Operation Market Garden and Operation Varsity. The unit flew its last combat mission on 25th April, 1945, by which time they had lost 127 aircraft shot down and 57 in other incidents over their 285 combat missions.

The base was used by the RAF after the war until it was closed in November 1961. During the period 1960 to 1964 there were USAF activities on the site when they used it as a radio base. The site was sold off in 1964 and then had a new lease of life as a turkey farm. The runways have large coops on them, but most of the other features have been demolished. There is a monument to the 392nd near the airfield, on the Beeston Road.

### Northamptonshire

### Chelveston, east of Wellingborough
When the airfield was opened in August 1941 it was used as a gunnery school and for experimental gliders. At this stage the landing

strips were grass, but it was identified as being ideal for the 8th and consequently construction got underway to bring it up to specification. Almost a year after its official opening in 1941 the 301st Bombardment Group (Heavy) arrived with their B-17s. However, they did not stay for very long and were assigned towards the end of November 1942 to Algeria. This led to the shifting of the 305th Bombardment Group (Heavy) from Grafton Underwood in the December. The 305th would fly a total of 337 missions for the loss of 154 aircraft.

The RAF took back possession of the base from October 1945 through to 1952. In 1952 it returned to US control and they authorised the construction of a new runway for jets. Many of the wartime buildings were torn down and replaced with more up-to-date facilities. The base was used by a number of different US units in the post-war period, but in March 1962 the runway was closed and it once again returned to RAF control. In the early 1970s they decided to sell off the base and in 2005 it was finally decided to dispose of what remained of the site to develop an industrial estate.

### Deenethorpe, east of Corby

This was a purpose built airfield for the 8th and the 401st Bombardment Group (Heavy) arrived there in November 1943, a month after the base opened. The four squadrons flew B-17s. One of the Flying Fortresses crashed into a cottage in Deenethorpe in

Buildings on the former technical site RAF Deenethorpe. [*Image courtesy of Chris Lowe*]

270

December 1943 but luckily everyone was evacuated before the bombs exploded. Apparently the blast could be heard nine miles away in Kettering.

The 401st flew a total of 255 combat missions for the loss of 95 aircraft. In the post-war years it was initially used by the RAF as a recruiting centre and the Royal Observer Corps made use of the control tower. The airfield was finally sold off in 1963 and returned to farmland. The tower was unfortunately demolished in 1996. Part of the airfield is still in use as a private airstrip.

### Harrington, west of Kettering

The airfield was originally designed to be a satellite station for RAF Desborough, situated between Market Harborough and Kettering. Instead, US engineers moved in and began construction, and the site completed in the first few months of 1944. The 801st Bombardment Group (Provisional) flew out of RAF Alconbury on 25th March, 1944 to set up at Harrington.

Originally they were just two squadrons but by the May they increased to four. They were quite a romantic group and became known as 'The Carpetbaggers'. Their main job was to use their aircraft to fly in agents and supplies for the resistance into France. They would also drop leaflets and safe passage documents over occupied Europe. In August 1944 the unit effectively became the 492nd Bombardment Group and were involved in conventional strategic bombing attacks. However, they continued to fly secret missions until as late as April 1945. The airfield fell into disrepair after the Second World War, but between 1958 and 1963 it operated as a site for RAF missiles.

The most prominent relic of its military use is the missile launch pads and some of the original roads. The Carpetbagger Aviation Museum was opened in 1993 and there are other exhibits that feature the history of the airfield over the years.

### Kings Cliffe, west of Peterborough

The airfield was still being built when the 347th Fighter Squadron and their P-39s flew in during December 1942. By January 1943 it had become the home of the 56th Fighter Group, but they did not fly any combat missions and were under training until they moved to Horsham St Faith in the April. The 20th Fighter Group came to the

**Did you know?**
In the large hangar at Kings Cliffe airfield Glenn Miller played his last airfield concert on 3rd October, 1944.

airfield in late August 1943 with their P-38s. One of their particular specialisms was knocking out trains and they received the nickname 'The Loco Group'. The unit began flying P-51s in July 1944.

The airfield returned to the RAF and was used primarily for storage until its sale in 1959. Some of the original buildings are used as part of the Bedford Purlieus National Nature Reserve. They use what used to be the cinema, chapel and gym.

### Polebrook, southeast of Oundle

The airfield began operations in June 1941 when it was used by RAF No 90 Squadron for test flying B-17s. Three of the aircraft were involved in a raid on Wilhelmshaven on 8th July, 1941 and they carried out further test raids through to 2nd September, by which time they had launched a total of 22 missions for the loss of eight aircraft.

It was then decided that Polebrook should become a US base and, as a result, the main runway was extended, along with the secondary runways. Between December 1943 and June 1945 it was the headquarters for the 94th Bombardment Wing. The first operational unit was the 97th Bombardment Group (Heavy), who began operations there on 17th August, 1942.

The 97th was transferred to the Mediterranean in late October 1942 and Polebrook remained empty until 15th April, 1943, with the arrival

**Did you know?**
The leading aircraft of the group was called Butchers Shop. Its pilot was the group commander, Colonel Frank A. Armstrong. He worked with the squadron commander, Major Paul W. Tibbets, who would go on to fly the Enola Gay, which would drop the first atomic bomb on Hiroshima on 6th August, 1945.

**Did you know?**
From July to September 1943 a certain Clark Gable was stationed at Polebrook. He produced a documentary entitled *Combat America*. Gable was actually on a mission on 4th May, 1943. In all he undertook five missions whilst making the documentary.

of the 351st Bombardment Group (Heavy). They were involved in a wide range of strategic bombing missions, completing 311 for the loss of 175 B-17s. One of the squadrons, the 509th, managed to carry out 54 missions without a single aircraft loss between June 1943 and January 1944.

A maintenance unit stayed on the base until October 1948 but Polebrook remained in RAF hands until 1959. It then became home for USAF ballistic missiles, which remained operational until August 1963. The grounds were then sold back to the Rothschild estate and a handful of buildings still remain, although much of the infrastructure was demolished during the 1970s.

## Suffolk

### Bungay (Flixton), southwest of Beccles
This airfield was opened during 1942, primarily as a satellite airfield for Hardwick. The airfield was not completed when B-25s belonging to the 310th Bombardment Group (Medium) temporarily stayed there *en route* to Morocco. In December 1942 through to March 1943 B-24 Liberators, belonging to the 329th Bombardment Squadron of the 93rd Bombardment Group (Heavy) operated out of Bungay.

There was more construction work to add to the main runway and the two other secondary runways in preparation for the arrival in November 1943 of the 704th, 705th, 706th and 707th Bombardment Squadrons of the 446th Bombardment Group (Heavy). They flew out of the airfield until April 1945. During this time they made attacks on U-boat installations, chemical plants, aircraft factories and oil refineries. They were also involved in supporting some of the western Allies major offensives throughout 1944 and 1945. The group flew some 273 missions for a loss of 86 aircraft.

Memorial to the fallen of the USAAF 446th Bomb Group at Bungay, near Flixton, Suffolk. [*Image courtesy of Keith Evans*]

The airfield temporarily became home to the Royal Navy and three Fleet Air Arm squadrons were based there. This was short-lived and in 1946 it was used by the RAF to store bombs and depth charges. In the period 1949 to 1955 the airfield was gradually cleared of munitions and it was put up for sale in 1962. Initially it was used as a base for private aircraft and then small air shows were presented there. The main runway was broken up in 1984. Although many of the original buildings have since been demolished, an aircraft museum was set up there in 1972. It now extends to several Nissen huts, portacabins and a large hangar, as well as an RAF Air-Sea Rescue and Coastal Command museum.

### Bury St Edmunds, east of Bury St Edmunds
This airfield is now known as Rougham airfield. Rougham was the airfield's original name and it was designed specifically for USAAF bombers, with accommodation for around 3,000 persons. It also operated as the headquarters for the 4th Combat Bombardment Wing. In September 1942 the 47th Bombardment Group (Light), flying Douglas A-20 aircraft, arrived but they were shifted first to Horham because the Bury St Edmunds airfield was not yet ready and subsequently, on 2nd November, they headed for Casablanca.

The more permanent arrivals came in December 1942 from Florida in the shape of the 322nd Bombardment Group. The airfield was still not ready, so only two of the four squadrons were based there; the other two were sent to Rattlesden. The 322nd shifted to Andrewsfield on 13th June, 1943 and two days later the 94th Bombardment Group (Heavy) moved in from Earls Colne. They flew B-17s and launched numerous missions against strategic targets. In all they flew 324 missions, losing 180 aircraft.

The airfield was handed back to the RAF in December 1945 and the following year the Air Ministry took it over. The site fell into disuse and was closed in 1948. Part of the site today is the Rougham industrial estate. The control tower, once a home, is now a museum and gliding still takes place on the grass runways.

### Eye, northeast of Stowmarket
This airfield was not ready to be used until May 1944 when the Idaho-based 490th Bombardment Group (Heavy) arrived in B-17s and B-24s. They were to fly 158 missions and lost 22 aircraft. This was the lowest

loss of all bomb units in the 8th. RAF Bomber Command took over the base in November 1945, but it was sold off in 1962. Part of the airfield is now a reprocessing plant and a handful of buildings can still be seen.

### Framlingham, southeast of Framlingham

This is the home of the museum to the 390th Bombardment Group, which was opened in 1981. The museum is based around the control tower. Although the rest of the base has largely been removed and there is an industrial estate making use of some of the old Nissen huts, much of the site was cleared after its resale to its original owner in 1964.

The base itself opened in 1943 with the arrival of the 95th Bombardment Group (Heavy). They were transferred to Horham in mid-June and on 4th July the 390th Bombardment Group (Heavy) arrived from Montana in their B-17s. They flew strategic bombing missions, as well as flying in support of ground offensives in the west. They continued flying until 20th April, 1945, by which time they had clocked up 300 missions for the loss of 714 crew and 181 aircraft.

### Great Ashfield, east of Bury St Edmunds

This airfield was originally used by the Royal Flying Corps during the First World War. In the Second World War it was known as RAF Elmswell and was briefly used by the RAF in May 1943, before the arrival from Montana of the 385th Bombardment Group (Heavy). They flew strategic bombing missions across Europe and in March 1944 they raided Berlin. From October 1945 until March 1957 the airfield was used by the RAF to store bombs but was sold off in 1960. The vast majority of the airfield has been removed, although a handful of dilapidated buildings can still be seen.

### Halesworth (Holton), west of Southwold

Initially this airfield was to be used as an RAF bomber base, but it was instead assigned to the USAAF. It had a main runway and two secondary runways, a pair of hangars and sufficient accommodation in Nissen huts for around 3,000 persons. On 9th July, 1943 three squadrons belonging to the 56th Fighter Group arrived from Horsham St Faith. The role of the 56th was to fly escort missions and low-level strafing attacks. The group transferred to Boxted on 19th April, 1944

**Did you know?**
Lieutenant Colonel Leon R. Vance Jr, who was deputy commander of the 489th, was forced to take over control of the aircraft he was flying in on 5th June, 1944. The pilot had been killed and Vance was severely wounded. He continued to fly the aircraft onto its target and then nursed the aircraft back towards Britain, ordering the rest of the crew to bail out. One of the crewmen was wounded and could not use his parachute. Vance ditched the aircraft into the English Channel and they were both rescued. For his bravery, Vance was awarded the Medal of Honor.

Memorial and flagpole at Halesworth Airfield. This is one of three memorials adjacent to Sparrowhawk Road and the airfield museum. [*Image courtesy of Glen Denny*]

to allow the 489th Bombardment Group (Heavy) to fly in from Utah on 1st May to take over Halesworth. They were in action by the end of the month and were directly involved in bombing missions in support of the Normandy landings.

The group left Halesworth in November 1944, and in January 1945 the 5th Emergency Rescue Squadron operated from the airfield. Later, until mid-1945, the base was used to train P-51 pilots. After being used by the Royal Navy Fleet Air Arm as a training base until the beginning of 1946, the site was closed and used for food storage until 1963, when it was then sold. A large turkey farm was established, which remains on the site until today.

### Honington, south of Thetford

The airfield was built between 1935 and 1937 but in the late 1930s and the early stages of the Second World War it was home to a number of different RAF squadrons. It was turned over to the use of the USAAF in June 1942 and was initially designated as an air depot dedicated to servicing and repairing B-17s. In fact if a B-17 was badly damaged but could limp back to Britain they were told to crash-land at Honington so that they could be more easily dealt with.

The 364th Fighter Group arrived at Honington in February 1944 and they were involved in escort work as well as combat patrols and ground attack missions. They covered part of the English Channel during Operation Overlord in June 1944. By the summer of 1944 they were flying P-51 Mustangs instead of their Lightnings and this meant that they could carry out long-range escort missions over Germany. They flew their last mission at the end of April 1945.

Honington was the last USAAF station to be returned to the RAF and this took place in February 1946. It was used by Transport Command for the Berlin airlift and for bomb storage between 1950 and 1956. From 1955 to 1957 RAF squadrons were based there, including those that took part in the Suez Crisis in 1956. It remained an important RAF airfield all the way through to 1994 when the last aircraft left. The base is now used primarily by the RAF Regiment.

### Horham, southeast of Eye

This was another airfield that the RAF intended to use, but in fact was only ever used during wartime by the USAAF. The first arrivals were the 47th Bombardment Group (Light), however they only used

> **Did you know?**
> A B-17 of the 95th was the very last B-17 to be shot down in Europe. They were dropping food supplies to Dutch civilians and passed over a German-held Dutch port on their way home. A ground-based machine gun hit one of the engines, which caught fire. The aircraft nearly made it home, but went down in the North Sea, just off Southwold. There were 13 onboard, but only four survived.

Horham as a stopping-off point *en route* to Morocco over the period October 1942 to January 1943. There was also a short stay by the 323rd Bombardment Group (Medium). They arrived from South Carolina in May 1943, but before they flew any combat missions they were transferred to Earls Colne in the June.

Far more permanent tenants were the 95th Bombardment Group (Heavy), who came from Framlingham in mid-June 1943, with their B-17s. They remained on the airfield until their last mission on 7th May, 1945.

The RAF made little use of the airfield in the post-war period and it was declared inactive in October 1946. For a short time in the 1960s it was used as a Bloodhound missile site by the RAF but was then sold off in the early 1960s. Today there is a museum on the site and several of the other buildings, now in a dilapidated state, can still be seen.

### Knettishall, southeast of Thetford
Originally this airfield was used in the first six months of 1943 by the RAF as a satellite airfield for Halesworth and Honington. In June 1943, flying out of Utah, came the B-17s of the 388th Bombardment Group (Heavy). They launched their first operation on 17th July. Their targets were predominantly strategic ones in Germany, Holland, France, Belgium and other countries. They flew 331 raids in total for the loss of 179 B-17s, losing 11 B-17s on just one mission. The RAF took over the base in 1945, but it was actually used as a depot by the British Army until 1948. In February 1957 it was sold off and much of the infrastructure was demolished. Some of the wartime buildings still exist and there is a small, grass airstrip that is still being used.

### Lavenham (Cockfield), north of Sudbury

This was another airfield that was developed late in the war, as it did not officially open until the arrival of the 487th Bombardment Group (Heavy) from New Mexico on 5th April, 1944. They flew B-24s and B-17s. In all, the group flew some 185 combat missions and lost some 77 aircraft.

---

**Did you know?**

Lieutenant Colonel Beirne Lay Jr was the first commander of the 487th. He was shot down on 11th May, 1944 over German-held territory. He managed to avoid being picked up and got back to his unit. He was already a famous Hollywood screenwriter and he wrote the screenplay for *Twelve O'clock High*, which was released in 1949.

---

Post-war, the airfield was mothballed until 1948 when it was sold off and the bulk of the runways were broken up. Some remain as farm roads, however there are several buildings still in existence, notably the control tower, which is in excellent condition.

### Leiston, northwest of Leiston

RAF Fighter Command originally intended to use this base, but in fact it was used by the 358th Fighter Group that came in from Goxhill in late November 1943. They began operations towards the end of

---

**Did you know?**

Perhaps the most famous member of the 357th Fighter Group was Chuck Yeager. He was stationed at Leiston flying P-51s and was shot down on 5th March, 1944, but managed to get to Spain and then back to Britain. He was able to knock down two German aircraft on one occasion without firing a shot, causing one of the German pilots to panic and collide with another German aircraft. He is best known for being the first man to break the sound barrier on 4th October, 1947.

---

December and at the end of January 1944 were shifted to Raydon. The 357th Fighter Group switched from Raydon to Leiston on the same day. They were involved in a wide variety of different missions, including fighter sweeps and dive-bombing attacks.

In October 1945, the RAF took the base back over and the site ran as a training centre until 1953. It was closed in 1955 and sold off a decade later. Only a handful of the wartime buildings still remain.

### Martlesham Heath, southwest of Woodbridge

The airfield was originally used in the First World War by the Royal Flying Corps but then served as an experimental station and then housed various RAF squadrons until the late 1930s. Although famous British pilots, such as Robert Stanford Tuck and Douglas Bader, were stationed there during the early stages of the war, the first Americans were actually pilots for the RAF and belonged to No 71 Eagle Squadron. They served at Martlesham Heath during 1941.

By 1943 it was decided that the 8th would use Martlesham Heath as a fighter base. The 356th Fighter Group arrived at the beginning of

The top half of the old Control Tower at Martlesham Heath is run as a museum by the Martlesham Heath Aviation Society. [*Image courtesy of Chris Holifield*]

October 1943 and initially they flew P-47s and then P-51s. Their main job was to escort bombers. By 1944 they had extended their repertoire to strafing missions across German-occupied Europe. They flew their last mission on 7th May, 1945.

The RAF took back the base, and the main runway was actually extended in 1955. In the meantime the site had been used for experimental work and for reserve pilots. The Battle of Britain memorial flight was stationed there between 1958 and 1961. The airfield was then formally closed on 25th April, 1963. Most of the site is now an industrial estate and it is also home to Suffolk Constabulary, but the control tower still exists and is now a museum and a preschool.

### Mendlesham, east of Stowmarket
Initially the airfield was used by Czech pilots flying RAF No 310 Squadron's Spitfires. They were active on the airfield between February and April 1944. From late March through to the end of the war the airfield was the headquarters of the 93rd Combat Bombardment Wing. The operational unit was the 34th Bombardment Group (Heavy), with their B-17s and B-24s. They were to fly some 170 missions. In the immediate post-war period the airfield was used to store ammunition, but it was sold off in the 1950s. Part of the site became an industrial estate and the rest of the airfield returned to farmland.

### Metfield, northwest of Halesworth
This airfield was built for the 8th in 1943 and was first the home of the 353rd Fighter Group, who flew in from Goxhill in the August. They flew P-47s and moved to Raydon in April 1944. This left the airfield free for the arrival of the 491st Bombardment Group (Heavy). They in turn moved to North Pickenham in August 1944.

**Did you know?**
A bomb went off in the munitions store on 15th July, 1944. This triggered off the explosion of 1,200 tons of bombs, destroying five B-24s and killing five men. At the time the crater that was left was never filled in and was used as a dump.

The 1409th Army Air Force Base Unit operated out of Metfield until the end of the war. They carried out secret missions. The RAF took over the station once more in May 1945 but never used it again. It was finally sold off in 1965 and by this stage the crater had become a lake. When this was emptied, a large number of unexploded bombs were found. There are scattered remnants of the airfield that can still be seen, including some of the concrete roads.

### Rattlesden, southeast of Bury St Edmunds

This airfield was always designed to be a USAAF base and it was designed as an offshoot of Bury St Edmunds airfield. Whilst it received two squadrons of the 322nd for a short period of time, it had to wait until the end of November 1943 before its long-term residents arrived. These were the 447th Bombardment Group (Heavy) who flew in from Nebraska in their B-17s. They launched their first mission on Christmas Eve 1943 and bombed a wide range of strategic targets across France and Germany.

The 447th flew 257 missions for the loss of 257 aircraft. The RAF used the airfield for a short time in 1945 to 1946 as a training base but after that it served as a depot for the Ministry of Food. In the 1960s the RAF sited anti-aircraft missiles on the airfield. It was then sold off in 1966. Only one major part of the airfield still remains intact, including a hangar, however near the main runway a gliding club operates and they use the control tower as their clubhouse.

**Did you know?**
Second Lieutenant Robert E. Femoyer was a navigator onboard one of the aircraft on a mission over Germany on 2nd November, 1944. Anti-aircraft fire shot up the B-17 and Femoyer had several shell fragments embedded in his body. He refused to take medication to ease the pain and instead was determined to get the aircraft out of danger and save his fellow crewmen. He got the B-17 home but shortly after a medical crew took him out of the aircraft he died. He was posthumously awarded the Medal of Honor.

## Raydon, southeast of Hadleigh

The airfield was built to house USAAF bombers but in fact one of the only bombers ever to use it was a B-17 that crash-landed onto the main runway before it was even finished. It was used as a fighter base by both the 8th and 9th USAAF. On 30th November, 1943 the 357th Fighter Group arrived, which were part of the 9th Air Force.

The next arrivals were the 358th Fighter Group, which came from Leiston in Suffolk. They were transferred to the 9th at the beginning of February 1944. In mid-April this unit was transferred to High Halden in Kent and the 353rd came in from Metfield. They were to fly some 447 missions in total. Fighter Command took over Raydon in December 1945 but rarely used it.

Part of the airfield was sold off in 1952 and it was closed as a base in 1958. More was sold off in the early 1960s and the final part in the 1980s. The site is now Notley industrial park.

Former RAF Raydon from the air. Raydon is to the left of the airfield. [*Image courtesy of Thomas Nugent*]

## Sudbury (Acton), east of Sudbury

This airfield opened relatively late, in 1944, and was home to the 486th Bombardment Group (Heavy), who flew in from Arizona in March. The group flew B-24s and then B-17s against a wide variety of targets in occupied Europe and against Germany itself. In all they flew 191 missions, with the loss of some 23 aircraft.

The station was closed down in 1945 and was used temporarily as a recruit centre until 1946. It was then sold and the majority of the runways were broken up. The control tower base can still be seen and for a time the hangars were used for grain storage.

## Chapter Five

# Support and Strike

A LTHOUGH most will associate the 8th as being the main USAAF force in Britain during the Second World War, there was in fact another entire air force. The 9th was established in 1941. At the time the USAAF was either strategic or tactical air forces. A strategic air force was designed to hit the enemy's ability to produce military materials. A tactical force was used to support any ground offensives against the enemy. Therefore, it was decided that the 9th Air Force would actually initially support the Allied effort in North Africa. It was officially activated in Kentucky on 11th September, 1941 and was then transferred to Cairo in November 1942. By the end of the year nearly 400 9th Air Force aircraft were operating in support of the Allies across Libya, Italy, Crete, the rest of Greece, Egypt and Tunisia.

Most of the 9th Air Force was operating under the command of RAF Middle East or Mediterranean. They were then involved in operations in Sicily and mainland Italy. However, some of the units were subsequently shifted to Britain in order to support the US forces that would be landing in Europe to help liberate France and the other countries that had been overrun by the Germans in 1940.

Officially the group was activated at Middle Wallop in Hampshire on 4th January, 1944. The group flew some 35,000 sorties between 1st May, 1944 and 6th June, 1944 alone. Significantly, they not only had bombers and fighters, but also gliders. These would be invaluable in landing airborne troops to seize vital strategic positions in the hours before the main forces arrived on the five D-Day beaches in Normandy.

## 9th Airfields

On D-Day alone the IX Troop Carrier Command flew around 2,000 sorties. Other units in the 9th Air Force also carried out huge attacks across northern France and their P-38 Lightning aircraft attacked German positions on and around the beaches at Normandy. As the 9th Air Force was designed to be mobile, some of the units ended up deploying into France just 10 days after the Normandy landings. Unlike the 8th, whose aircraft had a far longer operational range, the 9th needed to be as close to the front as possible. As a result they were shifted quickly to what were called 'advanced landing grounds'. In reality these were either former French airfields that had been used by the Germans for the past four years, or scratch built airfields on suitable former farmland.

By the beginning of August 1944 the vast majority of the 9th Air Force had left Britain and was in France.

## Berkshire

### *Aldermaston, southwest of Reading*

Part of the Aldermaston Court estate was designated as a site that could be developed for training bomber crews. In 1941 woodland was cleared away and three concrete runways laid and work continued into the summer of 1942, which included the construction of five hangars. One of the hangars was used to assemble Spitfires, which were then flight tested there.

Originally, Wellington bombers were due to operate from Aldermaston, but instead it was handed over to the USAAF in June 1942. Originally the 60th Troop Carrier Group of the 8th Air Force operated from Aldermaston from the August, but they shifted to Algeria in the November. An observation squadron operated there briefly over Christmas 1942 to 1943. The 315th Troop Carrier Group arrived from South Carolina in December 1942. They left for Algeria in May 1943.

Towards the end of 1943 the airfield was then transferred to the 9th Air Force. In December the 15th Tactical Reconnaissance Squadron arrived, but they were transferred to Middle Wallop in Hampshire. This left the airfield free for the arrival of the 370th Fighter Group, who arrived in February 1944. This was also only a temporary stay and they were transferred to RAF Andover, also in Hampshire. The 434th Troop Carrier Group arrived on 3rd March and they were under training with the 101st Airborne Division for their operations in Normandy in June 1944. The unit remained at Aldermaston until February 1945 when they moved to France.

The RAF took back the base in June 1945 and it was designated for use as a flying school. The school itself closed at the end of September 1948 and the base was considered as the third London airport. As it was, this did not take place and the Ministry of Supply took it over in 1950. It then became the base of the Atomic Weapons Establishment (AWE), which is its current use.

### Greenham Common, southeast of Newbury
Greenham Common is synonymous with the long-standing anti-nuclear camp that was established there in 1981 and remained until 2000. RAF Greenham Common was opened in 1942 and the RAF originally intended to use it for bombers. It operated as a satellite station for Aldermaston and in early 1943 it was used as an RAF training base. Towards the end of 1943 it was assigned to the 9th Air Force. The Americans used it initially as a staging post for their fighter squadrons.

In November 1943 the 354th Fighter Group, with their Mustangs, touched down at Greenham Common before moving on to RAF Boxted. In January 1944 the 368th Fighter Group flew in before moving on to Chilbolton. Between March 1944 and February 1945 the 438th Troop Carrier Group, designated for work with the 101st Airborne on D-Day, operated from Greenham Common. Elements of the unit moved to Italy in the late summer of 1944 and eventually the entire unit moved to France. The 316th Troop Carrier Group was briefly stationed there in July and August 1944.

In June 1945 the RAF began using the airfield for training ground units and this continued for a year. In 1951 the USAF, as it had now become, spent considerable sums updating the airfield to take jet bombers. The airfield came under the control of the 3909th Combat Support Group and the first bombers flew in during March 1954. It continued to be used by the USAF but its most significant period was when 96 cruise missiles were located there in response to the Russian deployment of missiles in Europe.

Greenham Common control tower. The control tower of the former airfield is now boarded up and fenced off. [*Image courtesy of Graham Horn*]

The USAF handed back Greenham Common in September 1992 and in the following year it was put up for sale. The peace camps stayed on the site until September 2000, mainly to ensure that the base would never again be used for military purposes.

### *Membury, north west of Hungerford*
Most of the construction work was done on this airfield in early 1942. It was still being built when the USAAF were allocated the site on 11th June, 1942. In order to accommodate their needs the runway was extended and more hangars were built. The first Americans arrived in early September 1942. It was then allocated to the 6th Tactical Air Depot for repairs and modifications on P-47 fighters. The first major operational unit arrived in January 1944. The 366th Fighter Group flew in from North Carolina and began to prepare for operations. The next arrivals were the 436th Troop Carrier Group. It was the 436th that would drop paratroopers of the 82nd Airborne into Normandy in June 1944. Detachments from the 436th were also involved in Operation Dragoon, which was the liberation of southern France. The unit was also involved in operations over Holland during Operation Market Garden.

The unit finally left for France in February 1945. The RAF took back control of the airfield and it was used to transport troops backwards and forwards from India. The two squadrons, the 187th and the 525th remained operational until October 1946 when Membury was closed. Flying continued until the late 1970s when the M4 cut straight through the airfield. Membury Services is actually on part of the old airfield and a repair and maintenance company run the remaining part, but the tower was demolished in 1998.

### Welford, northwest of Newbury

The construction of RAF Welford was begun in October 1941 and although it opened as an RAF base in June 1943, by the following month it was handed over to the USAAF. The first Americans arrived there on 6th September, 1943 and by the October it was allocated to the 9th Air Force. On 6th November the 315th Troop Carrier Group arrived from Aldermaston. They were later sent on to North Africa and the entire group eventually left for Sicily.

The new arrivals were the 435th Troop Carrier Group who flew in from RAF Langar on the Leicestershire/Nottinghamshire border at the end of January 1944. They were earmarked for use by the 101st Airborne and their operations in Normandy in June 1944. Part of the group was sent to Italy in the August but in the September they were involved in Operation Market Garden. In February 1945 they were transferred to France.

RAF Transport Command took back control of Welford at the end of June 1945 and by March 1946 the station was mothballed. But in October it became an important centre for signals units and it remained in this role until 1948. In 1955 the Americans took it over as a major logistics base for their 3rd Air Force. The station was home to the 3rd Air Force until the end of May 2004. It is still used by the Americans as a forward air station and many of the original wartime buildings are still being used.

## Cambridgeshire

### Snailwell, north of Newmarket

Very little remains of RAF Snailwell, although there are some pillboxes dotted around the perimeter. The site is now largely used by the

British Racing School. The airfield was in operation between March 1941 and April 1946. Interestingly, aside from the fact that it was used by the RAF and by the 9th USAAF, it was also used by the Enemy Aircraft Flight. This group of pilots flew captured German aircraft. Portions of the taxiway can still be seen at Snailwell, but the majority of the site is now farmland and paddocks for the school.

Before the construction of RAF Snailwell in 1939 there was an excavation of 10 ancient barrows on the site.

## Devon

### Exeter

This is the site of Exeter International Airport. It was originally opened as a flying club in 1938. The RAF requisitioned the site in 1939 and they made considerable improvements, particularly to the runway, perimeter track and hardstanding for the aircraft. In 1942 there were further improvements when the runway was extended and other features added. During the Battle of Britain it was home to three RAF squadrons, but in April 1944 the 440th Troop Carrier Group arrived. They had the mission of carrying elements of the 101st Airborne into France on D-Day. They later were involved in the liberation of southern France and the unit remained at Exeter until August 1944.

In the early part of 1945 Exeter was used by the RAF for air-sea rescue and glider training. Fighter Command took it over and remained there until November 1945. The last of the RAF units left the airfield in the summer of 1946 and it was returned to civilian use, although the RAF still flew some flights into the 1950s. Exeter began operating civilian charter flights in the 1950s and it is now an important international airport, catering for around one million passengers a year.

### Upottery, northeast of Honiton

Upottery, or Smeatharpe, was the western-most airfield allocated to the USAAF. It opened in 1944 and was first used by the 439th Troop Carrier Group, who would go on to fly paratroopers into Normandy in June. The mini-series *Band of Brothers*, released in 2001, featured a paratroop company from the 506th Parachute Infantry Regiment. They were based at Upottery and flew to Normandy from the airfield.

C-47 Skytrain (Dakota) at Upottery airfield. A Douglas C-47 Skytrain (Dakota), one of 82 that operated from this airfield during D-Night 5/6th June, 1944, stands towards the western end of the usable section of the main runway at Upottery 63 years after it was based here. It had been flown in for an air and fun day organised by the South West Airfields Heritage Trust. A reenactment group was on hand to replicate a scene from the film *Band of Brothers*. Some of the group's members stand in front of the aircraft, which is painted in its original 1944 markings of 92nd TCS, 439th TCG, complete with D-Day stripes. [*Image courtesy of Mac Hawkins*]

After the Normandy, operations the aircraft from Upottery delivered members of the 82nd Airborne onto Nijmegen during Operation Market Garden. They dropped supplies around Bastogne in early December 1944 to assist the 101st Airborne during the Battle of the Bulge. Their last work involved transporting displaced persons after Germany was defeated in May 1945. The base returned to RAF use in June 1945 and was used to store materials. They turned over the base to civilian use in November 1948. Very little remains, apart from hardstanding, and the concrete runways, but part of the airfield is still used by a flying club.

## Dorset

### *Christchurch, east of Bournemouth*
The airfield opened for civilian flyers in July 1926. In 1933 there was an aviation display there, which attracted around 8,000 people. In

April 1940 the RAF took over the airfield and the site was used by a special duties flight, operating a variety of different aircraft. Between March and April 1943 US engineers laid a concrete mesh runway and in the spring of 1944 the airfield was handed over formally to the USAAF.

The 405th Fighter Group arrived from South Carolina at the beginning of April 1944. They launched several operations against enemy targets in France before moving to an advanced landing ground in France towards the end of June 1944. The airfield was returned to RAF control and was used to repair gliders. In March 1945 Transport Command took over and then the Ministry of Aircraft Production in late January 1946.

It finally returned to civilian use towards the end of 1946, but a new flying club was only established there in 1948. During the post-war years there was a gliding school and it was used to build military aircraft, as there was a large factory on site. The factory closed in 1962 and the airfield itself in 1964. The present day airfield is being used by light industrial companies and many of the original buildings can still be seen, although most of the airfield is now covered with housing.

### Hurn, northeast of Christchurch

The RAF opened the airfield in July 1941 as a satellite station for RAF Ibsley, to the north of Ringwood. It was used for the Special Duties Flight and then by squadrons involved in towing gliders and then by night fighters and Typhoon fighter bombers. Between June and July 1944 US night fighter squadrons operated from here and then between August and September 1944 squadrons belonging to the 397th Bombardment Group, operating out of Rivenhall, also used Hurn. It was used as an airfield for flight testing in the post-war period and eventually it became Bournemouth Airport, with the first commercial flights going to Majorca in October 1958. It currently handles just over 600,000 passengers per year.

### Warmwell, east of Dorchester

Construction of the base began in 1936 and it was originally named Woodsford. In 1938 it was changed to Warmwell and at that stage consisted of grass runways. It was designed to house around 1,700 people. Warmwell was home to the only RAF fighter base during the Battle of Britain, when elements of RAF 609 Squadron operated from there. Over 30 RAF fighter squadrons were then based there at various times between 1940 and January 1944. The base, however, was destined to be used by American fighter aircraft, but these were delayed due to the fact that the RAF was still using the airfield.

The first 80 aircraft arrived on 12th March, 1944 in the shape of the 474th Fighter Group, who had flown in from California. The Americans actually called the airfield Moreton, due to the fact that it was the name of the nearest railway station. The 474th carried out operations from 25th April and continued to operate from Warmwell until early August 1944.

On 18th July, 1944 elements of the 474th, commanded by Lieutenant Colonel Henry Darling, intercepted a number of Fw 190s. They shot down 10 of them for the loss of one of their P-38 Lightnings.

During the American use of the base RAF Air-Sea Rescue operated from Warmwell, in the guise of No 275 Squadron. It was then used by RAF units in order for them to use the Chesil Bank bombing range. Warmwell was finally sold off in 1950. There is now a village called Crossways on the site. A tower has been converted into a house, the airfield cinema is the village hall and one of the housing blocks is a local shop.

### Winkton, north of Christchurch

The RAF built this airfield over the winter months of 1943 to 1944. The American 404th Fighter Group flew in on 4th April, 1944. They were involved in operations over Normandy and later the Ardennes and the crossing of the Rhine. Towards the end of 1944 the airfield was effectively returned to agriculture and officially it closed in January 1945. Until recently there was a small runway remaining for private use.

### Essex

### Birch, northeast of Tiptree

The airfield was opened in 1942 and originally allocated to the 8th Air Force, but due to the fact that extra construction work was necessary it was transferred to the 9th Air Force in October 1943. The 410th

Bombardment Group flew in from Florida in early April 1944 to discover that the airfield had not yet been completed. The unit was transferred to Gosfield, to the north of Braintree, whilst construction continued.

The base was handed back to the 8th for use as a reserve field. RAF Horsa gliders left RAF Birch from 0600 on 24th March, 1945 as part of Operation Varsity, which was a major airborne crossing of the Rhine. After this, Birch was barely used and in 1946 it was returned to agricultural use. Very little remains apart from part of the runway and sections of the perimeter track.

### Boreham, northeast of Chelmsford
This was another airfield that was designed for use by the USAAF. The land had actually been set aside since 1942, but it was the Americans that began construction in the spring of 1943. Due to a number of circumstances it took them the best part of a year to complete the construction work. The 394th Bombardment Group flew in from Michigan on 10th March, 1944. They flew many missions in their B-26 Marauders. They shifted to RAF Holmsley South in Hampshire on 24th July, 1944.

It was then used by Troop Carrier Command, and finally the Americans left in January 1945, but the last US operation was when aircraft belonging to the 315th Troop Carrier Group ferried the British 6th Airborne Division into Germany in March 1945. Soon after the airfield closed and it was initially used to house homeless people. It was then used for motor racing and by Ford for truck development, and Essex Police took over the control tower from 1990. Most of the airfield has been dismantled, although the northern side remains largely intact.

### Gosfield, north of Braintree
The site was set aside in around 1941, but construction did not begin until 1942, when it was allocated for use initially by the 8th USAAF. However the 8th did not end up operating from Gosfield and the first arrivals were actually the 365th Fighter Group, which flew in from Richmond, Virginia on 22nd December, 1943. They were involved in only a small number of operations until they moved to Beaulieu in Hampshire on 5th March, 1944. A month later, flying in from Georgia

via Africa, came the 397th Bombardment Group's B-26s. They only stayed for nine days before flying on to RAF Rivenhall.

On 15th April the 410th Bombardment Group came in to Gosfield from RAF Birch. They flew their first mission on 1st May. Their primary targets were V weapon sites, bridges, airfields and railways. In September they were shifted to France and although the Americans retained control of Gosfield it was rarely used, so in January 1945 the RAF took it over again until it was closed down in February 1946.

The airfield was retained until the land and buildings were sold off in 1955. It was used to test cars between 1965 and 1987 and the control tower has been added to in the post-war period and is now used as a light industrial unit.

### Matching, east of Harlow
This was allocated to the USAAF in August 1942. Construction was completed by December 1943 and on 26th January, 1944 the B-26s belonging to the 391st Bombardment Group arrived. Their first mission was on 15th February, 1944 and they remained at the base until the middle of September before moving to France. For a short time US troop carriers used the base, but towards the end of 1944 the RAF began using Matching again, but the airfield was closed and sold off in 1946. The original control tower was converted into a radar test station.

### Rivenhall, southeast of Braintree
Construction got underway at the beginning of 1943, with the airfield allocated to the 8th Air Force. As it was, the 363rd Fighter Group of the 9th Air Force flew in from RAF Keevil in Wiltshire on 22nd January, 1944. They supported raids over occupied Europe and Germany. In their short stay, until 14th April, they had flown 20 missions and lost 16 aircraft but had shot down 13 German fighters. On 15th April, the 397th Bombardment Group arrived and they stayed until 5th August, moving to Hurn so that they could be better used in Normandy.

In October 1944 RAF No 295 Squadron took over Rivenhall. They flew operations to supply the resistance movements in Denmark, Holland and Norway. They were also involved in other operations until they were disbanded in January 1946. At this stage the airfield was then used to house Polish servicemen who had been released from German prisoner of war camps but did not wish to return to Poland. Part of the airfield was leased to Marconi from 1956. The airfield has been largely dismantled, although there are still a handful of the buildings in existence. There were plans to turn the whole site into an incinerator and waste facility.

### Stansted Mountfitchet, now Stansted Airport
This is, of course, the site of Stansted Airport, where incredibly the original control tower from wartime days was not demolished until February 2008. The base was allocated to the Americans in August 1942 and construction was completed by the middle of 1943, so that it could be used by B-26s of the 9th Air Force, namely the 344th Bombardment Group. They arrived at the beginning of February 1944 and began operations in the March. They were involved in widespread operations across occupied Europe, including the Normandy landings. They shifted to France at the end of September 1944, by which time they had flown a hundred missions out of the airfield.

The 344th supported Patton's breakout from the Normandy beaches in mid-June 1944. Their support included the liberation of the village of Montfiquet, which was the ancestral home of the Norman family that gave its name to Stansted Mountfitchet.

The Americans continued to use the airfield until 12th August, 1954 then the RAF used it for storage. But between March 1946 and August 1947 it was used as a prisoner of war camp. After temporarily passing into civilian hands in 1949 the Americans returned and extended the runway in 1954, aiming to use it as a major NATO base. In the end this did not come to fruition and it passed into civilian use in 1957. Stansted Airport now handles over 18 million passengers a year.

### Wethersfield, north west of Braintree
It was originally planned that the airfield would be ready for use by December 1942, but a series of delays meant that it did not open until January 1944. The first tenants were the 416th Bombardment Group (Light). They flew in with their Douglas A-20G Havocs from Mississippi on 1st February, 1944. They would be involved in hitting targets across occupied Europe and supporting the advance across

France and towards the Rhine. The unit moved to France in September 1944.

The 416th launched an important mission on 6th August, 1944. Tens of thousands of German troops and all their equipment were trapped in what became known as the Falaise Pocket. This was to the west of the River Seine in France. The 416th destroyed the last bridge and, with it, 200,000 Germans became trapped. In the operation some 36 aircraft were launched, four of which were shot down and all of the others pockmarked by anti-aircraft shells.

The RAF used the base for their bombers until January 1945, by which time the runways needed work. In late March 1945 elements of the 316th Troop Carrier Group ferried British paratroopers to the east of the Rhine before flying back to RAF Cottesmore in Rutland. The airfield was effectively closed in July 1946 and was then used by Chipperfield's Circus as their winter camp, with the elephants being housed in the hangars. In 1951 the USAF earmarked Wethersfield for their fighter bombers.

US operations continued until 1990, with the base being officially handed back to the RAF, although the US retained housing on the site. Today the airfield is used by the Ministry of Defence Police and for fire investigation training, as well as by an engineering company. The airfield still retains many of its wartime buildings, as these have been maintained over the years by continued military presence.

Wethersfield Hangars. These are examples of the US Air Force hangars on the former RAF Wethersfield. The airbase is now home to the MOD Police & Guarding Agency HQ and Training Centre. [*Image courtesy of Glyn Baker*]

## Wormingford, northwest of Colchester

The only aviation links that this site still retains is its use by a gliding club. The airfield was originally designated as a landing ground during the First World War, but it was not opened as a proper airfield until 1942. It was to be used by the 8th Air Force, and the 362nd Fighter Group flew in on 30th November, 1943. The unit moved to RAF Headcorn in mid-April 1944, having supported American bombing attacks on German-occupied Europe.

The unit was also transferred to the 9th Air Force. The 55th Fighter Group moved in and they operated from the airfield until 21st April, 1945. The unit then shifted to Germany towards the end of July 1945. Wormingford was then handed to the RAF and used for training and transport aircraft. It was used for civil flying in the 1950s and then sold off in 1962. Little remains of the wartime airfield apart from a small section of the old runway.

## Hampshire

### Andover, west of Andover

German prisoners of war were deployed to build an airfield for the Royal Flying Corps in 1917. It had been intended to create an airfield on this site as early as 1912 and it was to be used as a training base. One of the first squadrons on site was 106, which was created at the end of September 1917. The RAF established their School of Navigation there in 1919 and then the RAF Staff College in 1922. It was also here that the Royal Air Force Association was created in 1929. In the 1920s and into the 1930s the RAF continued to use Andover to test new aircraft and to train pilots. In September 1939 it was transferred over to RAF Fighter Command for flight training.

On 13th August, 1940 German Ju 88s bombed Andover. They returned the following day, dropping bombs that destroyed some of the radio masts. During the raid WAF Corporal Josephine Robins was in a trench that received a direct hit. Two men were killed, but despite the danger Josephine tended to the wounded and made sure that they were evacuated. She would be only one of six WAFs to be awarded the Military Medal for her gallantry.

In February 1944 through to the July the USAAF's 370th Fighter Group operated from Andover in their P-38s. They moved to France on 20th July, 1944. Canadian units were created at Andover between December 1944 and March 1945. In January 1945 the first-ever British helicopter unit was created at Andover. The helicopter training school there would go on to train many pilots. Helicopter training continued in the post-war period. The RAF station was officially closed in June 1977 and the army would now be based at the site. In 2009 Andover became the headquarters for British Army Land Forces.

### Beaulieu, New Forest

Although Beaulieu had been used during the First World War for pilot training, there had been little development of the site. This all changed in the early 1940s and construction began to create a bomber base and work was completed at the beginning of August 1942. The RAF's No 224 Squadron with their Liberators moved into the base. They were involved in anti-submarine warfare. The unit left the airfield in April 1943 to be replaced by the Czech RAF unit, No 311 Squadron. Also

A memorial to all those who had served and worked in the New Forest Airfields. [*Image courtesy of Nigel Richardson*]

present from the September was No 53 Squadron. Shortly afterwards Beaulieu was earmarked for use by the USAAF.

The 9th Air Force's first unit, the 365th Fighter Group, came in from Gosfield in Essex on 1st March, 1944. The 365th, flying P-47s, would become one of the most successful fighter groups in the 9th Air Force. In their four months at Beaulieu they shot down 29 German aircraft. On one day alone, 25th June, 1944, they shot down eight German aircraft. The unit moved to France at the beginning of July and to replace them came the 323rd Bombardment Group. They arrived from Earls Colne in Essex. Some 60 B-26s belonging to the four squadrons flew 28 missions out of Beaulieu. By the end of August they too were gone and now based in France. For a short time Beaulieu was used as a staging post or refuelling depot.

In December 1944 experimental flights were staged from the airfield until the unit was transferred to Boscombe Down in Wiltshire. The Americans gained control of the airfield once again in April 1953. They carried out considerable construction work, but in the end the base was not used and it was handed back to the RAF in September 1955. It was mothballed until November 1959, when it was passed on to the Forestry Commission. None of the buildings exist today, although there is a small part of the perimeter track remaining and a water tower.

### Bisterne, south of Ringwood

Bisterne was something of an experiment. It was designed and constructed to replicate the kind of advanced landing ground airfields that the Allies would need to build in France once they had gained a foothold on the continent. The airfield was opened up in March 1944, although the site had been earmarked in 1942. US Army engineers carried out the bulk of the work and the first arrivals were the 371st Fighter Group. They carried out training and engaged in operations over France. There were problems with the airfield that taught the Allies some valuable lessons about rapid airfield construction.

The 371st had their first brush with the German air force on 8th May, 1944, which saw two German fighters shot down for the loss of a P-47. By the end of June 1944 the 371st had moved to France. Bisterne had proved to be a troublesome airfield and it was not used again. In fact it was effectively closed by the end of the summer of

1944. The land was returned to agriculture and very little remains of the original site. In 2004, however, a memorial was set up to commemorate those who flew from Bisterne during the war.

### Chilbolton, southeast of Andover

Chilbolton was originally created in September 1940 to be used as a satellite airfield for Middle Wallop. RAF Squadron No 238, with its Hurricanes, operated from Chilbolton during the Battle of Britain. The airfield saw some upgrades during 1941 and over that period, until 1943, several Spitfire and Hurricane units were stationed there. It was decided to upgrade Chilbolton by adding concrete runways in 1943. It would then be ideal for use by the USAAF. The first arrivals were members of the 5th Tactical Air Depot in January 1944. The base was used for maintenance and repairs of P-47s. Temporarily, elements of the 67th Reconnaissance Wing, flying Mustangs and Spitfires, used the base in March, but in the longer term it was to become home for the 368th Fighter Group who came in from Greenham Common. This meant that together with the tactical air depot there could be as many as 150 P-47s at Chilbolton at any one time. The 368th would go on to become the most successful P-47 unit of the 9th Air Force, shooting down 149 German aircraft. The 368th moved to France in mid-June 1944 and Chilbolton was then used as an air evacuation station. Later

Chilbolton Observatory. Satellite dish towering over recently cut fields. Built in the 1960s on site of the Second World War airfield for research in meteorology and radio engineering. [*Image courtesy of Colin Smith*]

it was used during Operation Market Garden and it was eventually handed back to the RAF in March 1945. The airfield was then used to train pilots, primarily in Spitfires and Hawker Tempests.

RAF No 247 Squadron, based at Chilbolton in March 1946, became the first unit to fly de Havilland Vampire jets. The aircraft would stay in front-line service until 1953 and be used as a trainer into the mid-1960s.

The airfield was then used to carry out development of aircraft until around 1961. At that point the bulk of the airfield was dismantled. Right at the very centre of the airfield is now the Chilbolton Observatory. Construction began in 1963 and it was opened in 1967. Nonetheless flying did continue at Chilbolton into the 1980s, primarily of crop sprayers and helicopters.

### Holmsley South, northeast of Christchurch

In the search for suitable airfields, land near to Holmsley was earmarked towards the end of the 1930s; however construction did not begin until 1942. It was first used by Coastal Command and by the USAAF 93rd Bombardment Group and their operations against German U-boats in the Bay of Biscay. No 547 Squadron then used the base and they specialised in attacking German ships. The site was also used by RAF Squadron Nos 58 and 502. Towards the end of July 1944 the B-26s belonging to the 394th Bombardment Group arrived from RAF Boreham in Essex. They were directly engaged in supporting ground units that had landed in Normandy.

The unit finally left the airfield at the end of August 1944 and it was then used by RAF Transport Command. But by October 1946 the airfield had been mothballed and rapidly became derelict. The Forestry Commission took over the site and removed the vestiges of the airfield, although some of the campsites are actually on original tracks and concreted areas.

### Ibsley, north of Ringwood

RAF Ibsley has quite a history even though it only opened in 1941. It was used by no fewer than 19 different RAF squadrons over the period February 1941 to June 1942. Therefore it saw Hurricanes, Spitfires, Typhoons, Mustangs and a host of other aircraft. The USAAF took control of the airfield in June 1942, with the 1st Fighter Group of

303

the 8th Air Force arriving them from RAF Goxhill towards the end of August. They only stayed there a short time, flying on to Algeria, at which point Ibsley was handed over to the 9th Air Force.

The 48th Fighter Group arrived on 29th March with their P-47 Thunderbolts. They flew their first mission on 20th April. For a time they were joined by the 371st Fighter Group, which doubled the number of P-47s operating from the base. The 48th were one of the very first units to move into the Normandy bridgehead, which they achieved on 18th June, 1944. Effectively they would follow the US 1st Army towards Germany over the course of the next 10 or so months. For a brief time elements of the 14th Liaison Squadron used Ibsley, but the base was allocated to the 367th Fighter Group who arrived from RAF Stoney Cross on 6th July, 1944. Within the month they too were in France.

The RAF took back control of Ibsley and used it as a flying school and then for transport aircraft. The hangars were by this stage being used for storage. RAF presence lingered towards the end of 1946, but in the spring it was sold off. For a time the site was used as a motor racing circuit but in 1955 it was sold for agricultural use and in the 1960s it was sold again to an aggregates company who quarried the site. This now means that Ibsley consists of a number of lakes and gravel pits and a forlorn, derelict control tower.

### Lymington, New Forest

Lymington was another of the prototype advanced landing fields that would need to be constructed in France once the Allies had achieved a bridgehead. The RAF began building the airfield towards the end of 1943. The 50th Fighter Group flew in from Florida at the beginning of April 1944 and they were directly involved in the support of the Normandy landings at the beginning of June. They moved to France themselves at the end of the month. For a time, until 1946, the Royal Navy used Lymington for storage, but in 1946 the airfield was dismantled. One hangar still exists and one of the runways is still being used by private aircraft.

### Middle Wallop, southwest of Andover

Today Middle Wallop is a British Army base, but it was originally opened in 1940 as a pilot training school. Construction had actually begun in 1938 and during the Battle of Britain 10 Group's RAF fighters operated from the airfield. In the autumn of 1940 night fighters moved in and until October 1943 some 30 different RAF squadrons were based at Middle Wallop at one time or another. The USAAF's 9th Air Force used Middle Wallop as their Fighter Command headquarters from November 1943. It was also used by the 67th Tactical Reconnaissance Group.

In May 1944 the 10th Photographic Reconnaissance Group also operated from the airfield. In July 1944 Royal Canadian Air Force night fighters used the airfield and in January 1945 control of Middle Wallop was passed to the Royal Navy. The following year the RAF took it back and Spitfires were based there. From around 1950 the army began using the airfield, but the RAF were still sited there until around 1957. It is now the home of the Army Air Corps and the Museum of Army Flying.

### Stoney Cross, west of Southampton

Stoney Cross opened in November 1942 but the site was still not completed, despite the fact that RAF No 239 and then 26 Squadrons were operating from there. Additional work was carried out between April and August 1943. The last RAF units were Nos 297 and 299 Squadrons, who remained there until March 1944. The 367th Fighter

A Puma helicopter takes off from Middle Wallop airfield. [*Image courtesy of Chris Talbot*]

Group, with P-38 Lightnings began arriving at the beginning of April 1944 and began operations on 9th May. To start with they attacked strategic targets, but were then used primarily to support the US 1st Army, which had landed in France and was pushing to breakout and seize Cherbourg.

At the beginning of July the fighter group moved to RAF Ibsley and Stoney Cross was taken over by the B-26 Marauders of the 387th Bombardment Group (Medium). They remained on the base until the beginning of September. On 5th September RAF Transport Command took Stoney Cross over and it was used to repair gliders. New transport squadrons were created at the airfield, namely Nos 232 and 242. In January 1945 RAF No 46 Squadron began operating from the base.

After Germany had surrendered in May 1945 the RAF used the base as a staging post to fly aircraft to the Far East. By December 1946 all of the remaining RAF units had been moved to RAF Manston in Kent. The RAF hung on to the airfield until January 1948 and in the 1960s the bulk of the airfield was broken up. The Forestry Commission took over the site.

### Thruxton, west of Andover

Thruxton is now better known as Thruxton Airport and as the site for motorcycle endurance races. It can trace its history back to 1941 when it was still under construction but being used by RAF No 225 Squadron. The construction involved building three concrete runways, a large number of Nissen huts and around 10 hangars. In 1942, 225 Squadron received Hurricanes and Mustangs. RAF No 297 Squadron also flew out of the base but towards the end of 1943 all RAF units were moved out in preparation for the 9th Air Force. Before it could be used by the Americans, additional reinforcement and construction was necessary.

The 366th Fighter Group came in from RAF Membury in Berkshire on 1st March, 1944. They flew P-47 Thunderbolts and entered combat on 14th March. The unit moved to France on 17th June. Thruxton was not used again by combat units and instead it was taken over for training and maintenance. The airfield was sold off in 1946 and was utilised by the Wiltshire School of Flying in 1947. It has now been developed into Thruxton Airport.

# Kent

## *Ashford, west of Ashford*

The British Army built this airfield for use by the 9th Air Force as a forward base. However the first arrivals were in fact the Royal Canadian Air Force, in the shape of Squadrons Nos 414 and 430, who arrived in August 1943 and left in the October. A pair of RAF squadrons and their Spitfires (65 and 122 Squadrons) then moved in. Ashford had proved to be problematic and the airfields were covered in puddles and damage had been caused to several aircraft due to the bumpy surface. US engineers came in to carry out vital work.

On 5th April, 1944 the 406th Fighter Group arrived from South Carolina. The men lived mainly in tents, but also in requisitioned houses in the vicinity. Some 90 aircraft operated from Ashford. The unit left for France and Ashford was only ever used as an emergency landing field from then on. In September 1944 the land was given back to agricultural use. There is little that remains of the airfield today.

## *Headcorn, west of Ashford*

This was another prototype advance landing ground. It opened in 1943 with the arrival of 403 and 421 Squadrons of the Royal Canadian Air Force. The USAAF engineers made considerable improvements to the airfield ready for its use by the 362nd Fighter Group, who was shifted from RAF Wormingford in Essex in April 1944. The 362nd remained at Headcorn until the beginning of July when they moved to France. US engineers then took up most of the runway to be shipped to Normandy and the site was returned to agricultural use.

## *High Halden, west of Ashford*

High Halden was another advanced landing ground prototype airfield. The RAF carried out basic construction in 1943. The first arrivals were the 358th Fighter Group who flew in from RAF Raydon in Suffolk on 13th April, 1944. The fighter group headed for France towards the end of June and officially the airfield was closed on 15th September. But the clearing of the site did not actually begin until January 1945.

There were two instances of considerable excitement at High Halden. On 9th August, 1944 a Gloster Meteor landed. It had arrived to see whether the runway was suitable for dealing with the V-1 threat. A very heavily damaged B-17 made an emergency landing at High Halden on 19th March, 1945. The crew was very fortunate, as engineers had removed much of the runway and only the main runway was still operational.

There is very little left of High Halden airfield but there is a memorial that is close to the northern end of the old runway.

### Kingsnorth, south of Ashford

Although there was an RAF Kingsnorth operational between 1918 and 1924 and located on the Isle of Grain, the Second World War base was another of the prototype temporary airfields. Woodland was cleared to make way for the main runway and it opened on 1st July, 1943. Kingsnorth was used by Fighter Command and Squadron Nos 19, 65, 122, 184 and 602 until around October 1943. US engineers arrived after this date to carry out additional work, notably on the runways. Their work was completed by 1st April, 1944 and this allowed the arrival of the 36th Fighter Group. They went into operation on 8th May and flew missions over occupied France. The unit moved to France at the beginning of July 1944. US engineers then moved in to pull up the pierced steel planking so that it could be relocated in France. This meant that the airfield effectively closed around September 1944. The base was turned over to agricultural land and there is very little that can now be seen of the airfield.

### Lashenden, west of Ashford

Confusingly, this is located very close to Headcorn and, as a result, it is the home to the Headcorn Parachute Club. It is a private airfield and home to the Lashenden Air Warfare Museum. It was another of the temporary landing grounds, which was opened in 1943 and remained operational until the autumn of 1945. Even before this it was known as Headcorn Aerodrome and used for private aircraft in the 1920s. The Royal Canadian Air Force's 403 and 421 Squadrons flew Spitfires out of Lashenden for a two-week period in August 1943. This was designed to evaluate the airfield for future use. On 17th April, 1944 the 354th Fighter Group flew in from RAF Boxted in Essex and began flying their P-51 Mustangs from the airfield.

Commemorative Plaque, Lashenden airfield. [*Image courtesy of Dave Skinner*]

The 354th was engaged in bomber escort duties and on 25th April, for the loss of two of their Mustangs, they shot down 18 German aircraft and possibly another five and damaged another 31. It only took them until 11th May to clock up their 100th victory.

The 354th left the airfield in mid-June 1944 and the runways were removed.

### Staplehurst, south of Maidstone

This was another advanced landing ground that opened in the late spring of 1943 and closed in September 1944. Once again it was first used by Spitfires from the Royal Canadian Air Force. The first US aircraft to land was a B-24 belonging to the 453rd Bomb Group operating out of Old Buckenham in Norfolk. It was a forced landing, as one of its engines had failed. The 363rd Fighter Group moved from RAF Rivenhall in Essex to Staplehurst on 14th April, 1944.

In the time they flew out of Staplehurst they shot down 41 German aircraft for the loss of 43 of their own. The unit began leaving in the July and work began soon after on removing the metal runways.

There is now very little left at the site, apart from a handful of wartime buildings now being used by local farmers. There is a memorial located near the old airfield, which was dedicated in June 2010.

## Woodchurch, southwest of Ashford

Another of the 9th Air Force's temporary advanced landing grounds, which also had a short life, with construction beginning in January 1943. The first arrivals were RAF Mustangs belonging to Squadron Nos 231 and 400. Some upgrades were carried out over the winter months ready for the arrival of the 373rd Fighter Group in April 1944. US engineers were still working on extending the runway, but this did not deter the group flying its first combat mission over Normandy on 8th May. In the short time that they operated from Woodchurch they shot down 30 German aircraft for the loss of 15 of their P-47s. Soon after, the Americans left for France the airfield was closed down and the steel planking moved to France. There is virtually no sign of the airfield today.

## Leicestershire

## Bottesford, east of Nottingham

Construction got underway in November 1940. It was designed to be used by RAF bombers. Construction was completed in 1942 and it became home to RAF No 207 Squadron. They remained at Bottesford until the September and two months later the Australians of RAF Squadron No 467 arrived. They began their operations in January 1943. Throughout this time additional hangars and other pieces of infrastructure were added to the site. There were also gliders housed there.

Eventually the airfield was set aside for the USAAF and additional work got underway so that it could be used by the US Troop Carrier Command. The 436th Troop Carrier Group arrived in the first few days of 1944. After carrying out training they moved to RAF Membury in the March. The airfield was then taken over by the 440th Troop Carrier Group and they would work in close operation with the 82nd Airborne Division. In July 1944 the airfield passed over to the RAF who ran Lancasters out of the base. The RAF retained the airfield until 1948. Some of the airfield is now used as a car assembly plant and the control tower has been fully restored and is used for offices.

## Saltby, south west of Grantham

Although most of the airfield is now farmland, a significant amount of the airfield still remains and it is still used by a gliding club. The airfield was built in 1942 and had Nissen huts and several hangars that could accommodate over 2,400 personnel. It was used between August 1942 and August 1943 as a training centre for the RAF. The runways were built specifically for the USAAF between August 1943 and the arrival of the 314th Troop Carrier Group in the December. They too worked with the 82nd Airborne Division and would drop them into Normandy and into Holland during Operation Market Garden. Later they would also drop British paratroopers into Holland. The unit moved to France in March 1945.

The last time the Americans used Saltby was in May 1945 when some aircraft belonging to the 349th Troop Carrier Group used it to take British paratroopers to Norway. The RAF made use of the airfield until August 1945 and then it effectively became a store area. The airfield was sold off in 1955.

## Lincolnshire

### Barkston Heath, northeast of Grantham

Originally this airfield was identified as an ideal place to be used as a landing ground for aircraft operating out of RAF Cranwell, near Sleaford. The airfield underwent improvements from 1939 and then in 1941 it was decided that it needed substantial further improvements. These continued until the arrival of the 61st Troop Carrier Group in February 1944. They had around 64 C-47 Skytrain aircraft, along with Horsa and Waco gliders. More hangars were built in the spring of 1944. The unit was involved in dropping troops from the 82nd Airborne Division during the Normandy landings.

In September they dropped paratroopers from the British 1st Airborne Division on Arnhem. They also resupplied US troops around Nijmegen. The unit moved to RAF Chipping Ongar in Essex in March 1945 and took part in Operation Varsity, which was the last major Allied airborne operation of the Second World War. In late

RAF Bomber and escorts. [*Image courtesy of Peter Baxter*]

March 1945 the 349th Troop Carrier Group had a three-week stay at Barkston before moving to France. Some of the aircraft returned in the May to move British paratroopers to Norway.

The airfield was returned to the RAF in June 1945. Initially it was used to store surplus equipment and then for training of the RAF Regiment. The airfield was still maintained into 1948 and in the same year the RAF College at Cranwell also started to use Barkston Heath. They retained their interest there until 1966. RAF Cranwell still uses the airfield today and in the 1980s it was also used by private aircraft. There is now a training school on site. In all, the airfield is extremely well preserved.

### Folkingham, east of Grantham
The airfield began life as a decoy field for RAF Grantham. It was designed to attract the interests of the Luftwaffe and did so on three

occasions. It was turned into a real airfield in 1943 when construction work began to build the runways and Nissen huts. There were also hangars built and accommodation for over 2,000 men. The first users of the airfield were the 313th Troop Carrier Group. They moved from Sicily and began to arrive in January 1944. They were involved in the Normandy landings and in Operation Market Garden. In February 1945 they began moving to France. By April the bulk of the Americans had left and the RAF used it for training for a short time, until 1946, but it was closed the following year.

Between 1959 and 1963 the RAF used the airfield as a ballistic missile base. The site had already been used by the British Racing Motors (BRM) to test their cars. They had been present in 1949, but now took over the site. It was short-lived, however, and the airfield was then sold off and returned to agriculture.

### Fulbeck, north of Grantham
This was another site that would be used to house missiles in the post-war period. The land was originally requisitioned in 1940 and was actually known as Fenton and used as a landing ground for RAF Cranwell. It became known as Fulbeck in 1942 when work got underway to turn it into a full airfield, together with Nissen huts and hangars. It was designed to house just over 2,800 men. The first users of the airfield were the 9th Air Force's 434th Troop Carrier Group. They flew in from Indiana in October 1943 but their stay was brief as they moved to Welford in Berkshire in the December.

In March 1944 the 442nd Troop Carrier Group arrived and they would be involved in the Normandy paratroop drops. By the middle of June they had moved on to Westonzoyland in Somerset. Fulbeck was used to some extent during Operation Market Garden in September 1944 when the 440th Troop Carrier Group used it to drop members of the 82nd Airborne Division.

The RAF then took over the base, notably the 189th Squadron, which flew some 40 missions and the 49th who flew 60. In all, the Lancasters operating from the base lost 38 aircraft. The closure of the airfield began in 1948 but it was still retained into the 1970s, by which time much of the original airfield had been removed. Fulbeck is now privately owned, but it is still used for some military training.

## Goxhill, south of Hull

The airfield was originally used during the First World War by the Royal Flying Corps. In the Second World War its original use was as a site for barrage balloons to help protect Hull. Bomber Command took it over in 1940 and construction began on building a bomber airfield. The first residents were No 1 Group who were involved in towing practice targets. 616 Squadron of Fighter Command also used the base between December 1941 and May 1942.

By the time it was assigned to the USAAF, the site had become a satellite field for RAF Kirmington. The US trained various fighter groups belonging to the 8th and 9th Air Force on the base. In all, around 2,400 fighter pilots were trained there. The RAF got back Goxhill in late January 1945. It was used to store bombs and ammunition and was effectively deactivated in mid-December 1953. Some of the hangars were retained when the site was sold off in 1962 but even these were disposed of in 1977. Several of the hangars do still exist, although the control tower was demolished in 2002. Today, there is a memorial that incorporates a P-38 propeller blade.

## North Witham, south of Grantham

This is now Twyford Wood, owned by the Forestry Commission. The airfield opened in 1943 and was only operational until late 1945. It had hangars, concrete runway and considerable amounts of accommodation. The Americans began arriving on 31st December, 1943 and the USAAF personnel lived in Nissen huts and, in addition, there were several hundred American soldiers on site.

It was used as the 1st Tactical Air Depot and was also home to the XI Troop Carrier Pathfinder Group (Provisional). They had a specialised job; their transport aircraft had to fly in the very first elements of the US 82nd and 101st Airborne into Normandy on the evening of 5th June and the early hours of 6th June, 1944. They were also used during the liberation of southern France and for Operation Market Garden. The USAAF continued to carry out repair activities on the airfield until at least March 1945. The following month it was handed back to the RAF who used it as a bomb dump. It was considered inactive by 1956 and was given to the Forestry Commission in February 1960.

## Northamptonshire

### Spanhoe, west of Peterborough

Spanhoe was originally known as Harringworth. The site opened in 1943, and in early February 1944 the 315th Troop Carrier Group arrived and began exercises with the 82nd Airborne Division. They would be involved in operations in Normandy, Holland and, later, airborne drops across the Rhine. The airfield remained in American hands until the beginning of July 1945. It was used as a concentration point for war materials that would be auctioned off. In the 1960s it was used by a gliding club, in the 1970s a great deal of the infrastructure was removed but flying returned and is still carried out by privately-owned aircraft.

## Nottinghamshire

### Balderton, southeast of Newark on Trent

A grass runway was constructed here in 1941 and it was first used by the Canadians of RAF No 408 Squadron in the December. At that stage it was not really suitable so it was decided that concrete runways would be built. Construction work was completed in March 1943 and alongside this were hangars and huts to accommodate 2,400 personnel. The 9th Air Force took over the airfield at the beginning of 1944. It would be used by the 437th Troop Carrier Group. They spent very little time there, arriving on 21st January and leaving for RAF Ramsbury at the beginning of February. A couple of weeks later the 439th Troop Carrier Group arrived from Indiana and they carried out exercises with American paratroopers until they were moved to Devon over the course of late-April and early May.

The Americans used the airfield during Operation Market Garden, but by the end of September it was handed back to the RAF. RAF No 227 Squadron, with their Lancaster, began operating from Balderton from 11th October, 1944. They remained there until around April 1945 and after this it was used to store bombs. In 1957 the airfield was sold off. Much of the concrete was used to become part of the A1 and after that open pit mining destroyed much of the airfield, but there are still some buildings, now on private land.

Balderton Hall. Built in 1840 for local banker Thomas Spragging Godfrey, it served as a family home until 1936 when work started on building a hospital in the parkland. It was officers' accommodation for RAF Balderton during the war and in October 1957 it became the administrative block of the hospital for patients with learning disabilities until it closed in 1993.

It is currently offices in a large development of over 1,000 new homes on the former hospital site. [*Image courtesy of Richard Croft*]

### Langar, west of Grantham

RAF Langar is home to the British Parachute School. The base was built in 1942 and was designed to house around 2,250 personnel. It had concrete runways, hangars and numerous huts. RAF No 207 Squadron's Lancasters used it in September 1942 and it was also used to repair and maintain Lancasters. The RAF moved out in October 1943, as the following month it was transferred to the USAAF's 9th Air Force. On 3rd November the four squadrons of the 435th Troop Carrier Group arrived and they remained there until the end of January 1944. In February 1944 the 438th Troop Carrier Group arrived but once they were organised they moved to Greenham Common. It was then home to the 441st Troop Carrier Group. They arrived on 17th March and flew off to RAF Merryfield in Somerset on 25th April.

The Americans then used the site for maintenance and supply and also to modify their gliders. However, in August, just as it was going to be handed back to the RAF, the 441st returned so that they could drop paratroopers around Nijmegen during Operation Market Garden in mid to late-September. The RAF did regain control in October 1944 and stationed Lancasters there until March 1945. It then became a centre for prisoners of war and displaced persons. The Royal Canadian Air Force took it over in 1952 and were based there for 11 years, making Langar the only Canadian base in Britain.

## Oxfordshire

### Chalgrove, southeast of Oxford

The airfield was constructed in 1943 and the first US personnel began arriving in January 1944. The first unit based there was the 10th Reconnaissance Group from Mississippi. They were engaged in photographing German installations, mainly in preparation for the Normandy landings. They moved to France in August 1944. Over the same period the 423rd Night Fighter Squadron used Chalgrove, as did the 15th Tactical Reconnaissance Squadron. Between September 1944 and March 1945 the XI Troop Carrier Pathfinder Group (Provisional) were based there. They were actively involved in the airborne operations in Holland and then the crossing of the Rhine.

Other US units that used the airfield included the 653rd Bombardment Squadron in August 1944 and squadrons of the 7th Reconnaissance Group in March 1945. The USAAF handed back the airfield officially on 1st December, 1945. Initially the RAF trained Spitfire and Mosquito pilots there. In 1946 the site was used to test ejector seats but today there is still flying carried out and some of the original buildings are now part of an industrial estate.

### Grove, southwest of Oxford

RAF Grove was opened in 1942 and originally designed for use by the RAF as a satellite field for RAF Harwell. It was also used to train glider pilots and for advanced flying. The 9th Air Force moved in during the middle of 1943, primarily to use the airfield for repairing aircraft. It was also home to photoreconnaissance aircraft and temporarily the 36th Bombardment Squadron. The Americans ended their association with the airfield in December 1945.

The RAF took the airfield back in 1946 and German prisoners of war as well as captured German aircraft were housed there. Consequently, work did take place to increase the length of the main runway. In 1955 part of the airfield was assigned to the United Kingdom Atomic Energy Authority. They remained there until the late-1960s but today there are still some of the original buildings, and part of the airfield may have a housing estate built on it in the near future.

### Kingston Bagpuize, west of Abingdon
This airfield was designed as a satellite field for RAF Abingdon. It was used between February and September 1944 by the 2nd and 42nd Air Depot Groups, based at Charmy Down airfield, to the north of Bath. It was to service aircraft. In December 1944 the airfield was closed down and briefly used by the army before disposal. The derelict control tower is still standing amidst farmland.

## Rutland

### Cottesmore, between Cottesmore and Market Overton
This airfield is due to close in 2013 but military interest began in 1935 when the area was earmarked for development. It opened in March 1938 and was used for training purposes until August 1943. In the following month the USAAF took it over, intending to use it for their troop transports. They promptly closed the airfield and began intensive reconstruction. US units began moving into the area in February 1944. Cottesmore received the 316th Troop Carrier Group. They had already been involved in the invasion of Sicily but now they were gearing up for their involvement in Operation Overlord. Later they would be involved in Operations Market Garden and Varsity.

On the night of 5th June, 1944 the 316th dropped 1,256 paratroopers of the 82nd Airborne Division to the west of Saint-Mère Église.

The RAF received the airfield back in July 1945. It was to become a base for RAF V bombers and in the 1980s as a training base for Tornado pilots. There was then a series of closures and mergers that threatened to end military interest in the base forever. RAF Cottesmore closed on

German Tornado at RAF Cottesmore. At the time this picture was taken RAF Cottesmore was being used as the Tri-national Tornado Training Establishment (TTTE) by the RAF, The German Airforce and the Italian Airforce. Nowadays the base is the home for Harrier Jump Jets. [*Image courtesy of Gary Radford*]

1st March, 2012 but it would continue to be used for at least another year or more by the British Army's East of England Multi-Role Brigade (MRB).

## Somerset

### *Charmy Down, northeast of Bath*

This was used as a base by RAF Fighter Command from late 1940. It was then decided to turn it into a major base. It was used by a variety of different RAF fighter squadrons, including 87, 125, 236, 137 and then by the Royal Canadian Air Force's 417 Squadron. In 1942, RAF Squadron No 533 and then 87 Squadron were housed on the site. The USAAF took it over in November 1943 and Charmy Down became a base for the 4th Tactical Air Depot, engaged in repairing P-38s and P-51s.

From March 1944 to the May it was home to the 422nd, 423rd and 425th Night Fighter Squadrons of the 9th USAAF. They all moved out of Charmy Down before being issued with the P-61 Black Widow night fighter. It then became home for the XI Troop Carrier Service

A Second World War brick building on Holts Down just off the Charmy Down, a Second World War airfield. It has six bays-like stable doors, half bricked up. Behind these brick doors are chutes out to the back and six holes in the roof. The sides have buttresses for strength as shown. [*Image courtesy of Rick Crowley*]

Wing. They carried out secret operations into German occupied France. They left in October 1944 and the airfield was the RAF then turned it into satellite field for South Cerney in Gloucestershire.

Between January and October 1946 it was a gliding school. Also using the airfield in the late 1940s was the Personnel Resettlement Centre for Australians. The airfield remained unused for many years and most of the buildings, except for the control tower, were demolished. There was talk of the site being used as a park-and-ride facility for Bath, but this does not appear to have come to fruition.

### Merryfield, southeast of Taunton

This airfield is now known as RNAS Merryfield, as from the 1970s it was used by the Royal Navy for assault helicopter training. Work on the airfield began in late 1942 and was originally called Isle Abbotts. It was formally opened on 9th February, 1944 and the Americans moved straight in to lay the main runway. The 441st Troop Carrier Group moved onto the airfield at the end of April 1944 and from Merryfield flew out to assist the Normandy landings before moving to France. A handful of American aircraft remained on the base until October 1944 when the RAF took it back. It was home to the RAF Transport Command's No 238 Squadron and then 187 Squadron.

In September 1945 53 Squadron and then 242 Squadron were based there. The airfield closed in October 1946 but was reopened five years later for pilot training on jets. The Royal Navy used it between 1958 and 1961 and for a decade the airfield fell into disrepair and a number of the buildings were sold. The Royal Navy moved back in during 1971.

### Westonzoyland, southeast of Bridgwater
The airfield was originally used in the 1920s, primarily so that targets could be towed for a gunnery range. In November 1939 RAF No 16 Squadron was based there and the airfield became important by September 1940 as a permanent station and the plans to generally improve the infrastructure.

The RAF had not originally intended to hand over this airfield to the Americans but in the end it was decided that the 50th Troop Carrier Wing could use this base to drop the 101st Airborne Division into Normandy. As it was, the 442nd Troop Carrier Group of the 50th was assigned to Westonzoyland. After Normandy three of the squadrons were sent off to Italy but they retained a presence until October 1944. The RAF then used the airfield until around 1947. Flying recommenced in 1952 when jet pilots were trained there. By 1958 it was again deserted and sold off in the 1960s.

### Wiltshire

### Keevil, east of Trowbridge
Although Keevil is a civilian site today, it is still used by the RAF and the Army Air Corps. The history of Keevil dates back to its identification as a base in the 1930s. It was requisitioned in 1941 and building got underway. In all, some 400 buildings were constructed. The USAAF was assigned the airfield in 1942 and elements of the 62nd Troop Carrier Group began arriving at the beginning of

## World War Two Memorial to 437th Troop Carrier Group

The memorial reads:

Dedicated to honour the members of the 437th Troop Carrier Group, United Stated Army Ninth Air Force World War Two who were stationed at Ramsbury Airfield and participated in the campaigns of Normandy, Ardennes Northern France Rome-Arno, Southern France, Rhineland and Central Europe.

Where the River Kennet flows over the small weir below this spot Major Donald E. Bradley and 1st Lt Gaylord Strong members of the 83rd Squadron 437th Troop Carrier Group died in the crash of a Dakota C47 aircraft on March 11th 1944.

They were attempting to retrieve a Horsa glider that had broken free in a practice mission and landed in the field above this spot.

Captain Lee Gilletre, 83rd squadron Flight Surgeon, although seriously injured survived the accident and returned to duty after five weeks in the US Army Hospital at Burderop Park, Wroughton Wilts. [*Image courtesy of Ben Hollier*]

September. They only stayed on the base until mid-November before flying out to Algeria.

Flying in from RAF Membury in Berkshire was the 153rd Observation Squadron. They arrived in December 1942 and remained there until they were disbanded in March 1944. Arriving from California on 20th December, 1943 was the 9th Air Force's 363rd Fighter Group. They would have to wait for their aircraft until late January, at which point they moved to Rivenhall in Essex. The RAF took over the base in March 1944 and used it to house RAF Squadron Nos 196 and 299. This was an interesting unit, as the aircraft were crewed not only by British pilots, but also Australians, New Zealanders and South Africans. They supported the clandestine activities of the Special Operations Executive and the Special Air Service.

Keevil became a training base in October 1944 and this purpose continued until July 1947. It was then used by the USAF to train airborne troops and then, in effect, it was put into reserve until 1965 when it was closed. On occasion, both the RAF and the British Army used the site after this date. It is now home to several gliding clubs and is used for motorsport.

## Ramsbury, south of Ramsbury

The construction of Ramsbury was finished in August 1942 and it was originally designed for use by the RAF to train pilots and crews. By the time it was completed it could house 2,300 people and had three concrete runways, a number of hangars and an array of huts. It was assigned to the USAAF and the first unit arriving was the 64th Troop Carrier Group from Massachusetts in mid-August 1942, but they were only passing through and headed out for Algeria on 9th November.

On another temporary basis, the RAF used the site as a training school between November 1942 and October 1943. It was then assigned to the 9th Air Force in November 1943. The units would work in close cooperation with the US 101st Airborne Division. On 5th February, 1944, flying in from RAF Balderton in Nottinghamshire came the 437th Troop Carrier Group. They would fly US paratroopers into Normandy for Operation Overlord. Later they would be involved in the liberation of southern France, Operation Market Garden, the Battle of the Bulge and the airborne landings across the Rhine in 1945.

RAF Transport Command was briefly housed at the airfield in August 1945 and it was then used for flight training in 1946. It was then decided to sell off the site and it was returned to agricultural use and a great deal of the airfield was demolished. There is now a poultry farm on part of the runway.

### Zeals, north of Zeals

This airfield had a relatively short life of just four years. Construction began in 1942 and it was used until July 1943 as a landing ground for RAF fighters. Between August 1943 and March 1944 the 9th USAAF maintained their C-47 aircraft on site. The problem with the airfield was that the site tended to flood in rainy conditions. The RAF took it back in March 1944 and Mosquito aircraft used it through to March 1945, although technically the unit had already moved into France shortly after D-Day and it was only then used for glider training.

The base was taken over in April 1945 by the Royal Navy, who called it HMS Hummingbird. Between May 1945 and September 1945 a number of squadrons were based temporarily at the airfield but it was officially closed in January 1946, with the Royal Navy finally relinquishing control in the June. The airfield was then returned to agricultural use. The control tower has been converted into a private home.

In February 1945 a Dakota transport crashed at Stourton. It had taken off from Zeals and was heading for Lincolnshire. Over 20 people on board were killed when the aircraft collided with beech trees in cloudy weather. There is a memorial at Beech Knoll in Wiltshire.

Conclusion

# The Legacy of Britain's Airfields

RECOGNITION of the incredible contribution that Britain's airfields have played, not only in the history of these islands but in the history of Europe and beyond, is being spearheaded today by the Airfields of Britain Conservation Trust (ABCT). It is the ABCT's intention to ensure that a memorial is erected at every disused airfield to act as a permanent reminder of the contribution the airfield, the personnel and the aircraft played in both world wars and other pivotal moments in British history.

Day by day, every one of the airfields is under threat. The demands of modern development, whether it is housing, road-building or simply the gradual decay of the buildings and infrastructure, threaten to wipe the remnants of the airfields away. Some have already been irretrievably lost, demolished, dismantled, broken up, buried under thousands of tons of concrete or have succumbed to decades of neglect.

Yet there is still an enduring passion for the airfields. The sites are of huge historical importance; they retain a unique place in the hearts and minds of the British people. Equally, their history transcends national boundaries, as they were the homes and workplaces of many nations in times of danger, despair and ultimate glory. Unbreakable links still exist with the personnel and descendents of countless Americans, Poles, Czechs, Australians, New Zealanders, French, Canadians, South Africans, Dutch, Belgians, Norwegians and many more. The history and legacy of the airfields belongs as much to them as to the former RAF and Royal Navy service personnel themselves.

Already too many irreplaceable sites and buildings have been lost and will never be seen by future generations. There is no overall plan to protect these historic sites that are of equal importance to an imposing castle, a significant country estate or a museum hosting artefacts. Some of the sites have been retained by the armed forces, others preserved by energetic charities, trusts and foundations, and others still have found a new use as industrial estates, recreation centres or part of a farm.

What will become of the airfields when the generations that served on them have gone? Will the desire to preserve them continue? Modern developments constantly encroach on the remnants of this significant part of our past. Today we can see the legacy of the airfields in every part of the British Isles, from the Shetlands and Orkneys down to Land's End and from the extreme fringes of East Anglia across to Northern Ireland. As each planning permission for development is granted, each road widened and concrete slab shattered for building material, the legacy is diminished and a fragment of history destroyed.

It may never be practical or desirable to retain every airfield, but the legacy must remain in some way, whether it is a repurposed control tower, a preserved pillbox, a stretch of runway or a Nissen hut. Above all, the legacy must mark the lives freely sacrificed, lives as precious and significant as those lost in other battles and wars that typify the history of Britain.

# Bibliography

**Websites**

Airfields of Britain Conservation Trust (http://www.abct.org.uk/)

Control Towers (http://www.controltowers.co.uk)

UK Airfields & Aviation Memorials
(http://www.ukairfields.org.uk/)

Aerial View of UK Airports and Airfields (http://www.content-delivery.co.uk/aviation/airfields/)

**Books**

Birtles, Phillip, *Battle of Britain Airfields* (Midland, 2010)

Blake, Ron; Hodgson, Mike and Taylor, Bill, *The Airfields of Lincolnshire since 1912* (Midland, 1984)

Chorlton, Martin, *Leicestershire & Rutland Airfields in the Second World War* (Countryside, 2003)

Chorlton, Martin, *Airfields of North-East England in the Second World War* (Countryside, 2005)

Copeland, Geoff, *Silksheen* (Midland, 1989)

Holmes, Malcolm, *RAF Beccles At War 1943–45* (Malcolm Holmes, 1994)

Smith, David, *Action Stations, Volume 7: Military airfields of Scotland, the North-East and Northern Ireland* (PSL, 1983)

Smith, David, *Britain's Military Airfields 1939–45* (PSL, 1989)

Smith, Graham, *Suffolk Airfields in the Second World War* (Countryside, 1995)

# Index